10 -6 -24

KU-112-551

Variant Sexuality: Research and Theory

The study of sexual behaviour is a subject that always attracts wide interest, but which is characterised more by sensational stories in the media than by scientific analysis. With variant sexuality and sexual deviation this is even more true. Some deviations, such as fetishes, may be trivial or at times amusing, but others may lead to horrific crimes. Although many forms of sexual behaviour such as homosexuality are now more widely discussed, others such as paedophilia are still largely taboo, and others may require clinical treatment.

This book presents contributions from major international authorities reviewing major themes in variant sexuality, and presenting new research. For example, there is evidence of neurological factors being identifiable in exhibitionists, who can be distinguished from normals on the basis of EEG repsonses to mental tasks. Genetic and evolutionary arguments are presented for the preponderance of paraphilia in males. Freudian and psychoanalytic theories are shown to have limited scientific explanatory power. These and other topics are reviewed in a book that should interest psychologists, biologists and psychiatrists in particular, as well as others fascinated by the social, behavioural and biological aspects of sexuality.

VARIANT SEXUALITY: RESEARCH AND THEORY

Edited by GLENN D. WILSON

CROOM HELM
London & Sydney

© 1987 Glenn D. Wilson
Croom Helm Ltd, Provident House, Burrell Row,
Beckenham, Kent BR3 1AT
Croom Helm Australia, 44-50 Waterloo Road,
North Ryde, 2113, New South Wales

British Library Cataloguing in Publication Data

Variant sexuality: research and theory
   1. Sexual deviation
   I. Wilson, Glenn, *1942–*
   306.7'7   HQ71

   ISBN 0-7099-3698-2

Phototypeset by Sunrise Setting, Torquay, Devon
Printed and bound in Great Britain
by Billing & Sons Limited, Worcester.

Contents

Contributors

Alex Comfort (MA, MB, BCh. Cantab. DSc, DCH Lond.) was formerly head of the MRC Group on Aging, University College, London and is now Adjunct Professor at the UCLA Neuropsychiatric Institute. His books include; *Practice of Geriatric Psychiatry*, *Sexual Problems of Disability*, *Reality and Empathy*, and the best-selling *Joy of Sex*.

Arthur W. Epstein (AB, MD Colombia) is Professor of Psychiatry and Neurology at Tulane University School of Medicine, New Orleans. A past-president of the Society of Biological Psychiatry, he is currently president-elect of the American Academy of Psychoanalysis.

Pierre Flor-Henry (MB, ChB, MD Edin., Acad. DPM, FRC Psych., CSPQ Psych) is Director of Admission Services and Clinical Professor at Alberta Hospital Psychiatric Treatment Centre, Edmonton, and an international expert on cerebral asymmetry and EEG diagnosis.

Raymond E. Goodman (MSc Salford, MRCS, LRCP, D.Obst, RCOG, MRCGP, C.Biol., MIBiol, London) is Specialist in Community Services and Psychosexual Therapist in the Salford District, Manchester. A member of the Institute of Psychosexual Medicine (London) and the Society for the Scientific Study of Sex (New York), Dr. Goodman has written extensively on the biological basis of sex.

Christopher C. Gosselin (BSc, MSc Chemistry, BSc PhD. Psychology, London) is a free-lance researcher and writer on human sex variations and difficulties. He has written many journal articles and book chapters on these topics and is co-author (with Glenn Wilson) of *Sexual Variations: Fetishism, Transvestism and Sadomasochism*.

Paul Kline (BA Reading, Dip.Ed. Swansea, MEd. Aberdeen, PhD, DSc Manchester) is Professor of Psychometrics at Exeter University. He is author of many articles and books, including *Fact and Fantasy in Freudian Theory* and *Personality Measurement and Theory*.

Reuben A. Lang (MSc Calgary, PhD London) is a forensic psychologist working in the Sex Offenders Programme at Alberta Hospital, Edmonton. Publications include studies of the measurement of sexual fantasy and a monograph on phases of recovery from depression.

Ron Langevin (PhD Toronto) is Senior Research Psychologist and Associate Professor at the Clarke Institute of Psychiatry, University of Toronto. A prolific researcher on sex deviation, his books include: *Sexual Strands* and *Erotic Preference, Gender Identity and Aggression in Men*.

Václav Pinkava (M Phil, PhD. Prague) previously practised as a clinical psychologist in Czechoslovakia and Britain and is now a free-lance writer and Honorary Research Fellow in The Department of Medicine, Kings College, London. A pioneer of computer applications in abnormal psychology, he is author of *Introduction to Logic for Systems Modelling*.

Frederick L. Whitam (BA Millsaps, AM, PhD Indiana) is Professor of Sociology at Arizona State University. A member of the International Academy of Sex Research he has conducted field work on variant sexuality in several different cultures and is author (with R.M. Mathy) of *Male Homosexuality in Four Societies: Brazil, Guatemala, The Philippines, and The United States*.

Glenn D. Wilson (BA, MA Canterbury, PhD London, FBPsS) is Senior Lecturer in Psychology at The Institute of Psychiatry, University of London. His writings on sex differences and deviations include: *Love and Instinct, The Psychology of Sex* (with H.J. Eysenck) and *Love and Attraction: An International Conference* (with M. Cook).

Preface

'There's nowt so queer as folk' is an observation that applies in the field of sexual behaviour as well as any. Newspapers abound in tales of eminent politicians who are whipped by women in their lunch hour and respectable clergymen who are dismissed for interfering with choirboys. These are intelligent men, who otherwise seem rational and well-adjusted, and who know what they stand to lose by discovery. Then why do they do it? Sexual proclivities are as compulsive as they appear absurd, and this is what makes them so interesting to the behavioural scientist. Curiosity alone might be sufficient reason for studying them, but there is more.

Some deviations, such as the tendency to get excited by high-heeled shoes or the urge to snatch spectacles off the faces of women in the street, might seem trivial or even laughable. But others, such as the ritual slashing of women in the stomach so as to create a wound reminiscent of the vagina or killing a succession of teenage boys in order to have sex with fresh corpses, are far from amusing — they are among the most horrific crimes known to human society. It is impossible to escape the impression that there is some kind of continuum between minor fetishistic and sadomasochistic 'kinks' and some of the ghastly serial crimes that culminate from an escalating chain of sexual fantasy and acting out. This is why the understanding of these phenomena is so important to clinical and forensic practitioners. Although many forms of sexual behaviour previously regarded as perverted have been legitimised in recent decades, there is bound to be a limit to the process.

In compiling this book I have not sought comprehensive coverage of the field. Rather, I have invited contributions from selected international experts who, in my view, have something new and important to say. The ten chapters are all original writings that update the author's ideas and that represent the leading edge of theory and research into sexual deviation. I make no apology about the fact that they are concerned almost exclusively with male sexuality, since deviation in this sphere is as much a male preserve as certain bars and clubs.

In Chapter 1, Alex Comfort discusses some issues of definition and 'diagnosis' with respect to variant sexuality and shows how sexual behaviour must be understood in the context of its meaning for the individual. While some behaviours are restrictive, distressing and unacceptable, others that have been viewed as pathological are better regarded as recreational, creative, expressive, and 'magical'.

Raymond Goodman (Chapter 2) traces the evolution of sexuality from bacteria to humans, showing the important role of chromosomes, genes, hormones, neurotransmitters and other biological factors in the determination of sexual behaviour, both normal and aberrant.

Pierre Flor-Henry (Chapter 3) considers the evidence for the involvement of neurological factors in deviant sexuality and presents new evidence that exhibitionists in particular can be distinguished from normal persons on the basis of EEG responses to standard mental tasks.

My own contribution (Chapter 4) examines sexuality in the light of ethological principles such as imprinting and dominance hierarchies, concluding that many of the facts concerning the paraphilias, most notably their male preponderance, can best be understood in these terms.

In Chapter 5, Václav Pinkava outlines some observations of he and his Czechoslovakian colleagues that led him to apply the mathematical theory of logical nets to sexual variation. Consistent with other authors in this volume (especially Comfort, Epstein and myself), he believes that distortions of innate and imprinted patterns of behaviour are an important basis of paraphilia and goes on to show how these can be modelled by computer.

Arthur Epstein (Chapter 6) discusses fetishism in the light of observations of similar behaviour in non-human primates, focussing on the characteristics of objects that attract fetishistic interest and the social experiences that render animals fetish-prone.

Since Freud and the psychoanalysts are so widely believed to have contributed important theories of sexual deviation, I invited Paul Kline to assess their current status in the light of the many empirical studies that have been inspired by them. His systematic review (Chapter 7) shows the difficulties that are encountered in testing Freudian theory scientifically and he concludes that that results so far are 'disappointing'.

Frederick Whitam (Chapter 8) compares samples of homosexuals and lesbians in the US, Philippines and Brazil, noting similarities in frequencies of occurrence, life style and behaviour that suggest to him a biological rather than social explanation. While his work with homosexual men has been reported previously, his cross-cultural comparison of lesbians has not.

Ron Langevin and Reuben Lang (Chapter 9) question the validity of the concept of 'courtship disorders' by examining the correlations between voyeurism, exhibitionism, obscene calls, toucherism, and rape. Some overlapping features are found, but also important differences, and the empirical evidence for various theories is reviewed.

Finally, Christopher Gosselin (Chapter 10) returns to a theme of Alex Comfort's, that an anthropological study of sadomasochistic practices that takes account of their meaning to the individuals involved is essential to full understanding. Specifically, he shows how s/m partners arrive at implicit 'contracts' that enhance their relationship.

I believe that these ten chapters cover the most significant developments in the understanding of variant sexuality to have emerged in recent years. The reader is left to judge to what extent the problem has been 'cracked' by these authors and how much mystery remains.

Glenn D. Wilson

1

Deviation and Variation

Alex Comfort

Psychiatry, like its predecessor moral theology, has generated much smoke over the issue of sexual deviance. Some of the most evident clinical expressions of this are now enshrined in the Diagnostic and Statistical Manual (DSM-3). Such a classification, which goes back to Krafft-Ebing, has been outdistanced in regard to clinical significance. Most of us now ask, at the practical level, not 'is this behaviour normal?' but rather 'what does this behaviour signify for this client? Is it reinforcing or handicapping?' and, of course, 'is the behaviour socially tolerable?'

This is a very different approach from Krafft-Ebing's tendency to characterise any behaviour he did not personally enjoy as a disease: we recognise that large and compulsive variations of emphasis, sex object, and arousing circumstances exist; we assess them, hopefully, without agitation, and help the patient to do the same. The biological extraordinariness of the instability of human sex-object formation tends to pass us by. Psychoanalysis was eager (a little too eager) to give a comprehensive origin for such variations. Biology, which is experimentally sophisticated over the formation of responses in lower animals, has still not really come to grips with the human system. Fascinating it certainly is — trigger responses of the lock-and-key type occur in humans, but when they occur in this form they are almost always unusual and present from an extremely early age. Gender perception alone — an issue far more fundamental than specific releasers — is complicated in humans not only by the potential to respond sexually to both sexes but by phenomena such as trans-vestitism and trans-sexualism. Faced with these, we have remarkably little hard evidence on how they come about.

It is clinically important that the psychiatrist, the physician and the sex counsellor make themselves familiar with the natural history of sexual variation and develop some personal criteria to distinguish variation from 'deviation' — meaning by this a degree of idiosyncracy that is symptomatic of something, that is causing interference with function, or that is socially intolerable or dangerous, and accordingly calls for intervention. Compulsive interest is probably not a sufficient criterion, since all sexual behaviour is at a certain level compulsive — compulsive, limiting idiosyncracy is a better test. In the final resort one should consider what role the behaviour plays in the patient's life style, whether it is a resource or a handicap, and whether the patient desires to be rid of it. One must also distinguish between behaviours that spring fully armed from the head of the patient and preoccupy him, and behaviours that are experimental, acquired from fashion, or tried at the instance of others: all these causes of variation exist, and I shall try to document some of them here.

Medical counselling has a rather bad record in dealing with unfamiliar manifestations in the sexual field (and even with familiar ones like masturbation) and much of this embarrassing record springs, and continues to spring, from lack of street wisdom — leading to gnomic remarks such as the statement that 'attempted autofellatio is diagnostic of schizophrenia' (a notion that would not survive a candid discussion with unschizophrenic schoolboys, most of whom attempt it but find it arduous or impossible). One also learns that psychodynamics can be real without being explanatory — most significant sexual behaviours hang on biological pegs.

One can also derive a certain amount of information from comparative anthropology and history: the prize offered by Helio-gabalus for a new and original deviation is still unclaimed after two millennia. There are behaviours of medical significance that appear to surface suddenly, however, and of which there is no comparative record. Extensive intrarectal manipulation in homosexuals ('fisting') is a case in point, important because it may have surgical and epidemiological effects. Is it a new behaviour spread by sexual fashion, e.g. in the San Francisco gay community, or was it always there, but undocumented because of the secrecy that was enforced on all homosexual behaviour between men? In cultures in which homosexuality was explicit, as in the epigrams of Martial, there is no mention of such a practice. One may assume that it is indeed new and expect new medical problems to arise from it.

The physician's sources of information are those of any human naturalist; direct discussion with patients, and if he has the courage and opportunity, direct observation, are the best. Failing these there is literature (popular and scientific — both these sources are potentially misleading). Much psychiatric classification is based on people with major problems who come for assistance, and on relative naiveté about the folklore of sex. Kinsey-type surveys are better, but give no indication of the significance, value or complications of the behaviours they describe, while rash classification of 'deviants' has been with us since Krafft-Ebing.

It is instructive, in regard to prevalence, that nearly all the off-diagonal sexual preferences and behaviours are now capable of generating, and therefore presumably sustaining, expensive and well-printed magazines. These cover everything from texture fetishes and shaved genitalia to paedophilia. Whether they play any exemplary part in popularising particular behaviours, rather than confirming pre-existing fantasies and giving them printed sanction, is doubtful. Pornography is a showcase, as it were, of the range of human preoccupations, but an unreliable index of the significance of the behaviours themselves — pornographers try to cover as many bases as possible (and sometimes give the impression of attempting to live up to psychiatric expectations by concentrating on very hostile male fantasies). By contrast the less-professional, cyclostyled productions of sexual hobbyists tend to convey a far more accurate picture of how the unusual preoccupation must feel from inside. The deviations that are most actively sanctioned and promoted in print with probable social effects are those that we traditionally do not class as deviations, such as obsessive sexual competitiveness and depersonalisation, together with gender-role fads of various kinds. This, however, is something that popular literature has always done. Whether the irresponsible cast is more objectionable than its predecessor, the moralistic, is open to argument. Out-of-culture *behaviours* as sexual techniques are beginning to appear in this popular literature, but in a very muted or coded form (sometimes under the guise of health advice — is swallowed semen fattening?)

It is a real, if humiliating, fact, that if we had been wise to what people actually do, we should have refrained from nearly all the interpretative medical comment that exists in the literature. At the same time, definite disorders of sexual expression exist (and are not removed by the political pretence that they are not disorders). They distress those who exhibit them and their potential partners, they are often very difficult to treat by approaches based on existing theoretical models, and in many cases the clinician will have the overwhelming though unproveable conviction that what he is dealing with is a neurological or biological problem, difficult to pin down because of the totality of its interaction with the patient's experience, but still basic to what has gone wrong. Some anomalies are wholly idiosyncratic — others are gross exaggerations of some component normally detectable in the spectrum of typical sexual behaviours, which appears to hypertrophy during the developmental process. In others, such as trans-sexualism, the patient's consciousness of an inborn anomaly carries more conviction than most going medical theories about its origin. What, meanwhile, do we make of the gentleman who published, at his own expense, books describing how, by tight corsetting, he got his wife's waist down to a minute size, and his fury when the doctor tried to discontinue the practice during pregnancy — 'all our achievement would have been lost'? What, for that matter, do we make of the wife's acquiescence? Few cases of obsession are luckily so extreme, but almost equally severe deformations of the female body have been socially promoted in some societies. What is the relation?

The Freudian view is that these anomalies arise as a by-product of the unusual childhood situation in humans. The Panglossian view is that if they are there, they must be in some way adaptive in terms of indirect selection, however reproductively disadvantageous to the individual a preference for boots or choirboys over fertile females may be.

We can see that a number of the behaviours which, in a pure culture, appear as 'deviant', are larvally present in the general population. The clinical 'deviants', however, look more like subgroups with special factors operating than simply the tail of a Gaussian distribution. There is *en masse* a roughly Gaussian distribution of homosexual traits in men: the wholly homosexual population is probably multifarious in origin and includes some individuals showing learned responses, but there is also a subgroup who have been solidly homosexual *ab initio*. Most well-developed fetishes have existed as long as the power of recall. It seems to me that unravelling the biology of these phenomena might open far wider neuropsychiatric vistas than those required to counsel people whose behaviours come up for medical advice.

The subject has therefore a fundamental importance going beyond both its psychiatric and its popular interest.

What — if it existed anywhere in the Edenic state, without any pressures from mores, peer groups or busybodies — would be the 'free-running' spectrum of human sexual activities? There are no such populations. Modern California, where I have done fieldwork, is anthropologically unusual, however, in containing a generation of candystore 'trisexuals' (who will try anything). The behaviour of this population is loudly explicit, and can even, with stamina, be inspected 'on the hoof'. Hardliners of all stripes would probably describe this subpopulation as deviant anyway: far more probably it represents an exaggerated version of what people do in private, or would do if they dared. It can be regarded with suitable precaution as a 'free-running' picture of sexual inclination, biased a little by peer pressure towards experimentation. At the same time, people do not persist in experimentation they find unrewarding.

One finds here that sexual deviation is real, i.e. that there are individuals whose releasers are basically unusual. The characteristics that define 'deviation' in this sense are that the atypical response is compulsive, that it substitutes largely or wholly for a more comprehensive sexuality, and that it cannot be cultivated experimentally or transferred to the general pool of sexual behaviours, except occasionally by conditioning in a partner. It resembles the lock-and-key response typical of instinctual patterns in animals and looks, to the psychobiologist, like a disorder of imprinting. Genuinely sadomasochistic behaviour patterns, when they are expressed in sexual activity, are usually also expressed in the subject's entire life style: these seem to be better candidates for a psychodynamic origin, though one cannot ignore the cerebral proximity of aggressive and arousal pathways, or the fact that, as Stoller (1976) has suggested, they tend to 'bleed over' in humans and work together. There is probably a great deal of phylogenetic complexity here, which accounts for the fine balance — the child who misreads the Primal Scene as aggressive can hardly be blamed, if the performance he witnesses is of concert standard, though a great many children, here and elsewhere, are exposed to the Primal Scene unscathed. American society also reinforces 'sadomasochistic' expressions, and makes the balance still more precarious, by containing a great deal of nonsexual, free-floating anger and dominance. At the same time, one has very little difficulty in

5

deciding at clinical interview if one is dealing with a clinical sadomasochist.

The one thing sexual deviants are not, however, is experimental. They are not 'trisexuals', but what the old French madames would have called 'des spécialistes'. If the speciality is not antisocial, the main justification for therapy is that it is limiting (and prevents the incorporation of sexuality into partner relationships – a major loss). What the dedicated rubber fetishist has is, effectively, a rather disabling and isolating hobby. By contrast the hardy recreationalists, while they incorporate behaviours that medicine has described as deviant, use them or drop them purely on a basis of whether or not they turn out to be enjoyable, either in the sense of increasing arousal or in the sense of functioning as play-therapy. In this group the repertoire of the sexually well-dressed individual includes oral sex (about which oceans of psychiatric ink were incautiously expended by the psychodynamic Ancestors before it was recognised as near-universal in mammals), anal experimentation, pseudoaggressive devices such as 'bondage' (a popular fantasy almost universally lumped by textbooks with sadomasochism), dressing up — but only rarely the compulsive range of object-specific behaviours. Incorporation of a third party into the couple can lead to bisexual experimentation: women tend to find this undisturbing, while men, under the persisting influence of homophobia, find it much less acceptable. Even if sexual activity between men is acceptable, affectional expression, such as kissing, is not. The growth of conscious attempts to 'explore the homosexual option' has now been nipped in the bud by the AIDS epidemic.

One can argue how far sophisticates among Californians, or among the Romans whose behaviours are referred to by Martial, can be treated as norms, let alone as socially desirable models. We do not classify irresponsibility, or for that matter compulsive prudery, as deviations, though they deserve a niche in DSM-3 because of their repercussions on the patient and others. California does, however, provide a population willing, and sometimes overwilling, to talk about its activities, and even to permit direct observation. This in itself is important — one cannot assess a sexual behaviour unless one ascertains exactly what is done and how it is done. Most normative literature in this area, it pays to recall, has been written on the basis of interviews with the disturbed by authors who never witnessed an act of sexual intercourse except possibly in a mirror — a very odd situation in the description of what is, in fact, human natural history. As with the nonsense written by our forebears about masturbation, nonplaying psychiatric coaches suffered, like their clients, from the convention of privacy — one that applies nowhere else in observational medicine.

The observable and sexually garrulous populations available today have to be approached with due psychiatric caution, but do, I think, give us a certain amount of evidence as to the way in which the off-diagonal behaviours traditionally called 'deviant' are used by less-vocal and more conventional couples (and will be so increasingly, given the availability of books that describe them).

Literature and counselling do now encourage sexual fantasy, verbalised if not acted-out: it has also become clear that patients brought up in a psychiatric culture, being profoundly unhappy with behaviours they desire or enjoy but do not fully understand, put disabling psychiatric labels on them. Of individuals who professed, sometimes defiantly, to being for instance 'into s and m', relatively few were in fact expressing the psychodynamics that we as professionals would associate with DSM-3:302/83 and 84 — the leading overdeterminants in the ritualised behaviour were very various, with physical arousal as the most important, and non-aggressive components such as trust, mutual pleasuring, excitement, and even magical ordeal coming before aggression-submission: the analogy to childhood play with the added reinforcement of orgasm was evident, especially when the behaviours were actually observed. The rituals used were sometimes spontaneous, and represented the fantasies of one partner (usually but not by any means always the male) but they were equally often tried on the recommendation of others and persisted in, or dropped, according to whether 'Tiggers do or don't like' the effects produced. Noticeably, object-fetishes were never acquired or learned in this way. When socially unscheduled behaviours figure in counselling, it is usually because the partners have read that they are 'abnormal', or one of them is put off by an activity, such as oral sex, that the other relishes.

This experience fits rather well with Maslow's (1942) idea that experimentation and what used to be called polymorphous-perverse sexuality correlate better with high dominance and a recreationally relaxed view of partner relations than with low dominance, neurosis or disturbance: counselling now proceeds on this assumption. It takes the line that off-diagonal sex behaviours, provided they are playful, non-dangerous, not antisocial, and reinforcing to both parties, are a part of mature sexual expression. Intervention is needed when they disturb one or both parties, and usually takes the form of reassurance. It is very specifically needed, however, when a behaviour variant is compulsive, limiting, stereotyped, antisocial or associated with deviant nonsexual behaviour. It is also clear that of sexual overemphases that fall into this category, some are exaggerations of universal human potentials (bisexuality, sexual pseudoaggression or submission) that can be reinforcing in small doses, while others (major fetishes, major gender disorders) are imprinting-disorders *sui generis*. Paedophilia, which greatly agitates America at the moment because of its social effects and its apparent prevalence, may be an imprinting disorder aggravated by low dominance. Rape, another grave issue in America and Britain, together with marital violence, has less to do with sexuality than with nonsexual anger and frustration. Exhibitionism, which is in its proper context an agreeable part of relationships between lovers, can similarly be inflated psychodynamically into a disorder. Moreover, deviant emphases, in their DSM-3 sense, tend to hang together in clusters, suggesting that when the mechanism of imprinting is experientially or neurologically upset, more than one off-diagonal 'releaser' may become set in concrete. This biological view describes the Freudian formulation — that deviations involve the avoidance of 'normal' coition — in different terms. Our choice of paradigm may well determine how we address these problems in treatment, though they are commonly hard to modify, either by depth psychology or by behaviour therapy. Predominant homosexuality in both sexes, although to most of us it seems almost certain to have neuroendocrine determinants, involves at the practical level nonresponse to the opposite sex rather than potential response to the same sex, which appears to be general in man, and perhaps in primates overall. How far this is a hardware problem and how far a software problem probably differs from case to case: one clinically unhelpful feature today is the insistence of society, and of those whose homosexual preoccupation is strong, that one must join one of two teams, gay or straight. The decision is commonly taken too early by the client, and is then self-reinforcing.

While DSM-3 gives a clinically adequate description of

unusual emphases, based on natural history, the biologist would be more inclined to a rather different division of exceptional or idiosyncratic behaviours. One group would cover imprinting disorders — in this case preoccupation with and erotic investment in textures, objects or behaviours is (a) excessive or exclusive, (b) required for potency, (c) preoccupying, (d) identifiably present from an extremely early age, or (e) not acquired by learning or by experimentation. The matter imprinted may be idiosyncratic (safety pins; Mitchell, Falconer and Hill, 1954) or something that is eroticised by most humans (hair, feet, skin texture, compression, restraint, etc.) at a non-exclusive level. Another group would include 'programmed plays' which chime with personality traits that are also expressed socially and are in consequence highly over-determined: 'sadomasochistic' behaviours are the most general example in this group, and these behaviours can be learned or acquired, especially if they fit the overall life-script of the acquirer. If we place imprinting deviations in the temporal lobe, which seems a reasonable evidential guess, these other behaviours exploit the adjacency of sexual and hostile arousal in the subcortical brain. Thirdly, we find purely acquired behaviours that presumably agree with the user's overall personality, but have been specifically learned. One might place here the interplay between fetish and fashion: corsets and masks were formerly fashionable and general, but are now seen as the materials of fetishistic emphasis; boots and leather suits, formerly fetishistic, are now fashionable. One notable omission from this classification is cross-dressing, which seems to belong in a category of its own, but appears very frequently along with a batch of other, more specifically imprinted, disorders. Often it seems to reflect the attempt to create an imaginary partner by identification, rather as the Lord Shiva created one by dividing himself into male and female, Ardhanarishvara.

The population I have studied was poor in major imprinting disorders: they were sexual experimentalists, not singleminded *spécialistes*. Such may well be locked into a hardware problem — in Mitchell, Falconer and Hill's case the safety-pin fetish was excised along with a temporal lobe focus. My classificatory experience has been chiefly with the second group ('programmed plays') and the third, behaviours acquired by learning, experiment, and persistence in sexual modes of expression that proved rewarding. The main observational lesson has been the bluntness

9

of conventional psychodynamic explanations in dealing with overdetermined behaviours that are physically effective in heightening arousal, and the consequent inutility of interpretative terms such as 'orality' or 'sadomasochism' if we treat them not as rough classes of overt behaviour, but also as implying a common significance for those behaviours in all cases.

Learned sexual behaviours are like political philosophies — in lean times they are kept alive by the preoccupied, who cannot function without them: given appropriate conditions, they may be experimented with by the unpreoccupied and persisted in if they work. The only unrewarding sexual behaviours in which people assiduously persist are those prescribed by moralists.

It is necessary, in a period of neuroamines and hormones, to remind residents on a psych. programme that while classical psychodynamics are not always therapeutically very helpful, they are still based on astute observation of human natural history, so that sexual style, not surprisingly, echoes personal style. What is new — apart from the growing information from ethology, neurochemistry and neurology, is the practical awareness of therapists of the play-value of sexual behaviour in the discharge of unacceptables, a form of treatment we cannot re-create in groups but which patients often discover for themselves. The one thing that the genuinely deviant person, as defined by DSM-3, cannot be is playful. His nearest approach is in becoming a preoccupied sexual hobbyist, like the collector of matchstick models or fishing flies. If motivated he may be enabled to break out of the imprinted preoccupation, but it is usually hard sledding all round. Most of the trouble we have had from the definition of deviance as against variation comes from our own professional virginity, our personal anxieties, and our lack of a sense of proportion. Sexuality between unanxious lovers contains large therapeutic resources of its own for containing unbiddables such as gender rivalry, low dominance, and childhood-based deformations of self-image, which we can use and encourage by reassurance but not emulate by any other psychiatric intervention. One is tempted to go on and assert that this is its programmed function, and that the large variability of human sexual expression is an evolved compensation for some of the problems created by infantile sexuality, a very odd biological phenomenon in its own right (Comfort 1960). Among the happily sexual, behaviour will vary from the very conventional to the very experimental — counselling has no brief for either so long as the result is mutually happy and satisfying — when it is not, our role is investigation, encouragement, permission, and the detection of more serious dysfunctions in the expressive mechanism.

At the biological and psychobiological level, there remains a great deal to learn about the diversity of human sexual releasers, and the interaction of experience and reinforcement with neurochemistry, temporal lobe function and 'windows' of imprinting. Evidence of true imprinting in humans would be significant, since we usually associate it with precocial rather than altricial animals. At the clinical level, the main risk we run is in underestimating the extent of overdetermination in behaviours and the resourcefulness of humans in adapting biological traits to symbolic and psychotherapeutic uses. The instability of human sex-object formation looks disadaptive in terms of ordinary evolutionary genetics — presumably, in accordance with Dr Pangloss, it has to be adaptive in other ways — the human capacity for male-male interaction may have served to counterpoise male-male competition for mates, for example. One sees male-male affectional bonding and ritualised mounting between males as a dominance-submission signal, in primates. In fact, human 'homosexuality' may well have more to do with restes of dominance behaviour than with sex, a not un-Freudian conclusion given that father-son competition is a special case of dominance behaviour in an animal that recognises gender by primary, not secondary, sex characters. Nobody suffers from beard envy in psychoanalytic practice.

Yet another layer that we need to consider is that addressed by the anthropologist. We do not usually think of sexual behaviours as 'religious' — rather, for historical reasons, the reverse, given the Judaeo-Christian background. The tendency has rather been to interpret magical or religious activities reductively in terms of sexuality: thus we tend to dismiss askesis as masochistic, etc. This is an example of tunnel vision. Listening to case histories of unusual sexual behaviours with an anthropological ear open, it becomes clear that some patients, when making love, are in these terms shamanising or practising *tapas* (yogic ordeal), using techniques that are shamanic or yogic, including ordeal, body-image confusion and even the wearing of masks as enhancers of orgasm (Eliade, 1964; Comfort, 1979). Bearing in mind that human religion is programmed around dissociative or ecstatic experiences at this level, and that orgasm is the only dissociative-

11

fusional experience widely available in our culture other than the use of drugs, this is hardly remarkable to an anthropologist, though non-Jungian psychiatry might find the idea novel. The yogi, who wants to implode the illusion of identity, and the masochist, who, according to Reich, wants to demolish the body image — in other words, to burst — are engaged in similar projects.

The 'variant' behaviours that figure in the practice of non-disturbed, non-DSM-3 clients include behaviours that are potentially universal but only recently decriminalised (oral and occasionally anal sex, masturbation, occasional bisexuality), pseudoaggressive behaviours (struggling, teasing, physical restraint of one partner by another: in some affectionate couples biting, scratching and slapping during arousal, as described in Hindu erotology, can be sufficiently vigorous to call for a word of caution, since pain responses are modified by arousal), and charismatic behaviours ('group' sex, for example), which are both human fantasies and, in some cultures, religious rituals. Aside from these, one occasionally encounters shared interest in even less typical activities such as urolagnia, which seem to represent reactivation of phylogenetic restes which, like the human pheromone system, are still there but in desuetude. Working out what this behaviour means to this patient is accordingly a daunting interpretative exercise, and an offputting one for the client if he is encouraged by the counsellor to attempt it. We would do well to recognise the range of possible over-determinants and keep quiet about them — what matters to the couple is that their bonding is enhanced. Examination of *why* precisely one enjoys football is equally complex and likely to spoil the game. We do not want to enhance the reputation of counsellors for making all the best turn-ons into hang-ups. Minor fetishes, if only at the level of preferring one complexion, or long or short hair in a partner, are universal in men (few really 'like them all' except at a level of specifically genital fetishism, which is itself a restrictive emphasis). When they include articles of clothing, etc. they may upset women — these being almost wholly a male phenomenon — who think that 'he is in love with gloves, boots, etc. rather than with me'. Prostitutes are occupationally sensitive to these idiosyncrasies of taste, and wives or lovers can be reassured that by knowing what he likes they can become invincible. One needs only to watch for the preoccupied individual in which the partialism tends to grow and displace relational sex.

Pseudoaggressive plays can disturb both a partner and the counsellor, the latter even when they are shared. Rather than looking at theoretical psychodynamics (which may well, of course, be present) it pays to listen carefully to what patients say about their conscious motives: a psychodynamically attractive behaviour that actually interferes with orgasm is likely to be persisted in only by the preoccupied, not by Joe and Jane Blow in search of kicks.

My own research and clinical experience with classical deviations has been limited. As an example of a sexual technique with both types of appeal, which is also relatively new to the polite repertoire, I have studied so-called 'bondage' or the playing of 'restraint games', in which one partner ties up the other with greater or less elaboration and then excites them, as it were, solo. The original aim was to determine what to say about this in a popular counselling book: it appeared with surprising frequency not only as a fantasy in both sexes, but as a 'required' skill among sexual sophisticates comparable to proficiency in oral sex, and a frequent ingredient of marital histories. One needed at the very least to ascertain whether the performance was dangerous as popularly current. Literature was of little help, lumping 'bondage' holus bolus with sadomasochism, confusing it with sexual servitude (*Hörigkeit*), or drawing cases from a population of very disturbed multideviants who were headed for trouble in any event (Littman and Swearingen, 1972). Pornography took the same view, emphasising humiliation or domination of a partner, and treating the transaction as overtly hostile and sadistic.

It proved rather easy to secure testimony on this sexual exercise, because users did not consider it embarrassing. The 'bondage' routine is a definite situational fetish for some individuals and a strong preference for others (of both sexes), but a high proportion of witnesses seemed to be incorporating it into a varied sexual repertoire as one more resource. For these, the physical effects (of Reik's 'suspense factor', of muscular eroticism) are experienced as primary and any psychosymbolic goodies as incidental. While pornography, to the anger of feminists, plays up an association with rape fantasies and a deal of hostility towards women, putting them always on the receiving end, in popular practice 'bondage' is a widespread female fantasy, in both the active and the passive role, surpassed only by ideal-partner fantasies, while the passive works equally well on the male, who loses traditional control over the tempo of arousal (and is incidentally relieved of performance anxiety). Humiliation and domination figured most often in the self-description of couples who had been reading psychiatric interpretations of their behaviour. Experiments with 'bondage' were variously intuitive, learned or introduced on the recommendation of others: while the result is potentially sadomasochistic if one cares to play it in that way, the same applies to sexual behaviour generally, and most practising couples I observed or interviewed were only minimally aroused by charades of domination, though women seemed to find satisfaction both in exaggeration of male control and in the opportunity to be the aggressor party. We were left with a few situational fetishists, a few obviously disturbed sadomasochists, and a large number of experimentally minded people who had discovered a new kind of foreplay.

Police authorities find 'bondage' alarming and selectively attack pornography depicting it, not only because of the aggressive tone of the published matter and the obvious risk if psychopaths become involved, but also because they associate it with accidental deaths. Some of these have occurred from carelessness: others involve fetishists who tie or chain themselves and are unable to escape. The vast majority of such accidents actually involve erotic strangulation or hanging — a common cause of accidental death in children, adolescents and multideviant adults, which is a serious cause of concern but has little to do with the erotisation of restraint.

The interest of this observationally neglected behaviour, apart from the obvious interaction of physical and psychodynamic overdeterminants, is its apparent novelty — not, perhaps, as a compulsive fantasy, but as a sexual technique: it is absent from most classical erotologies, and its surfacing much resembles the interaction of fetishisms and fashions, with the difference that fashion is not directly involved in the enhancement of orgasm. As to pseudoaggressive behaviours, the most popular in past European erotologies has been 'discipline', i.e. erotic flagellation, recognised long ago by Meibomius in his *De usu flagrorum*. In contrast to 'bondage', this behaviour has had a formative influence on psychiatric ideas of deviance culminating in Freud's '*A child is being beaten*'. At one time in the nineteenth century it was unquestionably fashionable. It is now relatively uncommon, though it persists in pornography and among the obsessed. The change of status reflects the fact that it is no longer recommended by word of mouth in sexual folklore. In Meibom's time it was actually prescribed as a remedy for impotence, not only by prostitutes but by the medical profession. It may or may not have owed a Victorian and eighteenth century upswing to the conditioning effects of child beating, but it has figured consistently in erotologies since Roman times. Much of the psychodynamic doctrine of sadomasochism has been shaped by this example, in which arousal is specifically conditioned by a pain stimulus. The physiology of muscular restraint, as well as its symbolism, are different, though the natural history of the behaviours has been confused by the use (chiefly by advertising prostitutes) of the phrase 'bondage and discipline' ('b and d'), implying the use of both.

'Bondage' appears in Chinese and Japanese erotic literature but not, until quite recently, in our own. One might connect this with the reification of the sex struggle in our society: actually it seems to owe its current popularity to the fact that the available pornography of a whole generation of American men was produced by two preoccupied bondage enthusiasts, Irving Klaw and John William Coutts, who 'got by' because their photographs and drawings of bondage situations were decent in the eyes of the law, while coition was not. The encounters between Coutts (who signed his work 'John Willie') and the censorship deserve a sociopsychiatric study on their own. His photographs, and an extremely funny high-camp cartoon cycle dealing with the Justine-like misfortunes of Sweet Gwendoline, in which Coutts caricatured himself as the moustachioed villain who repeatedly captured her, were not indecent. Censors, on the other hand, could perceive that they were in some way sexual, but did not know quite what to do with them. In the ensuing game of hide-and-seek, Coutts came as close as his fetishistic preoccupation permitted to a playfulness that he could not achieve in his own sexual relations. He also introduced a kind of style and aesthetic into the elaborate restraint-postures that he devised.

It is typical that out-of-culture sexual techniques originate with the preoccupied (who proselytise to reassure themselves) but it would not have caught on if it did not work, and would not have inspired T-shirts labelled 'John Willie Lives'. Few genuinely deviant behaviours work for non-fetishists, or even, except in fantasy, for the preoccupied themselves. One recalls an insightful cartoon showing a disappointed client and an elderly whore with a whip, who is remarking 'Well, you shouldn't believe everything you read in them books!' Such behaviours work for those they obsess in prospect and retrospect, but often poorly *in articulo*.

From this example one can learn that in order to assess the factors that influence the adoption of a novel or unusual sexual routine, one needs to listen to, and if possible observe, those who use it. A couple who told us they were 'into s and m' were found on enquiry to be quite uninterested in humiliation, guilt or aggression at any overt level. They had been initiated into bondage games by enthusiastic friends and selected the label they gave us as a result of their reading. They did seem to us, however, to make disproportionate use of them. On being asked to analyse the preference, the woman said that she liked the passive role because screaming and struggling enhanced her orgasm (normally they had to be controlled for practical reasons), because she enjoyed the charade of compulsion, and because she could not control the pace of arousal; and the active role because it was the first time she *had* been able to set the pace of arousal herself, without being controlled by the male. It also enabled her to insist on oral stimulation lasting as long as she wanted. The man enjoyed the active role because 'she looked sexy wriggling like that' and the passive because it appeared to him to generalise his sensations ('makes me feel like one big penis') and, incidentally, relieved him of performance anxiety. One could make psychoanalytic hay with this, of course, but the more superficial explanations appeared to have substance, and the couples were enjoying themselves without any signs of maladjustment in nonsexual areas. Sadomasochism seemed to have very little to do with this learned adjustment of sexual play. All sexual behaviours have their psychodynamic component, but they also have to pass the practical test of producing mutual arousal. There have been enthusiasts who interpreted sexual postures in wholly symbolic terms, and rejected the female-superior position as indicative of psychopathology — or in the days of moral theology as 'unnatural' and demeaning to the man.

While heterosexual couples clearly treated 'restraint games' as play, there was also a far more menacing tendency among homosexual men and the 'leather boys' culture to engage in dangerously severe sadomasochistic routines. At least one owner of a San Francisco leather bar spends his time warning his clients to keep this type of activity under the control of common prudence. How far this expresses the tendency of unusual sexual emphases to hang together in clusters, and how far guilt elements, assertion of masculinity, and communication of sexual practices by example, contribute to this sexual subculture requires study. It is clearly very different in motivation from heterosexual playfulness. One patient, dressed in leather and wearing Nazi insignia (which had little political association for him: he was not born by the end of World War Two), aggressively announced himself as a homosexual sadist. Asked what exactly this implied, he said that he cruised in Union Square, picked up submissive gay men, took them home, and subjected them to elaborate fetishistic preparation.

'What do you do then?'
Patient (pianissimo) 'I kiss them .'

In this case the elaborate facade of aggression seemed to be making tenderness towards another man compatible with a macho self-image. In other individuals the initial manic defence was less elaborate and the element of actual cruelty far more alarming. Unlike the heterosexual population, it is far more difficult for the physician-naturalist to study this population from the inside, but it needs to be studied sympathetically if only to minimise a rather evident danger of physical injury.

In heterosexual couples too, psychiatric assessment of an unusual behaviour calls for the awareness that 'it ain't what you do — it's the way that you do it', and the significance of sexual preferences in the context of the patient's personality and style.

Contrast with the matter-of-fact couple described above, another, also self-reported as 'into s and m'. Their sexual routines were very similar, and man and woman alternated in the passive role. But in this case the man had several mistresses whom he systematically humiliated; the woman had had three car accidents in two years and numerous accidental injuries, had been raped by an intruder, and while undergoing surgery to repair damage done by the assault she was persuaded by her lover to have a disfiguring lipectomy performed. When removing a dish from a top shelf she invariably pulled out the bottom item and brought the entire pile of crockery about her ears. Her choice of lovers was equally and consistently unfortunate. In this case our interpretation of the couple's range of preference would be very different. As Maslow said, there are no perverse behaviours, only perverse people: the first couple's playfulness was the second couple's symptomatology.

I pick this particular group of preoccupations because I happen to have studied them: they throw no light on the origins of sexual preference, but they do exhibit a range, from fetishistic compulsion to reinforcing play, and they show the influence of fashion, as well as the tendency of those with unusual preferences to proselytise. This most ingrained deviants cannot do, because a behaviour is only marketable if it actually works.

The biological interest of the unanswered questions that remain concerning the origin of sexual preferences is that more relaxed study, including ethology and neurobiology as well as the traditional psychodynamic approach, will both sharpen our clinical resources in dealing with those that are disabling, and give us a more sophisticated conception of the variety of overdeterminants that can operate. We do well to temper analytic enthusiasm with practicality, and the recognition that for the nondysfunctional sexual variation can be a therapeutic form of play, apt to the animal in which it has evolved. One may suspect that a change of orientation among sexual psychiatrists will alter their classificatory habits, limit the tendency to affix self-adhesive labels, and, if it includes more careful observation and assessment of the part that unusual behaviours play in the patient's overall life system, render us a good deal more helpful and less dangerous to clients than psychiatry has at times been in the past. At the same time, when the play becomes anxious or vicious, impairs relationships, or tends to sterile repetition of a compulsion, we need to recognise the signals and intervene *secundum artem*. In fact, DSM-3's categories cover the clinical signals for such intervention. Physicians encounter sexual behaviours when they go wrong or when they worry the patient or the partner — at the same time 'the physician who deprives patients of useful fantasies should be sued for malpractice' (Kaplan, 1980). Sexual behaviour that is *varied* is rarely clinically abnormal or deviant judged by these standards — an important qualifier in the DSM-3 categorisation is the word 'exclusive'. There is no diagnostic category, however, under which the rich range of constructive and rewarding sexual idiosyncracy can be subsumed, and patient and counsellor made to feel more comfortable about it. Nobody likes to be thought odd.

There remains a fruitful research field in determining experimentally and epidemiologically how exclusive unusual emphases are acquired. They are not simply genetic, but the vulnerability to imprinting might still conceivably be so. Psychodynamics are not to be discounted, but need to be assessed in the light of the capacity of patients to incorporate their responses into a life script, which makes it extremely hard to ascertain whether early experience is primary or a secondary use of material present from other sources. The resources of ethology have still not been fully incorporated here. Object preoccupations are most commonly — in fact, almost exclusively — seen in men, or were until recently. We now begin to see them in women, but the preoccupations involved tend to be situational rather than concrete. Is the difference real or factitious? Work on sexual reassignment (e.g. of intersexes or after mishandled circumcision) is beginning to throw more light on the inherent and learned components of gender identification, but in explaining trans-sexualism we are no better able to produce an investigable theory than those Hindu psychiatrists who attribute them to incomplete deletion of a 'past existence'. The acid test of classical psychodynamics is, or should be, the prospective study, but it is difficult to conduct. In a sense the general decriminalisation of sexual variation removes both clinical pressure to 'alter' the patient and pressure on the investigator to genuflect to social prescription, leaving the field open to more broadly based investigation on a par with the investigation of, say, digestion or immunocompetence. The basic problem is the complexity of humans, who display biology, psychodynamics, and an adaptable capacity to incorporate one into the other. Medicine can now look at this subject without the noises-off that hindered earlier investigation; it is likely to prove widely instructive.

REFERENCES

Comfort, A. (1960) 'Darwin and Freud'. *Lancet, ii*, 107–11
—— (1979) 'Sexual idiosyncrasy — deviation or magic?' *Journal of Operational Psychiatry*, *9* (2), 11–16
—— (1982) '"Bondage" in sexual histories — fantasy and enactment'. *Br. J. Sex. Med.*, *8*, 35–6
Diagnostic and Statistical Manual (1980), 3rd ed., Washington, D.C.: American Psychiatric Association
Eliade, M. (1964) *Shamanic Techniques of Ecstasy*. New York: Bollingnen Foundation
Kaplan, H.S. (1980) (Counselling column in) *Savvy Magazine*, April 1980, p. 66
Littman, R.E. and Swearingen, C. (1972) 'Bondage and suicide.' *Arch.*

Gen. Psychiatry, *33*, 80–5

Maslow, A.H. (1942) 'Selfesteem (dominance feeling) and sexuality in women.' *J. Soc. Psychol.*, *16*, 259–80

Mitchell, W., Falconer, M.A. and Hill, D. (1954) 'Epilepsy with fetishism relieved by temporal lobectomy.' *Lancet*, *ii*, 627–9

Stoller, R.J. (1976) 'Sexual excitement.' *Arch. Gen. Psychiatry*, *33*, 899–909

2

Genetic and Hormonal Factors in Human Sexuality: Evolutionary and Developmental Perspectives

Raymond E. Goodman

'What is precious, is never to forget
The essential delight of the blood drawn from ageless springs
Breaking through rocks in worlds before our earth.

Stephen Spender

BIOLOGICAL ORIGINS

The evolution of sex

Just as the Earth has moved from the centre of the Ptolemaic Universe to the outer edge of an insignificant galaxy in a turbulent universe, so the idea of man and his sexuality as being the apex of creation has likewise had to change. The origin of sex probably lies with the bacteria that arose about 3500 million years ago, some 100 million years before nucleated cells, the 'eukaryocytes' appeared, which eventually were to lead to man himself. Bombarded by ultraviolet light, before earth's protective ozone layer was formed, and short of nutriments, these primordial bacteria adopted a host of frenetic strategies to repair damage and to obtain food to ensure survival. These strategies included uneven fusions, with one cell squirting its genes into another, ingestion of conspecifics — cannibalism — to pool resources, and the evolution of DNA subsystems, in the form of viruses and plasmids, that could be taken into another bacterium and so modify the gene pool, throwing up new combinations to cope with the ever-changing conditions.

Whether sex arose from a common stock or separately in bacteria and eukaryocytes, is not known (see Bell, 1982, for discussion). Eventually, however, eukaryocytes did evolve, and

21

they faced the same environmental problems as had their bacterial predecessors. The earliest protocell, the forerunner of the modern cell, formed as a capsule containing strands of RNA. Once again the problem of dealing with damaged genes had to be overcome. If the organism carried spare genes, this would mean the diversion of precious energy resources, as well as necessitating an increase in size. This latter would make the organism more vulnerable to environmental hazards. To omit to carry such spares could lead to extinction. The most equitable solution adopted was for two such cells to fuse; not only could damaged genes be so repaired, but the resulting daughter cells could exhibit variation, as did their bacterial predecessors, to cope with any unforeseen adversity. Mitotic division created multicellular organisms, and from this process, in various ways, meiosis evolved, which, in animals, led to haploid germ cells. Thus sex became tied to reproduction; each putative parent contributed half the genes of the future individual. So sex in both bacteria and eukaryocytes probably evolved as a means to repair DNA and to offer variation to cope with unforeseen environmental factors (Margulis and Sagan, 1984; Bernstein, Byerly, Hope and Richard, 1984). As multicellular organisms developed, many new problems had to be overcome. One was the necessity to cope with microparasites, i.e. viruses, bacteria, fungi or protozoans. These have shorter generation times than the host and can adapt more quickly. Bremermann (1985) believes that sex in multicellular forms arose as a means of survival, to enable the host to keep ahead of its parasites by the recombination of genes thrown up by sexual fusions. The plasticity of the immune system in higher forms enhances this protection, although occasionally there is a breakthrough and an epidemic results, as in the influenza pandemic earlier this century or in the current outbreak of acquired immune deficiency syndrome (AIDS).

The evolution of the sex chromosomes

The X-chromosome

The whole process of gamete formation, fertilisation and early fetal development holds the key to the understanding of much adult sexuality. Right from the start of gamete formation, males and females differ with regard to chromosomal development. In males, each cell has one normally functioning X-chromosome which, at the start of spermatogenesis, becomes inactivated. In the female, on the other hand, the reverse happens, so that the previously inactive X-chromosome is reactivated as the developing oogonia are formed. Early female embryos, prior to the 8-cell stage, have twice the gene-linked enzyme activity levels as do males of comparable age. After this, the levels in both sexes approach one another, which indicates that the inactivation of one of the female X-chromosomes has occurred. Perhaps it is because so few genes are active in the early blastula that the female can tolerate the high enzyme levels without sustaining any deleterious aneuploidic effects.

The picture is complicated, however, by two factors. First, not all the gene systems on the inactivated X-chromosome are so affected. At least two genes escape this process, these are one coding for steroid sulphatase (STS) and one for the Xg Locus. The former is associated with congenital icthyosis and, on occasions, male hypogonadism, the latter with control of a red blood cell antigen. This escape of certain genes to inactivation goes far back in evolution, to before the time the Eutherians (placental mammals) separated from the Marsupials. Secondly, inactivation of the second X-chromosome does not occur uniformly throughout the whole blastocyst, but occurs in a specific series of steps, which varies from species to species. In Australian marsupials the paternal X-chromosome is preferentially inactivated throughout, whereas in humans the paternal X-chromosome is only preferentially inactivated in those cells that are due to form the extra-embryonic membranes. In those cells destined to form the fetus proper, random inactivation, involving both maternal and paternal X-chromosomes, occurs (Figure 2.1).

The molecular mechanisms for the various stages in X-chromosome inactivation and reactivation are being currently elucidated. For 'initiation' of the process many models have been suggested, of which the hypothesis that describes 'methylation of DNA', under the action of DNA cytosome, into DNA Z, a super-coiled form that spreads down the chromosome, currently seems plausible. There is a 'counting mechanism', as only one X-chromosome per autosomal unit is active, and a 'spreading process', the signal originating from one site on the chromosome then spreads by 'way stations', which amplify it and pass it on. These genes and mechanisms are conserved in mammalian evolution. These are current models for maintenance of inacti-

Figure 2.1: The cycle of X-chromosome activation and inactivation in the human female embryo

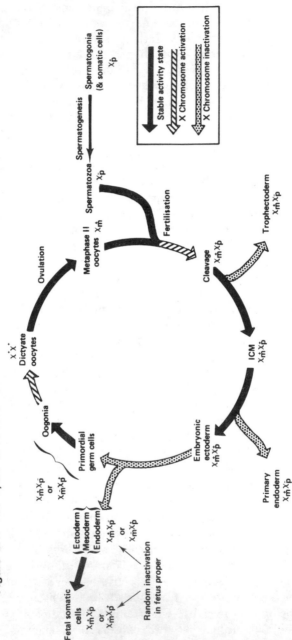

Xm and Xp, maternal and paternal X-chromosomes, respectively; X⁺ and X⁻, activated and inactivated X-chromosomes, respectively; ICM, inner cell mass.

Adapted from Vandeberg (1983), with permission.

vation and reactivation. The evolutionary relationships between dosage compensation and inactivation processes are not yet fully understood (Gartler and Riggs, 1983; Vandeberg, Johnson, Cooper and Robinson, 1983; Vandeberg, 1983).

The Y-chromosome and the HY-antigen system

The HY-antigen system was discovered by Eichwald and Silmser (1955) during transplant studies on mice. It has been suggested that this system forms the sex-determining process, or part of it, in many species including man (Ohno, Nagal, Ciccarese and Iwata, 1979). The HY-antigen system is always associated with the heterogametic sex chromosome, which is the Y in man and the W in birds. It forms part of a complex, associated with at least 24 genes on the X-chromosome and various ones on the autosomes, there being at least 48 genes involved in the sex-determining process in all (Polani, 1985). There may be more than one type or form of HY-antigen and indeed the transplant mechanisms may be separate from those that determine sex (McLaren, Simpson, Tomonai, Alexander and Hogg, 1984). Adinolfi, Polani and Zenthon (1982) suggest that HY-antigen exists in a precursor form, which is activated by gene dosage levels, and they use this model to explain various genetic discrepancies and cross-reactions.

The HY-antigen system is more than 300 million years old, and has been conserved throughout evolution. It is not used by the amphibia or by most reptiles but it is found in primitive snakes and is associated with the differentiation of separate sex chromosomes. In birds, the Z and W are not strictly homologous to the X and Y of mammals but are formed via a different route. Both birds and mammals use the HY-antigen system for sex differentiation, but whereas in mammals it differentiates the male, in birds it forms the female.

The Y-chromosome itself probably evolved from the X. In the process the X has lost most of its genes so that the Y has only those genes for sex-determination and tallness (Polani and Adinolfi, 1983); this suggests a scheme for the evolution of sex-determination. In primitive species the environment, e.g. temperature, controls hormones that activate the HY-antigen system to determine sex. As evolution progresses the animal's internal metabolism is able to dispense with the environment and itself controls the hormones. Eventually, as in man, the hormones themselves are put into a subsidiary role and the genes associated with the HY-antigen system have become the main controllers of sex.

Sex-determination in nature

In spite of genetic mechanisms discussed above, sex-determination in many species is not rigidly fixed in the embryo but often depends upon a host of environmental factors, of which the following are examples:

(1) In the wasp *Goniozus*, a parasite of moth larvae, the depositing female is able to modify the future sex of the eggs according to whether or not the larva is already parasitised. If the larva is free, more female eggs are laid, if it is parasitised, however, and eggs from another female are already present, the wasp lays more male eggs to fertilise these, and enhance its own genetic survival.

(2) If the marine worm larva, *Bonellia*, meets an adult female in the soil it becomes a male and fertilises her itself, if no such meeting takes place it grows into a female.

(3) In reptiles, such as turtles and crocodiles, sex depends on the temperature of incubation of the developing eggs. This temperature, as discussed above, affects the secretion of HY-antigen (Harvey and Slatkin, 1982; Daly and Wilson, 1983).

(4) In teleost fish, sex change can occur both from female to male and vice versa. If the male is removed from a male/female harem group, the dominant female becomes male and fertilises the other females. Sometimes these changes can be brought about by appropriate hormone injections (Reinboth, 1980).

(5) In the seal the mother will preferentially feed female pups rather than male in times of famine, as the latter take up too many resources due to their larger size.

The evolution of sex-determining mechanisms

Insect sex-determination, as seen in *Drosophila melanogaster* and some coccids, i.e. scale insects and mealey bugs, depends on the ratio of sex chromosomes (X) to autosomes (A). Haplodiploidy, i.e. unfertilised haploid eggs that form males and diploid fertilised eggs that form females, as occurs in bees and wasps, probably arose from this. Chandra (1985) has pointed out further the close inter-relationship that exists between the sex-determining systems of insects and that of female heterogamety as found in birds, and male heterogamety as occurs in mammals including man. A few gene mutations can turn the X/A system to the ZZ/ZW, while in some amphibians the ZZ/ZW and the XX/XY system may exist in the same family. Bull (1983) describes how such a system may coexist together in the same species in a dynamic equilibrium, which particular system is adopted at any one time depends upon a host of factors, which include the environment, the time of year, the availability of food supply, etc.

Human beginnings: evolution of the nervous system

The 'onion theory', in which the outer layers of humanity can be peeled off to leave a 'naked ape' has a lot wrong with it. First, the relation between man and his nearest primate relative with regard to the brain/body ratio is as large as that between the apes themselves and the insectivores, which have the lowest brain/body ratio of any primate. Secondly, as man separated from the ape stock 2 to 3 million years ago, not only his brain but also his cultural development has undergone extensive evolutionary changes. Man was originally a hunter/gatherer/primitive farmer and his biology was basically adapted to this *modus vivendi*. Modern changes, especially over recent times, have been too fast for evolution or adaptation to catch up, and one has to be very careful therefore of too glib explanations of behaviour (Martin, 1974).

Similar care has to be shown when dealing with inferences about the brain. The central nervous system in all vertebrates arises from a hollow fluid-filled tube, in contrast with invertebrates, which have a solid-core nervous system. With the coming onto land and the necessity of limbs, special senses, and sexual reproduction away from the sea, new motor/sensory/proprioceptive centres evolved in the brain. Older basic structures were supplemented rather than replaced in the process of 'cephalisation', in which progressive dependence of these phylogenetically older centres upon the newer forebrain structures occurred. However, the degree of cortical plasticity and the exact balance that occurs between these newer and the older structures varies between species, so that comparisons are not necessarily valid. In addition, different species may use different structures for the same function, e.g. the corpus striatum of birds incorporates some of the neocortex of mammals, and it is not therefore strictly comparable to that structure in the mammal. The higher centres, that is the phylogenetically most recent, are most vulnerable to many metabolic and degenerative diseases, e.g. subacute combined degeneration of the cord and Pick's disease, which affect only these newer parts of the spinal cord and cortex respectively. In contrast, developmental anomalies tend to affect midline structures in the older parts of the brain and nervous system, as do toxic and teratogenic factors (Mitchell, 1964; Sarnat and Netsky, 1974).

FETAL DEVELOPMENT

Historical background

Plato in his 'Symposium' describes three sexes — androgynes, males and females: split in half by an angry Zeus, each half forever seeks its partner, a neat explanation for heterosexual and homosexual attraction. The Marquis de Sade (1785) believed that sexuality was both innate and acquired (Gorer, 1953; Goodman, 1980). Many schools of thought lie between these two poles (Haire, 1968; Bancroft, 1974). Kaplan (1974) believes that female orgasmic response is innate and that orgasmic intensity is distributed on a normal distribution curve in the female population. Fisher (1973), who studied the orgasmic response of 300 women, as well as viewing the current literature, concluded that the orgasmic pattern was more or less constant for any particular woman, and that factors like background, religion, partner or sexual technique made relatively little difference to the response. Also, Eysenck's (1971) description of personality structure and Masters and Johnson's (1979) classification of fantasy structure hint at a biological background.

HY-antigen and its action in the fetus

The evolution of the HY-antigen system has been described previously, as has its role as the inducer of the heterogamous sex. The amount of HY-antigen is linked to the number of Y-chromosomes, so that individuals with more than one have correspondingly more HY-antigen. HY-antigen is a surface antigen that is attached to the short arm of the Y-chromosome. It diffuses from the cell to assert its effects elsewhere. This happens in freemartin cattle: a female twin is partially masculinised by HY-antigen that diffuses through the placenta from the male twin, some anastomotic communication having developed between them (Ohno, Christian, Wachtel and Koo, 1976). In addition to specific receptor sites for HY-antigen, there exist in many tissues nonspecific plasma membrane anchorage sites, usually associated with beta-2-microglobulins (Ohno et al., 1979). The HY-antigen complex is thought to consist of an HY-antigen gene on the Y-chromosome, a structural gene necessary for HY expression on an autosome, and a repressor gene linked to the X-chromosome. The latter is referred to as the testicular feminisation gene. This regulates the synthesis of protein receptors for androgenic steroids. (For further reviews see Polani, 1985; Brunner, Moreeira-Filho, Wachtel and Wachtel, 1984; Golimbu, 1984; Simpson, 1983; Meck, 1984; and Rao, Vaidya, Patel and Ambani, 1981.)

The Y-chromosome and fetal growth

Ounsted and Taylor (1972) suggest that the Y-chromosome slows down the growth rate in the male fetus. This allows more time for genomic information to be transcribed, and means that the male fetus is born relatively more immature compared with the female. This slowing of the growth rate has wide repercussions in all aspects of morbidity and mortality and it makes the male more vulnerable to a host of pathogenic factors. Thus males have a higher perinatal mortality, a higher incidence of accidental death, as well as a higher incidence of mental handicap, which includes autism and epilepsy, and later in life increased vulnerability to cardiac disease and certain forms of cancer. Overall, the development of a male brain involves more processes than that needed to create a female, and this increases the possibility of something going wrong. Perhaps the preponderance of the paraphilias in males is a reflection of this. On the credit side, the male is more likely to produce genius. To balance this excess male damage and loss 5% more males are born than females in the human population (Taylor, 1985).

29

The fetal genitalia

Jost (1953) showed that in the fetal rabbit, the testis, through testosterone (T), exerted a permanent imprinting action on both the internal and external genitalia. In a female fetus, with no testis, the Wolffian ducts atrophy, the Mullerian ducts develop into the uterus and Fallopian tubes, and the genital tubercle forms female external genitalia. In males, the Mullerian duct atrophies, the Wolffian duct forms the male internal duct system, i.e. vasa deferentia, epididymis and seminal vesicles, and the genital tubercle forms the penis and testicles. The testes exert an effect through T to form the internal duct system. Its conversion product, dihydrotestosterone (DHT) acts on the genital tubercle to form the external male genitalia. A substance called Mullerian inhibiting hormone (MIH), a polypeptide produced by the Sertoli cells, is responsible for the suppression of this duct. Occasionally it fails to act, and the individual, a phenotypic male, is born with a uterus. In man the process begins at about seven weeks of intra-uterine life, when chorionic gonadotrophin from the placenta is bound to receptors on the Leydig cells of the fetal testis, and stimulates T production. Later this is taken over by luteinising hormone (LH), via the hypothalamic/pituitary axis. Even in an anencephalic fetus the genitals are normally developed. For more detailed accounts see Anderson (1981); Wilson, George and Griffin (1981); and Winter, Fairman and Reyes (1981).

The brain and nervous system

Hormonal feedback studies

In humans, fetal T and its conversion products, DHT and oestrogen (E), together with fetal progesterone (P), react with the hypothalamus, limbic areas and cerebral cortex. Complicated new formations of, and modifications to, the receptor system occur at various critical times. Many of these changes are irreversible. The brain's neuronal structure and electrical response has been shown to be modified by the various processes. These changes signify a dimorphic change between male and female, for, in the latter, none of these interactions occur in the absence of T (Gorski, 1978; McEwen, 1981; Arnold, 1980).

Dörner (1976), has used the pattern of gonadotrophin release from the hypothalamic/pituitary axis as an indicator of the feminisation or masculinisation of the brain. Female rats show a cyclical pattern of hormonal release, but in the male the hormones are released in a tonic manner. With appropriate manipulations, i.e. by giving T to females and by castrating males at appropriate times, these responses can be reversed in the rat. Dörner has extended these ideas to humans and he claims that homosexual men and trans-sexuals show female-type LH feedback and surge values after exposure to E. This, he says, is evidence that they may have partially feminised brains; however, there are many objections to this theory. As previously mentioned, strict correlation between the brain structures of different species is not valid because, in the process of cephalisation, the various parts of the brain are incorporated differently in different species. This questions the validity of extrapolation of a particular hormonal response occurring in one species and applying it to another. As expected, therefore, the primate brain is different from that of the rodent.

If the fibres from outside the medial basal nuclei are cut in the female rat, the cyclical response is abolished, whereas in the female rhesus monkey, cutting the fibres leaves the response unaffected. Furthermore, studies with rhesus monkeys have shown both sexes to be capable of positive feedback and surge responses on exposure to E (Knobil, 1974). Our own study (Goodman, Anderson, Bu'lock, Sheffield, Lynch and Butt, 1985) demonstrated that normal men and trans-sexuals respond to E in the same way as rhesus monkeys. Likewise, Gooren, Rao, Van-Kessel and Harmsen-Louman (1984) and Gooren (1984), found no differences in the response to either E, LHRF (luteinising hormone releasing factor) or naloxone, between male-to-female trans-sexuals and normal men, and female-to-male trans-sexuals and normal women. Aiman and Boyar (1982), did report some differences in male-to-female trans-sexuals, however, while Gladue, Green and Hellman (1984), found the LH response to E in homosexual men to be in between that of normal men and women. Even if such different hormonal responses do occur, and most studies have not backed this up, there is no evidence that this gonadotrophin response necessarily implies 'feminisation' or 'masculinisation' of a brain. Indeed, Kawakami and Kimura (1978), have suggested that even in the rat, the male brain is formed independently of future LH response. Perhaps the genetic mechanisms previously described play some part here.

Enzymes and neurotransmitters

The two main enzymes involved in fetal development are aromatases (which convert T to E) and reductases (which convert T to DHT). Their distribution in the brain gives an indication of where these actions occur. In the rat, for example, over 50 per cent of E receptors do not have aromatase, so that they cannot receive E from T but must receive it directly. P can compete with T to form 5-alpha-reductase, and so can block the formation of DHT. E can also compete for hydroxylation enzymes to form catechol oestrogens, which are able to react with neurotransmitters. The neurotransmitters that are dimorphic to T, or E converted from T, involve the catecholamine system; those that are nonsensitive possibly involve cholinergic mechanisms. What part these neurotransmitters play in sexuality is not known; however, the dopamine system is stimulatory and the serotonin system is inhibitory (Gessa and Tegliamonte, 1974).

Brandon (1979) has pointed out the similarity between transsexuals and patients with monosymptomatic delusional states. It may be that both conditions have similar abnormalities in neurotransmitter mechanisms. Interestingly, male rats at 12 days of age have more serotonin than females, which perhaps reflects a dimorphic response to the influence of E. When given to animals, drugs that are known to interfere with neurotransmission, e.g. chlorpromazine or reserpine, also affect sexual development. The same is true of certain hormones, e.g. thyroxine, which alter the duration of critical phases.

Endogenous opiates are also involved both peripherally and centrally. They have been found in human semen, and in the prostate and seminal vesicles. Opiate receptors have been found in the vas deferens of the rat. Opiates depress sexual response and delay ejaculation by inhibiting the contractions of the vas deferens and seminal vesicles. Their central action is thought to occur through the hypothalamic/pituitary/testicular axis by inhibiting luteinising hormone releasing factor. However, it is possible that they also act through the dopamine-serotonin pathways. These opiates are released during sexual arousal and coitus and are responsible for the sexual anaesthesia and clouding of consciousness that occur then. Indeed, the use of opium to enhance sexual arousal has long been known. Nalorphine, the opiate antagonist, blocks many of these actions (McIntosh, Vallano and Barfield, 1980; Murphy, 1981). In the rat, E masculinises the fetal brain in the first week after birth. However, the female fetus is exposed to E from maternal sources, and protection of the female brain depends upon alphafetoprotein, an E-binding substance formed from the fetal yolk sac and liver. This mops up E, so that only T is able to reach the brain tissue, where some of it is bound to receptors and converted to E in situ. This means that only E from T can reach the brain in the rat. Alpha-fetoprotein shows species specificity; in man less than one per cent of oestrogen is bound to alphafetoprotein in this way, and masculinisation and defeminisation depend on the direct action of DHT. Women may be protected from these hormones by the action of P, which blocks DHT formation (MacLusky and Naftolin, 1981). An abnormality in this mechanism may be involved in the aetiology of lesbianism. The likely relevance of antibodies to alpha-fetoprotein and the effect of stress on fetal T are poorly understood (Mizejewski, Vonnegut and Simon, 1980; Bidling Maier, Knorr and Neuman, 1977; Ward and Weisz, 1980).

Masculinisation and defeminisation

In mammals the ability of the male to display masculine behaviour depends on two processes, masculinisation and defeminisation. These, although linked, are not mutually exclusive. Both, are dependent on T and its conversion products, and the interaction parallels the development of the genital ducts and organs. Masculinisation behaviours consist of mounting the female, penetrating her vagina, thrusting, and ejaculation, and depend on E (from T) and DHT. Defeminisation is the obliteration of feminine behaviours, e.g. presenting, lordosis, and allowing penetration, in a male.

Different species vary in the particular combination of T and its products that affect these processes. But between males and females of any one species there is an inverse degree of bisexuality, depending on which mechanisms predominate. In the rat the female is often exposed to small amounts of T in utero, so that some degree of masculinisation occurs, with the result that the adult female shows more bisexual behaviour than the male. By contrast, the rhesus monkey, like man, does not undergo defeminisation, and the male in both species shows more bisexuality than the female. Mounting behaviour, among some male primates, is a way of asserting dominance; but such homosexuality, certainly in some monkeys, has social value, and may serve as sublimation for those sub-dominant males who live on the periphery of the group, without access to females (Goy and Goldfoot, 1975). Lastly, separate neuronal primordia exist for both masculinisation and defeminisation, and the development of the penis, with all its nervous components, reinforces masculine behaviours (Goy and Goldfoot, 1975; Baum, 1979; MacLusky and Naftolin, 1981; Feder, 1981a, 1981b).

Genetic considerations

Common disorders

Only a few of the many genetic conditions will be mentioned. For fuller accounts see Polani (1981) and Wachtel and Koo (1981).

Congenital adrenal hyperplasia (CAH) in a female fetus leads to various degrees of masculinisation because the adrenal glands produce abnormal androgens due to an enzyme deficiency, usually 21-hydroxylase, on the pathway to cortisol. Baker (1980) found that girls with CAH had female gender identity patterns but male gender behaviour; they were tomboys with lots of energy. However, most studies have shown no increase in homosexual inclinations in these individuals.

Male partial pseudohermaphrodites were described by Imperato-McGinley, Peterson, Gautier and Sturla (1979). They lack 5-alpha-reductase, the enzyme necessary to convert T to DHT. The children were reared as girls until puberty, when under the surge in T, the enzyme block was overcome and male genitalia developed. Most individuals had no difficulty in assuming the male role at this time; the androgenised brain was able to overcome early learning experiences.

The androgen insensitivity syndrome occurs in a genotypically male fetus in which T fails to act because of abnormal or absent receptors. Such individuals look and think themselves to be female; but they have male levels of serum T and testicles in the form of herniae. They do not have a uterus because of the action of MIH.

Females with Turner's syndrome (46-XO) have dysgenic

ovaries and are therefore sterile. They may have other abnormalities such as small stature, webbed neck and coarctation of the aorta. This condition shows the importance of both X-chromosomes in normal female development. Wachtel (1979) has postulated the existence, in women, of ovarian inducers that interact with HY-antigen. Such patients with Turner's syndrome are weakly HY-antigen positive; Wolf, Fraccaro, Mayerova, Hech, Zuffardi and Hamiester (1980) believe this to be due to the absence of a repressor gene on the missing X-chromosome.

True hermaphrodites with different degrees of mosaicism have streak gonads (ovotestes) and imperfectly formed genitalia.

Twins

Kallmann's (1952) classic study on monozygotic (MZ) and dizygotic (DZ) twins and homosexuality had design flaws. His conclusions, however, that in general there is more concordance for homosexuality between MZ twins than between DZ ones, and more between DZ than in the general population, probably does have some validity. There are, however, many studies of MZ twins discordant for homosexuality (Davidson, Brierly and Smith, 1971; Zuger, 1976).

The placenta is extremely important in fetal development. Intimate contact between the trophoblast and the maternal uterine epithelium occurs during implantation and development, and in the male fetus there is a weak antigenic response from the mother due to the fetal HY-antigen that is present on the plasma membrane of the fetal cells (Mosley and Stan, 1984). Positioning of the fetuses in the uterus, certainly in rodents, may be important in regard to future sexual behaviour. Females situated near males have more aggression later in life, while those further away have less, due to their being exposed to T that is secreted from the fetal male testis (Vom Saal, 1982).

Melnick, Mynanthopoulos and Christian (1978) have shown that MZ populations are not in fact homogeneous if one considers the placenta, which may consist of one or two chorions. Identical twins that shared one chorion show higher concordance for I.Q., than those that had separate ones. Placental type probably has relevance to the future sexuality of the individual, and future studies on twins should include a placental assessment.

Homosexual genes — do they exist?

Homosexuality has been described in every culture and depicted in art from the beginning of history. Burton (1885), in his famous 'Terminal Essay', described a 'Sotadic Zone' named after the Greek poet Sotades who wrote verse about homosexuals; this zone covered most of the Mediterranean. Ancient Greece and Rome produced a plethora of writings on this theme (Licht, 1969; Keifer, 1969). Numerous sexologists in past times argued about the exact nature of homosexuality (Mantegazza, 1966; Haire, 1968).

Although no specifically homosexual genes have yet been demonstrated, it is possible that they do exist. Whether they act alone, in unifactorial manner or whether they need a specific environment to express the behaviour, in multifactorial fashion, is unknown. Both types of inheritance may coexist in the same individual or may occur separately in different individuals.

Many of the men who indulge in homosexual acts, perhaps as many as 40 per cent of all men at sometime in their lives (Kinsey, Pomeroy and Martin, 1948; Whitam, 1983; Langevin, 1985), are not true, exclusive homosexuals (i.e. Kinsey 5s and 6s) and do not have a homosexual gender identity. These people perform such behaviours for a variety of reasons, which may include the unavailability of women, as in prisons or institutions, or as a supplement to their more usual heterosexual behaviours. Only 4 per cent of people behaving so are in fact Kinsey type 5 and 6 homosexuals.

After reviewing many past studies and describing his own work in five contemporary societies, Whitam (1983; see also Chapter 8 of this volume) concludes that the appearance of homosexuality is inevitable in every culture, it is ubiquitous, and occurs in 5 per cent of any population. All homosexual groups show similar behavioural patterns, which include varying degrees of cross-dressing in childhood and a spectrum of behaviours ranging from effeminacy to ultra-masculinity in the adult. Many homosexuals show a strong affinity for the entertainment industry.

In a further paper (Whitam and Zent, 1984), the authors question the Freudian psychodynamic construct of the etiology of homosexuality. The classically distant, remote father and the smothering, over-protective mother, if they are present at all, seem to be a reaction to a child who is different, rather than a cause of same. In other cultures in which homosexuality is more readily accepted these dynamics are not in evidence. Similarly, Ross (1983) describes heterosexual marriages of male homosexuals in three different countries, each with very different attitudes to homosexuality. The incidence of divorce among such couples is much higher in the more intolerant countries. Ross believes this is because marriage in these societies is often undertaken by homosexuals to 'cure' their homosexuality, often at the advice of friends and doctors. In freer countries homosexuals are not under such pressure, and fewer Kinsey 5s and 6s marry. Just how homosexuality presents itself in a particular society depends on the current climate of tolerance and acceptance, rather than on variations in the nature of homosexuality itself.

Hutchinson (1959) advanced the idea that if homosexuality is indeed controlled by a gene, to prevent its being bred-out in evolution, the heterozygote who carries the gene would have to have some benefit. This is the so-called 'heterozygote superiority theory'. An analogy with sickle-cell disease, which occurs in Africa, has been drawn. Here the heterozygote who carries the sickle-cell gene does not show the disease, unless under extreme conditions, but does have resistance to malaria, which is endemic in Africa. In every Mendelian cross two heterozygotes result with immunity to malaria, while of the two homozygotes neither have such immunity and one has sickle-cell disease. If this does apply to homosexuals, one has to question what advantage the homosexual gene could possibly give to the heterozygote. Various ideas have been propounded. It has been suggested that such individuals have an increase in sexual desire or an ability under stress, e.g. in prison, to adopt a homosexual behaviour pattern as a survival strategy. There may be an advantage in having homosexual siblings. They would lessen reproductive competition and possibly enhance the breeding advantages of the others, rather like worker bees, who do not themselves breed but who work to guarantee the reproductive success of the queen by so-called altruistic behaviours. (For reviews see Pillard, Poumadere and Carreta, 1981; Ruse, 1984.)

Perhaps homosexual genes affect the brain, giving homosexuals different abilities than heterosexuals, rather like the differences between the male and female brains (see later). The pros and cons of having pre-programmed machines as against open neural nets in the construction of thinking machines is currently being explored (Aleksander and Burnett, 1984), but as far as the fetus goes there is probably some degree of compromise, for it would seem unnecessarily risky of nature not to put some basic patterns in the developing brain rather than to leave it all to learning. Nyborg's model, as discussed later, using genetic and hormonal variations, seems to support this view.

Criticism

There have been criticisms about using a genetic/hormonal model to try to understand the nature of homosexuality. Much of this has centred around the belief that such research considers homosexuality to be an illness, with the presumed aim of looking for aetiological factors being to 'cure' it. Other objections concern the validity of applying animal data to humans. (For detailed accounts see Birke, 1981; Futuyama and Risch, 1984; Hoult, 1984; Ricketts, 1984.) Hopefully most researchers accept homosexuality to be part of normal human sexuality, and any question of 'prevention' by genetic or hormonal means should be condemned. Of the other criticism, one should always keep in mind the problems of experimental validity and too-facile cross-species generalisations.

THE DIMORPHIC BRAIN

General observations

The following differences in behaviour between men and women are generally accepted:

(1) Girls have greater verbal ability than boys. They are friendlier and more communicative.
(2) Boys have greater visual/spatial ability than girls and are generally better at certain types of mathematics (perhaps these two factors are linked).
(3) Males are more aggressive; boys have more energy and play rougher games than girls.
(4) Girls are more maternal and in childhood play they rehearse maternal behaviours.
(5) Girls surpass boys on simple overlearned tasks, while boys excell in more complex tasks that require inhibition of immediate response (McGlone, 1980; Waber, 1985).

Laterality

This concept goes some way to offering an explanation of some of the above observations. The left cerebral hemisphere is involved in processing verbal and linguistic material, while the right deals with spatial and analytic processing. The brain is asymmetrically organised with regard to these functions, males having more specialised right brains while females are more bilaterally organised. Evidence for these ideas has been obtained from a host of sources, which include the differing effects of stroke, tumours, etc. on men and women as well as various psychological tests (McGlone, 1980; Inglis and Lawson, 1981).

Left handedness

This is commoner in men and is thought to reflect the effect of intrauterine T, which suppresses the growth of the left hemisphere and promotes that of the right. This process also affects the susceptibility to autoimmune disease. In populations with high mathematical abilities, there has been shown to occur a much higher percentage of men who are both left-handed and who suffer from various immune diseases than occurs in the general population (Geschwind and Behan, 1982).

Genetic and hormonal correlates of behaviour

Broverman, Klaider, Kobayashi and Vogel (1968) give an explanation of the interaction between adrenergic and cholinergic neural processes and hormonal background in an effort to understand the known differences in cognitive abilities between the sexes. The mechanisms behind these interactions have been further elucidated by Nyborg (1984), who offers a mathematical model, the 'curvilinear/covariance model' (Figure 2.2). This curve describes the interaction between spatial ability and level of E. The human male fetus is first exposed to T and later to E, designated T/E, its range is between A and D on the curve. The females first exposure is to E, so that she is designated E/T and ranges between E and H on the curve. Looking at a variety of behaviours in different genetic individuals, which include self-reliance, physical energy expenditure, maternal interests, etc.,

Figure 2.2: The curvilinear/covariance model (After Nyborg 1984)

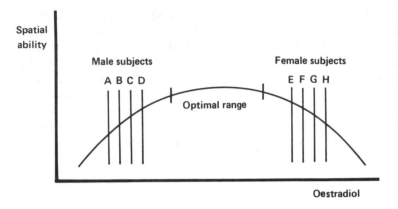

Depicting the 'optimal oestrogen range' for hormone level: spatial ability relationship. A to D, males primed with T — T/E, E to H, females primed with E — E/T, 'Masculine' man at A or 'Feminine' woman at H, low spatial ability androgynous men and women (range D to E), high spatial ability.

Nyborg is able to explain their occurrence by use of the model. The changes in cognition and spatial abilities that are known to occur at puberty, childbirth and menopause, or resulting from artificial hormone administration, can also be understood from this model.

SUMMARY AND CONCLUSIONS

It seems that sex first arose some $2\frac{1}{2}$ to 3 billion years ago in primitive bacteria, and consisted of frenetic acts of cannibalism in an effort to survive the harsh environment. Damaged genes were repaired and variation became possible. Eukaryocytes, cells that contain nuclei, did not appear until a billion years later. Whether their sexuality was a continuation from the bacteria or whether it arose separately is not known. The gene exchanges were now regularised and ordered as particular genes were preserved, first mitosis, and later meioisis, evolved, and sexual reproduction proper appeared.

Sex-determination was first controlled by the environment, as in crocodiles, where future sex depends upon the incubation temperature of the eggs. Later, with the evolution of the HY-antigen system, genes and hormones became relatively independent of the environment. Certain fish can undergo sex reversal with appropriate hormonal exposure, but higher up the scale sex becomes less reversible. The general tendency is that the hormones lose their primacy to genes. This can be seen in man, in whom fetal hormonal abnormalities, e.g. as in congenital adrenal hyperplasia, do affect the future individual in so far as the genitalia may be imperfectly formed but sexual identity and erotic preference seems relatively unaffected in the adult. There is no increase in paraphilia in such individuals. Perhaps this control of sexual identity and direction depends upon genetic factors, such as the patterns of inactivation of genes on the X-chromosome, variations in the HY-antigen systems, and the ratio in the brain of reductases to aromatases (Federman, 1981). Indeed, using human-rodent cell hybrids and electrophoretic techniques, Müller (1984) has shown that in the rat the male and female fetus have different polypeptides linked to reproductive genes, which have been detected very early on in the so-called 'indifferent gonad', well before the hormonal interactions occur. Drugs, hormones, antibodies and enzyme deficiencies may also play some role here.

Nyborg's (1984) curvilinear model offers a compromise in the current debate in cybernetics about the pros and cons of constructing a learning machine, using either pre-programming or having open neural nets. As has been described, much happens to the fetal hardware, the genes, from fertilisation up to the first few weeks of life, so that males and females undergo many different processes from conception onwards; and the fetus is really far from being 'neutral' or 'female' as has been claimed, up to the 7th week of intrauterine life, when the HY-antigen system becomes active. Once established, however, the genes act as a template upon which the hormones act. Priming with T first gives T/E and with E first E/T as represented by the male and female parts of Nyborg's curve and subsequent manipulations can be understood by using this model, so that neither environment nor genes alone have primacy.

The differing patterns between the behaviour of men and women (e.g., the increased spatial abilities and higher aggression levels of men and the maternal interests and better interpersonal skills of women) reflect a brain differentiation that seems to have been set for a nomadic/hunter/farmer life that occurred in Neolithic times some ten thousand or so years ago. This period is extremely short in evolutionary terms. Now that different demands are made on men and women it will be interesting to see if these variations cause changes in hormonal/genetic interactions. Perhaps these changes would only be evident over very long periods of time, far outside the life-span of any individual.

Much speculation exists as to the evolutionary advantages of having individuals who show variant sexual interests, e.g. homosexuals. The ideas of altruistic behaviour, heterozygote superiority, etc., have been discussed. Even if, as Sherman (1978) argues, the amount of variation in cognitive behaviour due to the sexual effect on the brain, i.e. as occurs in males and females, is less than 5 per cent and this possibility applies also to homosexuals, in a large population this will have considerable significance. Having individuals with different modes of thought and behaviour offers a plasticity that promotes the evolutionary possibilities and survival of that species.

Even Freud (1963), in his famous psychoanalytical construct of the homosexual genius of Leonardo da Vinci, admits that, however full the analysis, it can never completely explain Leonardo. Freud goes on to describe '. . . the chief features in a person's organic constitution as being the result of the blending of male and female dispositions, based on (chemical) substances. Leonardo's physical beauty and his left-handedness might be quoted in support of this view.' It is these constitutional factors that have been the concern of this chapter.

NOTE

This chapter is based in part on Goodman, R.E. (1983) 'Biology of sexuality: Inborn determinants of human sexual response.' *Br. J. Psychiatry*, *20*, 216–20

REFERENCES

Adinolfi, M., Polani, P. and Zenthon, J. (1982) 'Genetic control of HY synthesis: a hypothesis.' *Hum. Genet.*, *61*, 1–2

Aiman, J. and Boyar, R.M. (1982) 'Testicular function in transsexual men.' *Arch. Sex. Behav.*, *11* (2), 171–9

Aleksander, I. and Burnett, P. (1984) *Reinventing Man. The Robot becomes Reality*. Harmondsworth: Penguin Books

Anderson, D.C. (1981) 'Physiology of human fetal sex differentiation.' In *Clinical Paediatric Endocrinology* (ed. C.S.D. Brooke), Oxford: Blackwell Scientific Publications

Arnold, A.P. (1980) 'Sexual differences in the brain.' *American Science*, *68*, 165–73

Baker, S.W. (1980) 'Psychosexual differentiation in the human.' *Biol. Reprod.*, *22*, 61–72

Bancroft, J. (1974) *Deviant Sexual Behaviour: Modification and Assessment*, pp. 1–20. London: Oxford University Press

Baum, M.J. (1979) 'Differentiation of coital behaviour in mammals: a comparative analysis. *Neurosci. Biobehav. Rev.*, *3*, 265–84

Bell, G. (1982) *The Masterpiece of Nature: The Evolution and Genetics of Sexuality*. London: Croom Helm/Los Angeles: University of California Press

Bernstein, H., Byerly, H.C., Hope, F.A. and Richard, E.M. (1984) 'Origin of sex.' *J. Theor. Biol.*, *110*, 323–51

Bidling Maier, F., Knorr, D. and Neuman, F. (1977) 'Inhibition of masculine differentiation in male offspring of rabbits actively immunised against testosterone before pregnancy.' *Nature*, *266*, 647–8

Birke, Lia (1981) 'Is homosexuality hormonally determined?' *J. Homosex.*, *6* (4), 35–49

Brandon, S. (1979) *Aspects of psychosexual problems*. Paper given to a symposium organized by the Department of Psychiatry, University of Liverpool.

Bremermann, H.J. (1985) 'The adaptive significance of sexuality.' *Experientia*, *41*, 1245–54

Broverman, D.M., Klaider, E.L., Kobayashi, Y. and Vogel, W. (1968) 'Roles of activation and inhibition in sex differences in cognitive abilities.' *Psychol. Rev.*, *75* (1), 23–50

Brunner, M., Moreeira-Filho, C.A., Wachtel, G. and Wachtel, S. (1984) 'On the secretion of HY-antigen.' *Cell*, *37* (2), 615–19

Bull, J.J. (1983) *Evolution of Sex-Determining Mechanisms*. California: Benjamin/Cummings

Burton, R.E. (1885) *Thousand Nights and a Night*. Kameshastra Society. Copyright Vols. 1 and 2. Ellis Spear, Vols. 3–10 and Supplemented Vols. Philip Justice. 10 vols. plus 6 Supplemented Vols. *See Terminal Essay*: Pornography (vol. 10).

Chandra, H.S. (1985) 'Sex-determination: a hypothesis based on noncoding DNA.' *Proc. Natl. Acad. Sci. USA*, *82*, 1165–9

Daly, M. and Wilson, M. (1983) *Sex Evolution and Behavior*, 2nd edn. Boston: William Grant Press

Davidson, K.J., Brierley, H. and Smith, C. (1971) 'A male monozygote twinship discordant for homosexuality.' *Br. J. Psychiatry*, *118*, 675–82

De Sade, The Marquis (1785) *120 Days of Sodom and Other Writings*. (Compiled and translated in 1966 by A. Wainhouse and R. Seaver). New York: Grove Press

Dörner, G. (1976) *Hormones and Brain Differentiation*. Amsterdam: Elsevier

Eicher, W. (1981) *HY-Antigen in Transsexuality*. Paper given to the fifth World Congress of Sexology, Jerusalem

Eichwald, E.J. and Silmser, C.R. (1955) Untitled communication. *Transplant Bulletin*, *2*, 148–9

Eysenck, H.J. (1971) 'Personality and sexual adjustment.' *Br. J. Psychiatry*, *118*, 593–608

Feder, H.H. (1981a) 'Hormonal actions on the sexual differentiation of the genitalia and the gonadotrophin-regulation system.' In *Neuroendocrinology of Reproduction* (ed. N.T. Adler), New York: Plenum

—— (1981b) 'Perinatal hormones and their role in the development of sexually dimorphic behaviors.' In *Neuro-endocrinology of Reproduction* (ed. N.T. Adler), New York: Plenum

Federman, D.D. (1981) 'The requirements for sexual reproduction.' *Hum. Gen.*, *58*, 3–5

Fisher, S. (1973) *The Female Orgasm: Psychology, Physiology, Fantasy.* London: Allen Lane

Freud, S. (1963) *Leonardo da Vinci, And a Memory of his Childhood.* Transl. by Alan Tyson. Harmondsworth: Penguin Books

Futuyama, D.J. and Risch, S.J. (1983/4) 'Sexual orientation, sociobiology and evolution.' *J. Homosex.*, *9* (2–3), 157–68

Gartler, S. and Riggs, A.D. (1983) 'Mammalian X-chromosome inactivation.' *Annu. Rev. Genet.*, *17*, 155–90

Geschwind, N. and Behan, P. (1982) 'Left handedness: association with immune disease, migraine and developmental learning disorder.' *Proc. Natl. Acad. Sci. USA*, *79*, 5097–100

Gessa, G.L. and Tegliamonte, A. (1974) 'Possible role of brain serotonin and dopamine in controlling male sexual behaviour.' In *Serotonin–New Vistas* (eds. E. Costa, G.L. Gessa and M. Sandler), New York: Raven Press

Gladue, B.A., Green, R. and Hellman, R.E. (1984) 'Neuroendocrine response to estrogen and sexual orientation.' *Science*, 225, 1496–9

Goodman, R.E. (1980) 'Photoquiz: The Marquis de Sade.' *Br. J. Sex. Med.*, *59*, 57–8, 60, 75–6

——, Anderson, D.C., Bu'Lock, D.E., Sheffield, B., Lynch, S.S. and Butt, W.R. (1985) 'Study of the effect of estradiol on gonadotrophin levels in untreated male to female transsexuals.' *Arch. Sex. Behav.*, *14* (2),141–6

Golimbu, M.D. (1984) 'HY-antigen: genetic control and role in testicular differentiation.' *Urology*, *24* (2), 115–21

Gooren, L. (1984) 'The naloxone-induced LH release in male to female transsexuals.' *Neuroendocrinology Letter,*, *6* (2), 89–93

Gooren, L.J.G., Rao, B.R., Van-Kessel, H. and Harmsen-Louman, W. (1984) 'Estrogen positive feedback on LH secretion in transsexuality.' *Psychoneuroendocrinology*, *9* (3), 249–59

Gorer, G. (1953) *The Life and Ideas of the Marquis de Sade.* London: Peter Owen

Gorski, R.A. (1978) 'Sexual differentiation of the brain.' *Hospital Practice*, *13*, 55–62

Goy, R.W. and Goldfoot, D.A. (1975) 'Neuroendocrinology: animal models and problems of human sexuality.' *Arch. Sex. Behav.*, *4*, 405–20

Haire, N. (1968) *Encyclopaedia of Sexual Knowledge*, pp. 672–708. London: Encyclopaedic Press Ltd.

Harvey, P.H. and Slatkin, M. (1982) 'Some like it hot: temperature-determined sex.' *Nature*, *296*, 807–8

Haseltine, R.P. and Ohno, S. (1981) 'Mechanism of gonadal differentiation.' *Science*, *21*, 1272–84

Hoult, T.F. (1983/4) 'Human sexuality in biological perspective: theoretical and methodological considerations.' *J. Homosex.*, *9* (2–3), 137–55

Hutchinson, G.E. (1959) 'A speculative consideration of certain possible forms of sexual selection in man.' *American Naturalist*, *93* (869), 81–91

Imperato-McGinley, J., Peterson, R.E., Gautier, T. and Sturla, E. (1979) 'Androgens and the evolution of male gender identity among male pseudo-hermaphrodites with 5-alpha-reductase deficiency.' *N. Engl. J. Med.*, *300*, 1233–7

Inglis, J. and Lawson, J.S. (1981) 'Sex differences in the effects of unilateral brain damage on intelligence.' *Science*, *212* (4495), 693–5

Jost, A. (1953) 'Studies on sex differentiation in mammals.' *Rec. Prog. Horm. Res.*, *29*, 1–35

Kallman, F.J. (1952) 'Comparative twin study on the genetic aspects of male homosexuality.' *J. Nerv. Ment. Dis.*, *115*, 283–98

Kaplan, H.S. (1974) *The New Sex Therapy: Active Treatment of Sexual Dysfunction*. London: Baillière Tindall

Kawakami, M. and Kimura, F. (1978) 'The limbic forebrain structures and reproduction.' *Perspectives in Endocrine Psychobiology* (eds. F. Brambilla *et al.*) *3*: 101–56

Keifer, O. (1969) *Sexual Life in Ancient Rome*. London: Panther Books

Kinsey, A.C., Pomeroy, W.B. and Martin, C.E. (1948) *Sexual Behavior in the Human Male*. Philadelphia: W.B. Saunders

Knobil, E. (1974) 'On the control of gonadotrophin secretion in the rhesus monkey.' *Recent Prog. Horm. Res.*, *30*, 1–43

Langevin, R. (1985) *Erotic Preference, Gender Identity, and Aggression in Men. New Research Studies* (ed. R. Langevin), Hillsdale, N.J.: Lawrence Erlbaum Associates

Licht, H. (1969) *Sexual Life in Ancient Greece*. London: Panther Books

MacLusky, N.J. and Naftolin, F. (1981) 'Sexual differentiation of the central nervous system.' *Science*, *211*, 1294–303

Mantegazza, P. (1966) *The Sexual Relations of Mankind*. California: Brandon House

Margulis, L. and Sagan, D. (1984) 'Evolutionary origins of sex.' In *Oxford Surveys in Evolutionary Biology* (eds R. Dawkins and M. Ridley), pp. 16–17, London: Oxford University Press

Martin, R.D. (1974) 'The biological basis of human behavior.' In *The Biology of Brains* (ed. W.B. Broughton) Symposium of the Institute of Biology, No. 21, Institute of Biology, *12*, 215–50

Masters, W.H. and Johnson, V.E. (1979) 'Incidents and comparison of fantasy patterns.' In *Homosexuality in Perspective*. Boston: Little, Brown & Co

McEwan, B.S. (1981) 'Neural gonadal steroid actions.' *Science*, *211*, 1303–11

McGlone, J. (1980) 'Sex differences in human brain asymmetry: a critical review.' *Behavioral and Brain Sciences*, *3* (2), 215–24

McIntosh, T.K., Vallano, M.L. and Barfield, R.J. (1980) 'Effects of morphine B-endorphin and naloxone on catecholamine levels and sexual behavior in the male rat.' *Pharmacol. Biochem. Behav.*, *13*, 435–41

McLaren, A., Simpson, E., Tomonai, E., Alexander, P. and Hogg, H. (1984) 'Male sexual differentiation in mice lacking HY-antigen.' *Nature*, *312*, 352–5

Meck, J.M. (1984) 'The genetics of the HY-antigen system and its role in sex determination.' *Perspect. Biol. Med.*, *27* (4), 560–84

Melnick, M., Mynanthopoulos, N.C. and Christian, J.C. (1978) 'The effects of chorion type on variation in I.Q. in the NCPP twin population.' *Am. J. Hum. Genet.*, *30*, 425–33

Mitchell, G.A.G. (1969) *The Essentials of Neuroanatomy*. Edinburgh: E & S Livingstone

Mizejewski, G.J., Vonnegut, M. and Simon, R. (1980) 'Neonatal androgenisation using antibodies to alpha-feto protein.' *Brain Res.*, *188*, 273–7

Mosley, J.L. and Stan, E.A. (1984) 'Human sexual dimorphism, its cost and benefit.' *Adv. Child Dev. Behav.*, *18*, 148–85

Muller, U. (1984) 'Chromosomes and sex differentiation in eutherians.' *J. Embryol. Exp. Morphol.*, *83* (Suppl.), 41–9

Murphy, M.R. (1981) 'Methadone reduces sexual performance and sexual motivation in the male Syrian golden hamster.' *Pharmacol. Biochem. Behav.*, *14*, 561–7

Nyborg, H. (1984) 'Performance and intelligence in hormonally different groups.' *Prog. Brain Res.*, *61*, 491–508

Ohno, S., Christian, L.C., Wachtel, S.S. and Koo, G.C. (1976) 'Hormone-like role of HY-antigen in bovine freemartin gonad.' *Nature*, *261*, 597–9

Ohno, S., Nagal, Y., Ciccarese, S. and Iwata, H. (1979) 'Testis-organising HY-antigen and the primary sex-determining of mammals.' *Recent Prog. Horm. Res.*, *35*, 449–75

Ounsted, C. and Taylor, D.C. (1972) 'The Y-Chromosome Message: A point of view.' In *Gender Differences: Their Ontogeny and Significance* (eds C. Ounsted and D.C. Taylor), pp. 241–262, Edinburgh: Churchill-Livingstone

Pillard, R.C., Poumadere, J. and Carreta, R.A. (1981) 'Is homosexuality familial? A review, some data, and a suggestion.' *Arch. Sex. Behav.*, *10*, 465–75

Polani, P.E. (1981) 'Abnormal sex development in man: (1) anomalies in sex-determining mechanisms and (2) anomalies of sex-differentiating mechanisms.' In *Mechanisms of Sex Differentiation in Animals and Man* (eds C.R. Austin and R.G. Edwards). New York: Academic Press

Polani, P.E. and Adinolfi, M. (1983) 'The HY-antigen and its functions: a review and a hypothesis.' *J. Immunogenet.*, *10*, 85–102

Polani, P.E. (1985) 'The genetic basis of embryonic sexual dimorphism.' In *Human Sexual Dimorphism* (eds. J. Ghesquiere, R.D. Martin, and F. Newcombe), Symposia of the Society for the study of Human

Biology, *24*, 125–50, London: Taylor and Francis

Rao, C.S., Vaidya, R.A., Patel, Z.M. and Ambani, L.M. (1981) 'Role of HY-antigen in gonadal differentiation.' *Indian J. Med. Res.*, *73*, 342–9

Reinboth, R. (1980) 'Can sex inversion be environmentally induced?' *Biol. Reprod.*, *22* (1), 49–59

Ricketts, W. (1984) 'Biological research on homosexuality: Ansell's cow or Occam's razor?' *J. Homosex.*, *9* (4), 65–93

Ross, M.W. (1983) *The Married Homosexual Man. A Psychological Study*. London: Routledge and Kegan Paul

Ruse, M. (1981) 'Are there gay genes? Sociobiology and homosexuality.' *J. Homosex.*, *6* (4), 5–34

Sarnat, H.B. and Netsky, M.C. (1974) *Evolution of the Nervous System*. London: Oxford University Press

Sherman, J.A. (1978) *Sex-related Cognitive Differences*. Springfield, Ill.: Charles C. Thomas

Simpson, E. (1983) 'Immunology of HY-antigen and its role in sex-determination. Review lecture.' *Proc. R. Soc. Lon. [B]*, *220*, 31–46

Taylor, D.C. (1985) 'Mechanisms of sex differentiation: Evidence from disease.' In *Human Sexual Dimorphism* (eds. J. Ghesquire *et al.*), *24*, 169–89, London: Taylor and Francis

Vandeberg, J.L. (1983) 'Developmental aspects of X-chromosome inactivation in eutherian and metatherian mammals.' *J. Exp. Zool.*, *228*, 271–86

——, Johnson, P.G., Cooper, D.W. and Robinson, E.S. (1983) 'X-chromosome inactivation and evolution in marsupials and other mammals.' In *Isozymes: Current Topics in Biological and Medical Research*, *9*, *Gene Expression and Development*, pp. 201–218, New York: Alan R. Liss

Vom Saal, F.S. (1982) 'Intrauterine positioning of male and female fetuses: influences on prenatal hormone titers and adult behavior.' *Sexology, Sexual Biology, Behavior and Therapy* (eds. Z. Hock and H.I. Lief), pp. 48–52, Amsterdam: Excerpta Medica

Waber, D.P. (1985) 'The search for biological correlates of behavioral sex differences in humans.' In *Human Sexual Dimorphism* (eds. J. Ghesquire *et al.*), pp. 257–82, London: Taylor and Francis

Wachtel, S.S. (1979) 'Immunogenetic aspects of abnormal sexual differentiation.' *Cell*, *16*, 691–5

Wachtel, S.S. and Koo, G.C. (1981) 'HY-antigen in gonadal differentiation.' In *Mechanisms of Sex Differentiation in Animals and Man* (eds. C.R. Austin and R. J. Edwards), New York: Academic Press

Ward, I.L. and Weisz, J. (1980) 'Maternal stress alters plasma testosterone in foetal males.' *Science*, *207*, 328–9

Whitam, F.L. (1983) 'Culturally invariable properties of male homosexuality: tentative conclusions from cross-cultural research.' *Arch. Sex. Behav.*, *12* (3), 207–26

Whitam, F.L. and Zent, M. (1984) 'A cross-cultural assessment of early cross-gender behaviour and familial factors in male homosexuality.' *Arch. Sex. Behav.*, *13* (5), 427–39

Wilson, J.D., George, F.W. and Griffin, J.F. (1981) 'The hormonal control of sexual development. *Science*, *211*, 1278–84

Winter, J.S.D., Fairman, C. and Reyes, F. (1981) 'Sexual endocrinology and foetal and perinatal life.' In *Mechanisms of Sex Differentiation in Animals and Man* (eds. C.R. Austin and R.G. Edwards). New York: Academic Press.

Wolf, U., Fraccaro, M., Mayerova, A., Hech, T., Zuffardi, O. and Hamiester, H. (1980) 'Turner's syndrome patients are HY-positive.' *Hum. Genet.*, *54*, 315–18

Zuger, B. (1976) 'Monozygote twins discordant for homosexuality: Report of a pair and significance of the phenomenon.' *Compr. Psychiatry*, *17*, 661–9

3

Cerebral Aspects of Sexual Deviation

Pierre Flor-Henry

Langevin (1983, 1985) has reviewed the empirical evidence that indicates that the presence of a sexual deviation increases the probability of occurrence of other sexual deviations in the affected individual. Let us examine in greater detail these associations:

Transvestism = fetishism
Heterosexual paedophilia = exhibitionism
Exhibitionism = voyeurism (with orgasm) and solitary outdoor masturbation
Voyeurism = heterosexual paedophilia, obscene telephone calls, transvestism, exhibitionism
Sexual aggression and rape = heterosexual hebephilia (13-to 15-year-old), exhibitionism, voyeurism, frottage and transvestism (orgasm)
Sadomasochism (majority 'versatile': only 15% exclusively sadist or masochist = $\frac{1}{3}$ heterosexual, $\frac{1}{3}$ bisexual and $\frac{1}{3}$ homosexual)
Sadism = exhibitionism, orgasmic cross-dressing, feminine gender identity
Paedophiles = ($\frac{1}{3}$ heterosexual, $\frac{1}{3}$ bisexual, $\frac{1}{3}$ homosexual) — exhibitionism, cross-dressing, voyeurism, frottage, rape
Incest offenders = similar to heterosexual paedophiles on erotic preference questionnaire
Fetishism = homosexuality and transvestism
Male homosexuality — (indifference about gender identity) = sadomasochism, paedophilia, fetishism
Trans-sexuality — (gender identity of the opposite sex) = some association with sadomasochism

MacCulloch, Snowden, Wood and Mills (1983) emphasise in a study of a group of sadistic psychopaths, the extreme importance of fantasy, the frequent impotence and the common association with cross-dressing, fetishism and homosexuality. Indeed, the contrast between quasi-obsessional ruminations over the preferred deviant sexual act and its (relatively) rare actualisation appears to be a general characteristic of all sexual deviations. De Clerambault was also impressed by this phenomenon: he wrote in 1908, discussing fetishism, sadism, masochism and homosexuality: 'A remarkable feature in sexual deviation is the extreme prominence of fantasy related to the object of their passions.' Spengler's finding (1977) that in 245 sadomasochistic men one-third are heterosexual, one-third bisexual and one-third homosexual illustrates how profoundly intertwined are the sexual deviations. Excepting female homosexuality, trans-sexuality and masochism (yet these last two are still more frequent in men) it is a remarkable fact that sexual deviations occur exclusively in men. For example, in the 48 cases of sexual fetishism described by Chalkley and Powell (1983) there is only one woman: a homosexual with a fetish for breasts. The fundamental reason for this susceptibility of men to sexual deviation has been well expressed by Taylor (1981): 'since . . . the male sex syndrome must be promoted from the neutral (female) condition then we can expect more variety in maleness than in femaleness in any of the senses of those terms as used above, and more sex/gender problems in males than in females.' Furthermore since male specialisation hinges on testosterone/left hemisphere interactions whereby the developmental pace of the left hemisphere is slowed, it follows, theoretically, that the cerebral locus of sexual deviations is probably determined by unusual patterns of neural organisation in the dominant hemisphere.

Traditionally the subcortical components of the complex, integrated neural network mediating sexual behaviour has been emphasised: for example, electrical stimulation of the pre-optic area, lateral hypothalamus or dorsomedial nucleus of the hypothalamus produces sexual responses in male rhesus monkeys (Perachio, Marr and Alexander, 1979). Also, lesional studies in the male rat indicate that the medial-lateral or dorsal fibre connections of the medial pre-optic anterior hypothalamus exercise two regulatory functions: the initiation of copulation through lateral connections with the medial forebrain bundle and ejaculation (with subsequent refractory period) through amygdaloid and hippocampal projections (Szechtman, Caggiula and Wulkan, 1978). The medial forebrain bundle is the point of articulation, in the brain stem, of the limbic system, and the amygdala and hippocampus are key components of lateralised limbic organisation. Rogers (1980) showed that the injection of cycloheximide (an antibiotic that inhibits ribosomal protein synthesis and indirectly increases the levels of intracerebral glutamate and aspartate), when injected into the left forebrain of chicks dramatically increases their copulatory and aggressive behaviours, whereas with right-sided injections the animals did not differ from intact birds. These authors also found (Howard, Rogers and Boura, 1980) that administration of glutamate (an inhibitory neurotransmitter) in the left forebrain of chicks produced a 'remarkable increase in attack and copulation'. Injections in the right brain or of both hemispheres led to behavioural states similar to that of animals with intact brains. Experimental studies carried out by Denenberg (1981) investigating emotionality (lithium-induced taste aversion) and aggression (muricidal attacks) in the rat showed, in the same way, that emotionality and aggression were derivative of right-brain systems, under inhibitory regulation from the left brain in the intact animal. Thus a fundamental principle of organisation in double brain systems emerges, common to both avian and mammalian evolution: neural systems in the right hemisphere determine emotionality, aggression and sexual arousal under regulatory inhibition from the left hemisphere (see Figure 3.1). There is evidence that indicates the same principle of cerebral organisation is present in man.

Disturbances of hypothalamic/neuroendocrine interactions lead to perturbation of sexual behaviour. In a remarkable series of experiments (in the rat), Gerendai (1984) has demonstrated the importance of laterality in neuroendocrinology and of asymmetries in hypothalamic regulation. There is a higher concentration of luteinising hormone releasing hormone (LHRH) in the right side of the hypothalamus in intact female rats. Ablations of the right hypothalamus influence gonadal functions, whereas similar lesions on the left side are without effect. Further, unilateral lesions of the locus coeruleus on the right or section of the vagus on the left side, interfere with ovarian functions: similar interventions on the opposite side are without effect. Posterior hypothalamic lesions on the left side alter thyroid functions, similar lesions on the right side are

Figure 3.1: Effects of left and right cortical excisions vs intact brain on behaviour

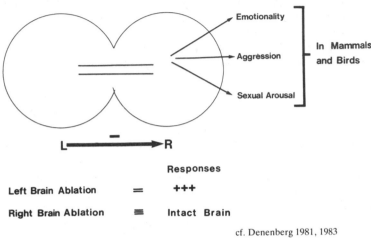

cf. Denenberg 1981, 1983

without effect. Left-sided vagotomy (with or without unilateral ovariectomy) delays the onset of puberty whereas right-sided vagotomy is without effect. On the other hand, right-sided vagotomy with right ovariectomy results in precocious puberty and compensatory ovarian hypertrophy. It is well known that women, after unilateral mastectomy for breast carcinoma, may develop hyperprolactinaemia and galactorrhea. Gerendai and her collaborators found that pituitary prolactin secretion is modified in opposite directions by left- or right-sided mastectomy in the male rat: right-sided excisions producing hyperprolactinaemia, left-sided lesions hypoprolactinaemia. These illustrations of asymmetric regulation of hypothalamic functions and of laterality in neuroendocrinology are but special examples of a fundamental principle, well expressed by Geschwind and Galaburda (1985a): 'Asymmetries of structure and function far from being confined to the human are widespread and possibly even universal properties of living things in both the plant and animal kingdoms. They are present in unicellular organisms as well as in the most complex multicellular forms.'

Nordeen and Yahr (1982) demonstrated the importance of hemispheric asymmetries in the sexual differentiation of the mammalian brain. Oestrogen exposure to the right and left hypothalamus of newborn female rats had different effects: oestrogen implants on the left side produced defeminised, and on the right, masculinised development. Furthermore, the critical period of masculinisation was found to begin and end earlier than the critical period for defeminisation. It was noted earlier that Gerendai (1984) found a greater concentration of LHRH in the right mediobasal hypothalamus of female rats than in the left. Bilateral ovariectomy produced a drop in total LHRH because of a decrease on the right side and in addition unilateral ovariectomy induced a significant increase in LHRH in the hypothalamic region ipsilateral to the resected ovary: thus right-sided ovariectomy enhanced the right>left LHRH asymmetry characteristic of intact female rats while left-sided ovariectomy shifted the balance to the more symmetrical state, which is that of the intact male rat. In the male rat, however, the compensatory increase in follicle stimulating hormone following hemi-orchidectomy can only be blocked by unilateral hypothalamic de-afferentiation when isolation of the right side of the hypothalamus is combined with right hemicastration. Thus male and female patterns of behaviour at the level of hypothalamic/pituitary functions seem to be determined by extremely complex asymmetrical hypothalamic/pituitary/endrocrine interactions.

It is therefore noteworthy that Boyar and Aiman (1982), in the study of 13 male-to-female trans-sexuals, observed that in a number of these subjects the mean serum concentration of LH, the LH pulse frequency (when an LH value exceeds the previous one by at least 20%) and the LH half life were all greater than the 95% confidence limit of normal men. Also the maximum concentration of LH and FSH following the administration of 100 μg of LHRH was significantly greater than in heterosexual men in half of the trans-sexuals. In all these endocrinological characteristics the trans-sexuals shift towards values found in normal heterosexual women. Trans-sexual men would appear to be genetic and morphological men who subjectively feel that they are women because of the particular direction of their hypothalamic/pituitary/endocrine asymmetry of organisation. A similar pattern has been found in paedophiles — Gaffney and Berlin (1984) reported a significant increase in LH response to LHRH in paedophiles compared with nonpaedophilic para-philiacs and normal control men, a result indicating hypothalamic/pituitary/gonadal dysfunction in paedophiles.

Evans (1974) showed in the anthropometric study of 44 homosexual men compared with 111 heterosexual men that the bi-iliac/bi-acromial ratio (3 × bi-acromial −1 × bi-iliac) of the homosexuals was significantly smaller than that of the heterosexuals and in the direction of a female pattern, with narrower shoulders in relation to pelvic width. The scores of the homosexuals were much more variable than those of the heterosexuals and also they were considerably weaker in dynamometric hand strength for the preferred hand. Anthropometric measurements carried out by Coppen (1959) in 31 homosexuals also found that they had decreased androgyny scores and bi-acromial diameters, although this author concluded that this was nonspecific as neurotic patients differed from normal persons in a similar way. Interestingly, Perkins (1981), collecting anthropometric data on 241 homosexual women compared with almost 2000 heterosexual women, observed that homosexual women were significantly narrower in the hips, had less subcutaneous fat and more muscle than the controls. These changes were more pronounced in women showing 'inversion' but were also present in 'passive' homosexual women. These anthropometric considerations suggest that homosexuality, in both men and women, is the consequence of subtle disruptions in the brain mechanisms determining sexual differentiation, maleness and femaleness. Here cerebral lateral organisation is of paramount importance.

Fundamentally, in mammals the male specialisation hinges on testosterone slowing the developmental pace of the left hemisphere: there is evidence that homosexual men have not fully differentiated from the female infrastructure common to both sexes. In mammals the positive oestrogen feedback response is characteristic of female organisation. Following the injection of oestrogens (i.e. premarin) through pituitary feedback inhibition there is a fall in plasma LH concentration after 24 hours with respect to baseline levels. Over the next 48, 72 and 96 hours there is a 200 per cent overshoot above baseline in females. Normal men do not show a rebound increase above baseline at any time following the single injection of oestrogens. Dörner, Rhode, Stahl, Krell and Masius (1975) reported that homosexual men (and some trans-sexuals) exhibited the positive oestrogen feedback characteristic of female mammalian organisation. This was confirmed by Gladue, Green and Hellman (1984) in the comparison of 12 heterosexual women, 14 homosexual men and

17 heterosexual men. The homosexual men showed a positive feedback, intermediate between the heterosexual women and men. That critical brain-testosterone interactions are essential for complete male development is demonstrated by the androgen insensitivity syndrome, in which genetic males with male levels of plasma testosterone develop as females, with normal female external morphological sexual characteristics (although with absence of ovaries and uterus), who are feminine in their psychological and sexual orientation and, cognitively, have an exaggerated female configuration. The syndrome arises because of the complete cellular conversion of endogenous testosterone into oestrogens. There are anecdotal reports of a high incidence of sinistrality in homosexuals (Geschwind and Galaburda, 1985a and b) consistent with altered testosterone/left hemisphere neurohumoral organisation, and in trans-sexual men Werneke (1986, personal communication) reports over 50 per cent strong sinistrality.

There are important interactions between the gonadal steroids and the immune system. Grossman (1985), reviewing the evidence in this field, concludes that the reproductive-immunological interactions are hormonally regulated, the hormones originating from the thymus, hypothalamic/pituitary axis and the gonads. Gonadotrophin releasing hormone from the hypothalamus stimulates LH release from the pituitary and LH stimulates hypothalamic sex steroids release. In turn, increased sex steroid levels depress (and depressed levels stimulate) thymic thymosins, which modulate T-cell functions, since T-cells have both androgen and oestrogen receptors. The ratio of circulating androgens/oestrogens appears to determine whether the effects of circulating steroids will be immunostimulatory or immuno-inhibitory. Remarkably, it has been shown that in mice, T-cell and killer phagocytic activity is under left brain regulatory control. Left neocortical lesions in mice lead to a 50% reduction in T-cells and to a severe depression of T-cell mediated responses; similarly, killer phagocytic reactivity of mouse spleen cells is exclusively controlled by the left brain neocortex. Lesions of the symmetrical right neocortical areas are totally without effect on these immunological modulations (Renoux, Biziere, Renoux and Guillaumin, 1983a and b; Biziere, Guillaumin, Degenne, Bardos, Renoux and Renoux, 1985). Geschwind and Behan (1982) have attributed an increased incidence of auto-immune diseases found in sinistrals (11% vs 4% in dextrals) to testosterone supersensitivity slowing the developmental pace of the left hemisphere and simultaneously suppressing fetal thymus and T lymphocytic reactivity. By an analogous reasoning it is not to be excluded that homosexual men, with a CNS organisation that has remained partially feminised as a result of testosterone/ left brain interactions and sex steroid/pituitary balances not seen in heterosexual men (with consequent dysregulation of immunological balances on two counts: interference in the left-brain regulation of immunological systems and altered pituitary/ sex steroid/thymic peptide hormonal/hypothalamic GnRH hormone interactions) are for those reasons particularly predisposed to acquired immunodeficiency syndrome (AIDS).

An intriguing clue into the possible etiology of male homosexuality is provided by the studies of Ward (1984) on the prenatal stress syndrome in the rat. Exposure of female rats to stressors during pregnancy (last week) results in selective feminisation and demasculinisation of adult sexual behaviours in the male offspring. There are no behavioural consequences in the female offspring and the reproductive morphological structures are normal in both sexes. Ward was able to show that the feminisation of the male offspring occurred only when the female rats were stressed in the last week of pregnancy. The normal rise in fetal male plasma testosterone that takes place on days 17 and 18 after conception did not occur; instead, there was a sharp decline. Similar mechanisms during critical periods of sexual differentiation in intrauterine life may well arise in humans.

In recent years the neurotransmitter modulation of sexual behaviour has been clarified. Rodriguez, Castro, Hernandez and Mas (1984), by making selective lesions of catecholaminergic and serotoninergic neurons in the medial forebrain bundle of the male rat have shown that dopaminergic systems facilitate and serotoninergic systems inhibit male sexual behaviour. Similar findings in the male rat were reported by McIntosh and Barfield (1984a, b and c). In addition, these authors observed that disruption of central noradrenergic systems in the locus coeruleus reduced sexual arousal, without affecting other parameters of sexual behaviour, such as the number of intromissions required to achieve ejaculation or the length of the post-ejaculatory refractory pause. These neurochemical effects on sexual behaviour operate in the same way in female mammals. Indeed, Meyerson (1964; Meyerson, Carrer and Eliasson, 1974) were the first to report the serotonin-mediated inhibition of 'heat' display in female rats and, conversely, its enhancement by inhibiting serotonin. In an editorial, Everitt (1983) reviewed the numerous studies that led to the recognition of these relationships. He notes that the nigrostriatal (and mesolimbic) dopaminergic neurons project to the septal nuclei, amygdala and frontal cortex; the noradrenergic neurons from the medullary ventrolateral reticular formation innervate the hypothalamus and septal and amygdaloid nuclei; the pontine noradrenergic projection is to the hippocampus and neocortex while the serotoninergic cells in the raphé nuclei project to the hypothalamus, thalamus, striate, septum, hippocampus and neocortex. Everitt remarks that since the striatal dopaminergic system (and its projections) is essential to goal-directed (and sexual) behaviour and is *not* hormone dependent, 'we must come to terms with the fact that dopaminergic manipulations can affect the expression of sexual behavior without directly affecting its hormonal determinants.'

If we consider that dopamine, noradrenergic and serotoninergic systems have bilateral projections to essential limbic/cortical structures (hippocampal, amygdaloid, septal and frontal), the question of the hemispheric regulation of sexual behaviour immediately arises. This has been curiously neglected, in spite of the investigations of Denenberg and others earlier discussed. McIntosh and Barfield (1984b), in their conclusions on the excitatory effect of dopamine and inhibitory effect of serotonin on sexual behaviour, refer to the experimental evidence showing that there is a reciprocal central antagonism between these two neurotransmitter systems. I have reviewed elsewhere (Flor-Henry, Koles and Reddon, 1985) the further evidence that in man, these neurotransmitters are bilaterally asymmetrically organised: dopaminergic biased towards the dominant and serotonin and noradrenergic towards the non-dominant hemisphere, as well as linked by *complex* reciprocal relationships (see Figure 3.2). Thus the question of lateral cerebral organisation in the determination of sexual behaviour arises at the level of its neurotransmitter regulation. I have also reviewed (Flor-Henry, 1980) the evidence derived largely, but not exclusively, from epileptic studies, which indicates that sexual deviation is the result of lateralised, often astonishingly specific disturbances of temporal/limbic neural sets. Kolarsky, Freund, Machek *et al.* (1967), in a study of 86 males, have noted that sexual deviation was significantly associated with temporal

Figure 3.2: Reciprocal relationships between neurotransmitter systems and their bilaterally asymmetrical corticolimbic distributions

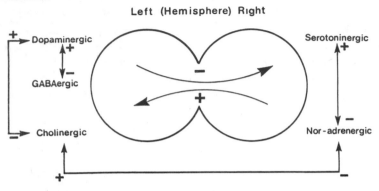

Left (Hemisphere) Right

lobe epilepsy occurring before the first year of life. All categories of sexual deviations were found: voyeurism, exhibitionism, homosexuality, heterosexual and homosexual paedophilia, sadism and masochism, as well as fetishism and transvestism. Hyposexuality was also significantly associated with temporal lesions. Many other authors have described the presence of fetishism in temporal lobe epilepsy and have provided remarkable descriptions of orgasmic epilepsy and of unusual cases of hypersexuality found with parasagittal lesions, often with involvement of the paracentral lobule (Flor-Henry, 1980 for review). Ten years ago I reviewed the international literature searching for published cases of orgasmic epilepsy (Flor-Henry, 1976): without a single exception, all related to focal epilepsies of the non-dominant hemisphere. A later series confirmed this lateralisation (Remillard, Andermann, Testa, Gloor, Aube, Martin, Feindel, Guberman and Simpson, 1983).

We have seen earlier that in the general mammalian brain organisation erotic arousal is a function of neural networks of the right hemisphere under inhibitory regulation from the left brain. There is evidence that the same is true in man. Cohen, Rosen and Goldstein (1976) demonstrated that in both male and female normal volunteers who masturbated to orgasm under EEG monitoring, the orgasmic response was associated with a large increase in EEG amplitudes in the theta range, localised in the right parietal region. Cohen, Rosen and Goldstein (1985) replicated these findings, showing a pattern of right temporal EEG activation during sexual arousal in normal men who exhibited high penile tumescence responses to visual and auditory erotic stimuli. Tucker (1983), investigating erotic arousal in normal subjects, found a significant increase in right parietal EEG coherence during sexual excitement in these subjects. Sexual arousal during sleep is also related to right hemisphere activation. Karacan, Goodenough, Shapiro *et al.* (1966) reported that REM sleep is associated with penile erections in 80 per cent of instances in normal males. Analogous vaginal excitatory changes have been described in women during REM phase. Bakan (1975) reviewed the evidence suggesting that REM sleep was related to right hemisphere activation and partial interhemispheric disconnection. Lewis and Oswald (1969) noted that the rebound REM sleep that follows overdosage with tricyclics (after an interval of about 5 days) is typically linked to unpleasant erotic stimulation. Banquet (1983), investigating inter-hemispheric and intra-hemispheric EEG activity during sleep in man, found that the REM phase of sleep was characterised by an increase in intra-hemispheric and a decrease in inter-hemispheric EEG coherence, a result confirming the presence of partial disconnection in REM sleep. Hirshkowitz, Ware, Turner and Karacan (1979) had also shown that the onset of nocturnal erections during REM sleep was correlated with right-hemispheric EEG activation. Thus it seems well established from these convergent lines of evidence that the orgasmic response is mediated by neural systems in the non-dominant hemisphere and that (during sleep) this activation is paralleled by decreased inter-hemispheric synchronisation, i.e. the result of release from left hemisphere regulatory inhibition.

A number of observations showed that cerebral representation of pain perception was lateralised to the non-dominant hemisphere. In 1937, Halliday noted the preponderance of pain in the left shoulder and left arm in 21 patients with rheumatism. Earlier, in 1924, Purves-Stewart had described the left-sided predominance of tender spots in hysteria, a lateralisation that has recently been confirmed by several recent studies which indicate a strong excess of left-sided symptomatology in patients with unilateral conversion symptoms. Morgenstern (1970) showed that in 154 patients with unilateral or bilateral limb amputations pain was significantly greater for left-sided amputations, even in bilateral amputations. The effect was independent of sex, marital status, arm-vs-leg section, causes of amputation, the state of the stump, and past or present medical disorders. Agnew and

Merskey (1976), analysing chronic pain in 128 patients, found a significant excess of pain on the left side in both organically based and psychologically derived illnesses. Haslam (1970) established the physiologic generality of these phenomena when she demonstrated in normal persons that the dominant hand has a higher pain threshold than the non-dominant and that the pain threshold was inversely correlated with manipulospatial ability (of the hand).

The intimate interrelation of pain and mood is thus the reflection of their common lateralisation to non-dominant, limbic/cortical structures. The above inter-relationships suggest that masochistic sexual deviation is the result of abnormal fusion of cerebral systems related to pain and orgasmic response, as both are lateralised in the same hemisphere. That the neurophysiological systems subtending pain perception and orgasmic physiology are deeply interconnected is also suggested by the studies of Whipple and Komisaruk (1985) on the action of vaginal stimulation in rats, with reference to orgasm and analgesia in women. In the rat, vaginal mechanostimulation blocks withdrawal reflexes to noxious stimulation applied to the body surface. There is evidence that a descending monoaminergic system is activated as well as a (partially) glycinergic spinal mechanism. Non-painful self-applied vaginal pressure elevates the pain threshold — but not the tactile threshold — in women. When the vaginal stimulation led to orgasm the pain detection threshold increased by over 100 per cent and the pain tolerance threshold by 75 per cent compared with the baseline.

A few years ago (Flor-Henry, 1980), consideration of the cerebral aspects of the normal and deviational orgasmic response suggested the following propositions:

(1) Sexual deviation is gender-dependent and not only much more frequent but also much more varied in its manifestations in the male than in the female. Certain deviations such as voyeurism, exhibitionism[1], homicidal sadism and fetishism are virtually never encountered in women. Thus the possibility arises that sexual deviation is linked to the differential cerebral organisation of the male and female brains, which, in turn, is the result of neurochemical interactions that are testosterone-dependent, that occur during critical epochs of embryogenesis, and that determine a

different organisation of lateralised cognitive systems in males and females. It would appear that the male pattern — more lateralised for both verbal and visuospatial cognitive modes and also more vulnerable in its verbal/linguistic dominant axis — carries with it an increased susceptibility to aberrant sexual programming. In this perspective a fundamental component of sexual deviation would hinge on abnormal ideational representations derivative of altered dominant hemispheric functions. The other side of the problem relates to neurophysiologic mechanisms underlying the orgasmic state in the non-dominant hemisphere.

(2) These considerations lead to the following neuro-physiological hypothesis for sexual deviations: normal sexuality is determined by the presence of normal verbal/ideational sexual representations, which depend essentially on intact dominant hemispheric systems and on their (normal) ability to trigger the orgasmic response in the non-dominant hemisphere. This implies intact inter-hemispheric connections. It has been shown that under certain circumstances lateralised cerebral dysfunction alters the organisation of the opposite hemisphere. Pathological neural organisation of the dominant hemisphere provides the substrate for the abnormal ideational representations of the sexual deviations and leads to (or is associated with) perturbed inter-hemispheric relationships, so that only these abnormal ideas are capable of eliciting or have the highest probability of inducing the orgasmic response.

Neuropsychological studies of a variety of sexual offenders carried out at the Alberta Hospital by Yeudall, Fedora, Schopflocher, Reddon and Hyatt (1986) confirm the presence of dominant hemispheric dysfunction in sexual deviation. Table 3.1 shows the composite neuropsychological profile of 109 sexual offenders: homicidal rapists, aggressive sexual criminals, heterosexual and homosexual paedophiles, fetishists and incest offenders as well as of exhibitionists. Their neuropsychological scores are expressed in terms of standard deviations against normal controls corrected for age and sex ($n=192$). As a group these court-referred sexual deviants are most impaired for the following neuropsychological variables: William's Verbal Learning; Colored Progressive Matrices and Trail-Making B.

Table 3.1: Neuropsychological characteristics of sex offenders (*n* = 109)

| | | STANDARD DEVIATIONS: | | | | | | |
| | | IMPAIRED | | | NORMAL | ABOVE NORMAL | | |
		-3	-2	-1	0	1	2	3
APHASIA TEST	2.81			X				
ORAL WORD FLUENCY	11.38			X				
WRITTEN WORD FLUENCY	9.54			X				
SPEECH SOUNDS PERCEPTION	7.72			X				
WILLIAM'S VERBAL LEARNING	13.96	X						
SEASHORE RHYTHM	5.24			X				
COLORED PROGRESSIVE MATRICES	4.72	X						
ORGANIC INTEGRITY	74.94					X		
MEMORY-FOR-DESIGNS	42.65			X				
TRAIL MAKING A	38.06			X				
TRAIL MAKING B	95.06	X						
SYMBOL GESTALT	0.07			X				
PURDUE PEGBOARD: RIGHT	13.91				X			
TACTUAL PERFORMANCE: RIGHT	359.39				X			
PURDUE PEGBOARD: LEFT	13.64				X			
TACTUAL PERFORMANCE: LEFT	279.63				X			
PURDUE PEGBOARD: BOTH	11.52				X			
PURDUE PEGBOARD: ASSEMBLIES	33.19			X				
TACTUAL PERFORMANCE: BOTH	163.16				X			
HALSTEAD CATEGORY	56.12			X				
WISCONSIN CARD SORT: ERRORS	24.86				X			
WISCONSIN CARD SORT: SUBTESTS	4.48			X				
TACTUAL PERF.: MEMORY	7.41			X				
TACTUAL PERF.: LOCALISATION	4.80				X			
TACTUAL PERF.: BOTH	163.16			X				
WILLIAM'S: NONVERBAL: T1	2.13				X			
WILLIAM'S: NONVERBAL: T2	2.25				X			
DYNAMOMETER: RIGHT	47.79				X			
FINGER TAPPING: RIGHT	48.07				X			
NAME WRITING: RIGHT	9.25				X			
DYNAMOMETER: LEFT	44.20				X			
FINGER TAPPING: LEFT	42.90				X			
NAME WRITING: LEFT	24.46				X			
FINGER LOCALISATION: RIGHT	5.61			X				
FINGERTIP # WRITING: RIGHT	3.06			X				
TACTILE FORM RECOG.: RIGHT	0.04				X			
L.J. TACTILE RECOG.: RIGHT	39.77				X			
FACE-HAND: RIGHT	0.16				X			
FINGER LOCALISATION: LEFT	6.78			X				
FINGERTIP # WRITING: LEFT	2.68				X			
TACTILE FORM RECOG.: LEFT	0.06				X			
L.J. TACTILE RECOG.: LEFT	35.61					X		
FACE-HAND: LEFT	0.25				X			
L.J. TACTILE RECOG.: BOTH	29.45				X			

cf. Yeudall et al., 1986 In Preparation.

Their scores for Aphasia Screening test, Oral Word Fluency, Written Word Fluency, Seashore Rhythm, Memory For Designs, Trail-Making A, Halstead Category and Wisconsin Card Sorting are also impaired. The overall pattern of cerebral dysfunction is thus clearly bilateral frontotemporal, left>right. A remarkably similar pattern is seen in a group of 18 incest offenders (father/daughter) as indicated in Table 3.2. The neuropsychological characteristics of 23 exhibitionists are shown in Table 3.3. Here the dysfunction is much more discrete, involving Oral Word Fluency, Speech Sounds Perception and William's Verbal Learning, i.e. focal left frontotemporal dysfunction. It should be emphasised that the neuropsychological profile in exhibitionism is more than a statistical group effect: this very configuration, without exception, was seen in every subject.

Nineteen of these 23 exhibitionists were studied neurophysiologically (Flor-Henry, Koles, Reddon and Baker, 1986a). The EEG was recorded at locations P_4, P_3, T_4, T_3, F_8, F_7, T_6, T_5, referred to Cz (International 10–20 system) for two minutes during the following mental conditions: at rest with eyes open, at rest with eyes closed, during verbal processing (Vocabulary subtest of the WAIS and Oral Word Fluency) and during spatial processing (Block Design subtest of the WAIS). These 19 subjects were matched against a healthy control group ($n=19$) in terms of age, sex and handedness. Characteristically all were men and 20 per cent were sinistral (consistent and inconsistent in the Annett (1970) classification). Taking consistent dextrality as criterion, 50 per cent of the exhibitionists were non-dextrals (as opposed to 35 per cent in the general population). The EEG characteristics of the exhibitionists were compared with those of the controls in terms of previously established norms on five fundamental EEG parameters (Power, Coherence, Phase, Log of right/left Power Ratio and Oscillations) derived from a larger sample of normal controls (Flor-Henry, Koles and Reddon, 1986b).

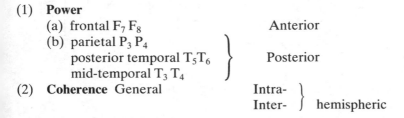

(1) **Power**
    (a) frontal F_7 F_8 Anterior
    (b) parietal P_3 P_4
         posterior temporal $T_5 T_6$ Posterior
         mid-temporal T_3 T_4
(2) **Coherence** General   Intra-
                             Inter-   hemispheric

Table 3.2: Neuropsychological characteristics of incest (*n* = 18)

		STANDARD DEVIATIONS: IMPAIRED			NORMAL	ABOVE NORMAL		
		-3	-2	-1	0	1	2	3
APHASIA TEST	2.89		X					
ORAL WORD FLUENCY	8.84		X					
WRITTEN WORD FLUENCY	8.58		X					
SPEECH SOUNDS PERCEPTION	8.44		X					
WILLIAM'S VERBAL LEARNING	13.88	X						
SEASHORE RHYTHM	5.67		X					
COLORED PROGRESSIVE MATRICES	5.11	X						
ORGANIC INTEGRITY	71.78				X			
MEMORY-FOR-DESIGNS	42.50		X					
TRAIL MAKING A	37.58		X					
TRAIL MAKING B	93.29	X						
SYMBOL GESTALT	0.08			X				
PURDUE PEGBOARD: RIGHT	14.18				X			
TACTUAL PERFORMANCE: RIGHT	347.41				X			
PURDUE PEGBOARD: LEFT	14.06				X			
TACTUAL PERFORMANCE: LEFT	240.89				X			
PURDUE PEGBOARD: BOTH	11.53				X			
PURDUE PEGBOARD: ASSEMBLIES	32.94			X				
TACTUAL PERFORMANCE: BOTH	146.44				X			
HALSTEAD CATEGORY	54.22			X				
WISCONSIN CARD SORT: ERRORS	21.73				X			
WISCONSIN CARD SORT: SUBTESTS	4.73			X				
TACTUAL PERF.: MEMORY	7.50			X				
TACTUAL PERF.: LOCALISATION	4.94				X			
TACTUAL PERF.: BOTH	146.44				X			
WILLIAM'S: NONVERBAL: T1	1.94				X			
WILLIAM'S: NONVERBAL: T2	2.00			X				
DYNAMOMETER: RIGHT	46.02			X				
FINGER TAPPING: RIGHT	49.63				X			
NAME WRITING: RIGHT	11.29		X					
DYNAMOMETER: LEFT	42.30			X				
FINGER TAPPING: LEFT	43.80				X			
NAME WRITING: LEFT	26.90				X			
FINGER LOCALISATION: RIGHT	5.56			X				
FINGERTIP # WRITING: RIGHT	2.65				X			
TACTILE FORM RECOG.: RIGHT	0.0					X		
L.J. TACTILE RECOG.: RIGHT	35.16					X		
FACE-HAND: RIGHT	0.0					X		
FINGER LOCALISATION: LEFT	6.33			X				
FINGERTIP # WRITING: LEFT	2.41			X				
TACTILE FORM RECOG.: LEFT	0.07				X			
L.J. TACTILE RECOG.: LEFT	29.15					X		
FACE-HAND: LEFT	0.0					X		
L.J. TACTILE RECOG.: BOTH	26.39					X		

cf. Yeudall et al., 1986 In Preparation.

Table 3.3: Neuropsychological characteristics of exhibitionists (*n* = 23)

STANDARD DEVIATIONS:

		IMPAIRED			NORMAL	ABOVE NORMAL		
		-3	-2	-1	0	1	2	3
ORAL WORD FLUENCY	12.32			X				
WRITTEN WORD FLUENCY	10.67		X					
SPEECH SOUNDS PERCEPTION	6.87		X					
WILLIAM'S VERBAL LEARNING	12.65	X						
SEASHORE RHYTHM	3.13				X			
TRAIL MAKING A	28.28				X			
TRAIL MAKING B	60.24				X			
PURDUE PEGBOARD: RIGHT	15.52				X			
TACTUAL PERFORMANCE: RIGHT	336.55				X			
PURDUE PEGBOARD: LEFT	14.70				X			
TACTUAL PERFORMANCE: LEFT	232.37				X			
PURDUE PEGBOARD: BOTH	12.22				X			
PURDUE PEGBOARD: ASSEMBLIES	38.30				X			
TACTUAL PERFORMANCE: BOTH	159.04			X				
HALSTEAD CATEGORY	46.96			X				
WISCONSIN CARD SORT: ERRORS	23.83			X				
WISCONSIN CARD SORT: SUBTESTS	5.17			X				
TACTUAL PERF.: BOTH	159.04			X				
WILLIAM'S: NONVERBAL: T1	1.83				X			
WILLIAM'S: NONVERBAL: T2	1.91			X				
DYNAMOMETER: RIGHT	52.38					X		
FINGER TAPPING: RIGHT	50.90					X		
NAME WRITING: RIGHT	10.05			X				
DYNAMOMETER: LEFT	51.01					X		
FINGER TAPPING: LEFT	45.05				X			
NAME WRITING: LEFT	25.20				X			
TACTILE FORM RECOG.: RIGHT	0.04				X			
L.J. TACTILE RECOG.: RIGHT	29.53					X		
FACE-HAND: RIGHT	0.26				X			
TACTILE FORM RECOG.: LEFT	0.0				X			
L.J. TACTILE RECOG.: LEFT	25.22					X		
FACE-HAND: LEFT	0.26				X			
L.J. TACTILE RECOG.: BOTH	23.86					X		

cf. Yeudall et al., 1986 In Preparation.

Figure 3.3: EEG factors: (1–3), (4–7), (8–13), (20–40) Hz normals (phase'A')

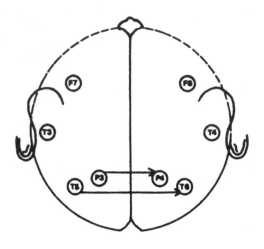

Figure 3.4: EEG factors: (1–3), (4–7), (8–13), (20–40) Hz normals (phase 'B')

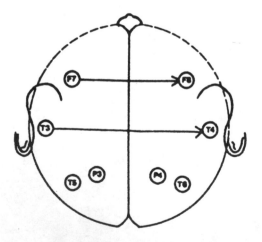

Figure 3.5: EEG factors: (1–3), (4–7), (8–13), (20–40) Hz normals (phase 'C')

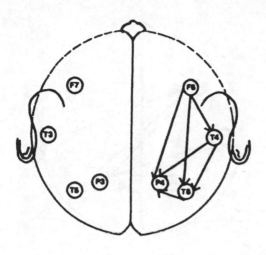

Figure 3.6: EEG factors: (1–3), (4–7), (8–13), (20–40) Hz normals (phase 'D')

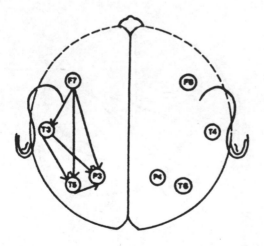

Figure 3.7: EEG factors: (1–3), (4–7), (8–13), (20–40) Hz normals (phase 'E')

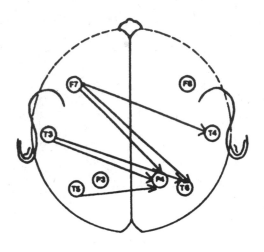

Figure 3.8: EEG factors: (1–3), (4–7), (8–13), (20–40) Hz normals (phase 'F')

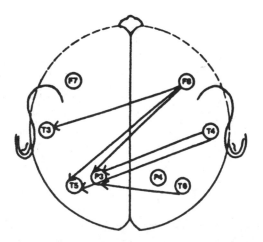

(3) **Phase**: (See Figures 3.3–3.8)
    (a) $(T_5 > T_6)$; $P_3 > P_4)$
    (b) $(F_7 > F_8)$; $(T_3 > T_4)$
    (c) $(T_4 > P_4)$; $(F_8 > T_4)$; $(F_8 > P_4)$; $(T_6 > P_4)$; $(F_8 > T_6)$; $(T_4 > T_6)$
    (d) $(F_7 > P_3)$; $(F_7 > T_3)$; $(T_3 > P_3)$; $(T_5 > P_3)$; $(F_7 > T_5)$; $(T_3 > T_5)$
    (e) $(F_7 > P_4)$; $(F_7 > T_4)$; $(T_3 > P_4)$; $(T_5 > P_4)$; $(F_7 > T_6)$; $(T_3 > T_6)$
    (f) $(F_8 > P_3)$; $(T_4 > P_3)$; $(F_8 > T_3)$; $(T_6 > P_3)$; $(F_8 > T_5)$; $(T_4 > T_5)$

(4) (a) Log right/left **frontal power ratio**
    (b) Log right/left **temporal/parietal power ratio**
(5) **Oscillations**[2]
    (a) Temporal-parietal
    (b) Frontal

The 13 measures were obtained for each of the five tasks and analysed by repeated measures analysis of variance. Elsewhere (Flor-Henry *et al.*, 1985, 1986b) we reported task effects for these measures and hence the task effects in the present analysis were not pursued further. Only effects due to group membership and group by task interaction were evaluated further with *post hoc* evaluation of mean differences. The results were as follows:

EXHIBITIONISTS, GROUP 1 (*n* = 19) VS MATCHED CONTROLS

Repeated measures analysis of variance revealed the following significant differences ($P < 0.05$):

Main effects	*Hz*
Log right/left frontal power ratio	(1–3)
	(4–7)
	(8–13)
Phase	
Right Intra-hemispheric	(8–13)
Anterior > Posterior	
Left Intra-hemispheric	(8–13)
Anterior > Posterior	
Left > Right Inter-hemispheric	(8–13)

69

Task × diagnosis interaction

Eyes Open	Power (Posterior)	(8–13)
Eyes Closed	Power (Posterior)	(8–13)

Both the right and left anterior ➤ posterior intra-hemispheric phase relationships were reduced in the exhibitionists, compared with the controls, as was the left ➤ right inter-hemspheric phase lead. During the cognitively neutral condition (eyes open, closed), power in the more posterior cerebral regions was increased in the sexual deviation. The right/left frontal power ratio was reduced in exhibitionists. It should be noted that the significant findings are all in the slower frequency bands — the majority in the alpha frequency — and none in the beta range.

Eighty per cent correct classification between the two populations was achieved, as the following discriminant function analysis (Jackknife) shows.

DISCRIMINANT FUNCTION ANALYSIS (JACKKNIFE)

Theta (4–7) Hz = 81.6% Correct Classification:

Log right/left Frontal Power Ratio	Block Design
Frontal Oscillations	Block Design

Alpha (8–13) Hz = 78.9% Correct Classification:

Left intra-hemispheric	Block Design
Anterior ➤ Posterior Phase	
Log right/left Frontal Power Ratio	Block Design

It should be noted that the best discrimination occurred during the visual processing condition, again in the lower frequencies, theta and alpha. Univariate follow up analysis for the EEG measures in the four frequency bands showed that the phase relations: left intra-hemispheric anterior ➤ posterior, left ➤ right inter-hemispheric and the log of the right/left power ratios were all significantly different interactions, which differentiated the exhibitionists from the controls in all four frequency bands but with the highest probability ($P < 0.005$) in the alpha frequencies.

A second group consisting of 20 exhibitionists (again, all men) was subjected to quantitative EEG analysis according to the same procedure. Once more 20% of the second group were sinistrals. Having shown that the two sexually deviant groups did not differ in age or handedness, but only in severity of EEG changes on some EEG variables (see Flor-Henry *et al.*, 1986a) the two groups were combined ($n=39$) and compared against the controls. Repeated measures analysis of variance revealed the following:

Main effects		*Hz*
Coherence	$P < 0.02$	1–3
	$P < 0.04$	4–7
Oscillations (posterior)	$P < 0.02$	1–3
	$P < 0.02$	8–13
Oscillations (frontal)	$P < 0.05$	8–13
Right Intra-hemispheric Anterior ➤ Posterior	$P < 0.01$	8–13
Left Intra-hemispheric Anterior ➤ Posterior	$P < 0.007$	8–13
Left ➤ Right Inter-hemispheric	$P < 0.006$	8–13
Right ➤ Left Inter-hemispheric	$P < 0.02$	8–13

Task × diagnosis interactions		*Hz*
Left Intra-hemispheric Anterior ➤ Posterior	$P < 0.02$	4–7
Posterior Power	$P < 0.03$	8–13
Log of right/left Posterior Power Ratio	$P < 0.03$	8–13
Oscillations (frontal)	$P < 0.04$	8–13

The main effects show that the exhibitionists, when compared with the controls, have reduced coherence in the delta and theta ranges, slower oscillations posteriorly in the delta and both frontal and posterior in the alpha range. Still in the alpha, anteroposterior intra-hemispheric phase is bilaterally less pronounced and left ➤ right and right ➤ left inter-hemispheric phase relations are also significantly reduced, particularly the former. The significant task by diagnosis interactions again emphasise the left intra-hemispheric anterior ➤ posterior phase (theta), increased posterior cerebral power, smaller log of right/left power ratio and slow frontal oscillations — all in the alpha frequencies.

Delta (1–3) Hz = 72.4% Correct Classification:

Left Intra-hemispheric Anterior ➤ Posterior	Eyes closed
Left ➤ Right Inter-hemispheric	Eyes closed
Posterior Oscillations	Eyes closed

Theta (4–7) Hz = 70.7% Correct Classification:
Left ➤ Right Inter-hemispheric (homologous)
	Oral Word Fluency

Right Intra-hemispheric — Oral Word Fluency
  Anterior ➤ Posterior
Left ➤ Right Inter-hemispheric — Oral Word Fluency
Right ➤ Left Inter-hemispheric — Oral Word Fluency
Frontal Oscillations — Oral Word Fluency

Theta (4–7) Hz = 72.4% Correct Classification:
Frontal Power — Block Design
Left ➤ Right Inter-hemispheric — Block Design
Log of right/left frontal power ratio — Block Design
Log of right/left temporal/parietal power ratio — Block Design

Alpha (8–13) Hz = 75.9% Correct Classification:
Left ➤ Right Inter-hemispheric (Posterior) — Eyes open
Coherence — Eyes open
Left ➤ Right Inter-hemispheric (Anterior) — Eyes open
Left ➤ Right Inter-hemispheric (Posterior) — Eyes open

Alpha (8–13) Hz = 72.4% Correct Classification:
Frontal Power — Vocabulary
Left ➤ Right Inter-hemispheric — Vocabulary
Temporal-Parietal Oscillations — Vocabulary

Alpha (8–13) Hz = 74.1% Correct Classification:
Right Intra-hemispheric — Oral Word Fluency
  Anterior ➤ Posterior
Temporal/parietal Oscillations — Oral Word Fluency

Beta (20–40) Hz
No separation between groups at 70% Correct Classification or above.

The essential findings in this neurophysiological investigation of the EEG characteristics of exhibitionism may be summarised in the following way: the evidence from the first group indicates that there is in these subjects a smaller right/left frontal power ratio; a less pronounced anteroposterior phase lead in the left hemisphere and a reduced left ➤ right (homologous) inter-hemispheric phase lead. Further, the discriminant function analysis and *post hoc* univariate follow up verifications showed that the presence of visuospatial cognitive activation (Block Design condition) was the most important for the EEG differentiation of the exhibitionists from the controls. The task × diagnosis interactions identified the same EEG factors, revealing, in addition, increased power in the exhibitionists. The alpha frequency band was the most critical in the separation of the sexual deviation from the normal controls, but the delta and theta bands were also important. Although the Hotelling T^2 (in group 1) showed that in the beta frequencies the same general relationships differentiating exhibitionism from normal subjects held, the fact that the faster frequency characteristics were not significantly different in the populations suggests that there is little or no artifactual myogenic contamination in these results, as does the fact that the alpha band is the most relevant frequency.

The evidence from the combined group of exhibitionists shows that they are characterised by reduced overall EEG coherence, slower oscillations and reduced intra- and inter-hemispheric phase relations bilaterally. The majority of the effects took place in the alpha band and none emerged in the beta frequencies. Except for power, which was increased, all the other EEG variables above were reduced in the exhibitionists. The discriminant function analysis in the combined group of exhibitionists vs the controls confirmed the importance of increased frontal power, the left hemispheric phase deaccentuation, reduced coherence and slower frontal oscillations in the neurophysiological organisation of exhibitionism.

In a different analysis, bipolar montage was reconstructed and bipolar coherences were determined between the following regions:

$$\left.\begin{array}{l} F_7 - F_8 \\ T_5 - T_4 \\ P_3 - P_4 \\ T_5 - T_6 \end{array}\right\} \text{Inter-hemispheric}$$

$$\left.\begin{array}{l} F_7 - T_3 \\ T_5 - P_3 \\ F_8 - T_4 \\ T_6 - P_4 \end{array}\right\} \text{Intra-hemispheric}$$

As Figure 3.9 illustrates there are no electrodes common to any pairs of electrodes from which coherence values are measured. The 31 exhibitionists, all dextrals, were compared with 57 normal dextral males of comparable age ($X = 33$ years) derived from another series of normal subjects studied in the development of normative data. The eight coherence derivations give rise to 20

Figure 3.9: EEG recording derivations

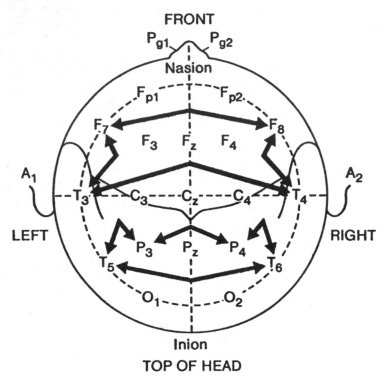

possible combinations in each of the four frequency bands, i.e. to a total of 80. The 10 best were chosen for each task (eyes open, Oral Word Fluency and Block Design) by univariate analysis of variance and a stepwise discriminant function was calculated by maximising a between groups/within groups separation index.

STEPWISE DISCRIMINANT FUNCTION ANALYSIS (BIPOLAR COHERENCE) SHOWING SEPARATION BETWEEN EXHIBITIONISM AND CONTROLS

Task	Weights	Derivations	Band
Eyes open	5.1	P_3-T_5/T_3-F_7	Delta
	− 2.2	T_4-F_8/T_3-F_7	Theta
	10.2	F_8-F_7/T_6-T_5	Alpha
	−4.5	T_4-T_3/T_6-T_5	Alpha

Oral Word Fluency	-6.1	$T_3 - F_7/T_6 - T_5$	Delta
	5.3	$T_4 - F_8/T_6 - T_5$	Theta
	6.9	$F_8 - F_7/T_6 - T_5$	Beta
Block Design	4.7	$P_4 - T_6/F_8 - F_7$	Delta
	-3.4	$P_3 - T_5/T_4 - T_3$	Alpha
	-10.0	$P_4 - T_6/F_8 - F_7$	Beta
	6.3	$T_4 - F_8/P_4 - P_3$	Beta
	8.6	$F_8 - F_7/T_6 - T_5$	Beta

(Note: Normals = 57, Exhibitionists = 31, all dextrals: Positive discriminant coefficients indicate that normals have higher coherence in that derivation.)

In all three conditions, eyes open, Oral Word Fluency and Block Design, the anteroposterior coherences $(F_7 - F_8)$ $-$ $(T_5 - T_6)$ are reduced in exhibitionism. In the resting condition there is a reduction in left intrahemispheric coherence in the delta frequencies $(F_7 - T_3)$ $-$ $(T_5 - P_3)$. During verbal processing there is an increase in left frontotemporal/posterotemporal coherence $(F_7 - T_3)$ $-$ $(T_5 - T_6)$ in the delta band, while in spatial processing the right temporoparietal-frontal coherence $(F_7 - F_8)$ $-$ $(T_6 - P_4)$ is reduced in the delta band. However, in spatial processing the right temporoparietal/frontal coherence $(T_6 - P_4)$ $-$ $(F_7 - F_8)$ is increased in the beta frequencies. The two most discriminating sets of coherences differentiating the exhibitionists from normals are as follows:

(1) Reduction in anteroposterior coherence (alpha) in the resting state and
(2) Increase in right temporoparietal/frontal coherence (beta) during spatial processing.

Further, given the left intra-hemispheric coherence reduction in the resting state, it would appear that the general pattern of coherence disregulation in exhibitionism is characterised by:

(1) A dislocation of frontal/temporoparietal relationships;
(2) Intra-hemispheric disorganisation of the dominant hemisphere;
(3) Alterations of right hemisphere neuroelectric organisation during spatial processing. It should be noted that during verbal tasks left intra-hemispheric coherences are increased and that, correspondingly, right hemispheric coherences are

increased during spatial tasks. This is consistent with the findings of Tucker, Dawson, Roth, Bair and Sawler (1982) who have shown in normal subjects a local increase in left frontal coherence during verbal and in right parietal coherence during spatial processing. In exhibitionists these cognitively determined coherence patterns are accentuated.

Given the importance of left-brain inhibition of right brain systems in both the avian and mammalian brain (Denenberg, 1981), these results are consistent with a left hemispheric deficit (phase) interfering with left hemispheric neural inhibition (increased power) and left brain inhibitory regulation of the right hemisphere (frontal power ratio reduction indicating greater relative activation of the right hemisphere) in exhibitionism. A perturbation of inter-hemispheric relationships is further suggested by the reduced general coherence and the slower frontal oscillations seen in the deviation.

Central to the exhibitionist deviation is a disturbance of visual/erotic/genital arousal in the triggering of the orgasmic response. The subject has to be seen while looking at an adult woman, who is unfamiliar and sexually neutral in behaviour. Indeed, Fedora, Reddon and Yeudall (1986) have shown in the measurement of sexual arousal (penile plethysmography) that exhibitionists differ from normal persons, and those with other sexual deviations in becoming sexually aroused to scenes of fully clothed, erotically neutral females. Similarly, Langevin's observation (Langevin, Paitich, Ramsay, Anderson, Kamrad, Pope, Geller, Pearl and Newman, 1979) that voyeurism associated with orgasm and outdoor masturbation is specifically linked to exhibitionism emphasises the crucial importance of the visual mode in the deviation. The abnormal right frontal activation reflects, presumably, this component of the deviation but the fundamental locus of dysregulation hinges on altered left hemispheric systems. The excess of sinistrality in both exhibitionist groups (20.5 per cent) — a pathological male population — in itself directly suggests the presence of left hemisphere dysfunction.

The EEG configuration in exhibitionism, with perturbation of anteroposterior phase relationships in the left hemisphere, of left ➤ right inter-hemispheric phase lead and with excessive right frontal activation, reduced coherence and slowing of frontal oscillations, is abnormal. The abnormality is predominantly frontal and is most evident in the alpha frequency band. It is accentuated by visual cognitive processing. The findings are generally consistent with the neurophysiological model for sexual deviation developed, because of other evidence, prior to the investigation. A clue into the nature of the lateralised cerebral interactions that determine sexual behaviour is perhaps provided by the opposite changes in sexual drive encountered in the bipolar psychoses: the hyposexuality of depression and the hypersexuality of mania together with the disordered sexuality not infrequently seen in schizophrenia. In schizophrenia, hyposexuality consistent with generalised disturbance of limbic function is common. However bizarre, polymorphous deviational sexuality consistent with dominant hemisphere disorganisation is not infrequent. As reviewed elsewhere (Flor-Henry, 1985) there is evidence that supports the view that the depressive phase of the bipolar syndrome is associated with dysfunctional overactivation of right frontotemporal systems; deeper depressions leading to depressive mutism and stupor through contralateral left brain inhibition, while mania, with a greater degree of right hemisphere disorganisation, evokes, through disruption of right-brain inhibition of left-frontal systems, the characteristic speech acceleration and euphoric mood of mania.

Thus, with a starting point in the right hemisphere, contralateral inhibition of dominant hemispheric systems produces hyposexuality, while contralateral excitation induces hypersexuality. Recalling that dopaminergic systems, which have a left-hemisphere bias, activate sexual drive, while serotoninergic systems, which are right-hemisphere biased, inhibit sexual drive. If we also accept that mania is a hyperdopaminergic state while depression (hypodopaminergic) has been associated with a functional hypercatecholaminergic state (antidepressants producing a subsensitivity of beta-adrenergic post-synaptic receptors), an integration between the bilaterally asymmetrical distribution of the neurotransmitters responsible for positive and negative emotions, sexual excitation and inhibition and dominant/non-dominant hemispheric interactions becomes possible. The importance of laterality in the neuroendocrinology of sexual behaviour in mammals and the corresponding asymmetries in hypothalamic regulation was reviewed and it is not surprising that there should be complex correspondences between these and hemispheric cortical systems of regulation of sexual drive in humans. The fact that sexual deviations are, overwhelmingly, a consequence of the male pattern of cerebral organisation has been repeatedly emphasised in this discussion. The general phenomenological characteristics of sexual deviations, their ruminative, quasi-obsessional ideational intrusive qualities, often against a background of relative hyposexuality, have immediate brain implications relating to altered limbic mechanisms that involve the dominant cortical/limbic axis. A striking aspect of sexual deviations is that, for the most part, they represent fragments of normal sexuality, which become abnormal because only the isolated, exaggerated fragment becomes optimal for eliciting erotic arousal and the orgasmic response. Voyeurism, exhibitionism, fetishism, gentle forms of sadomasochism, the attraction of adolescent forms are all to some extent part of normal sexual experience — but they are peripheral. In deviation they become central. This explains why the sexual deviations are inter-related, the presence of one increasing the probability of others in the affected individual.[3] Fundamentally the male susceptibility to sexual deviations is an expression of the vissicitudes of male specialisation — and hence relates inevitably to the functional (dis)organisation of the dominant hemisphere and its cerebral repercussions.

NOTES

1. Grob (1985) indeed describes a single case of a woman with exhibitionism: driving in an open car she would undress having caught the eye of passing truck drivers or of low flying airplanes and when her genitals were exposed would experience a spontaneous orgasm. That her central nervous system was unusual is suggested by the fact that she was capable of experiencing up to 50 orgasms in a single night with her lover. Similarly de Clerambault (1908–1910) has described unusual examples of fetishism in women whose preferred method of reaching orgasm was by friction of the vagina with velvet material. Such exceptional cases should be considered as examples that 'prove the rule'.

2. (Flor-Henry, Koles and Sussman, 1984). A measure estimating the frequency of right/left hemispheric energy shifts through time.

3. A striking illustration of this is provided by the single case described by Lesniak, Szymusik and Chrzanowski (1972). A man, previously normal, between the ages of 56 and 60 years began to show the following aberrations: 'harlotry, incestuous pedophilia, hetero- and homosexual pedophilia, bestiality (sodomy), masochism, sadism, coprolalia and exhibitionism'. His mental state during these four years changed to one of disinhibited euphoria, and impulsive, explosive aggressivity. He was found to have a neoplasm of the basal regions of the right frontal lobe. Relevant to the pathophysiology in this case is the evidence that non-irritative lesions on the right hemisphere (anterior)

through contralateral disinhibition induce abnormal activation of the left hemisphere (Sackeim, Greenberg, Weiman, Gur, Hungerbuhler and Geschwind, 1982; Flor-Henry, 1985).

REFERENCES

Agnew, U.C. and Merskey, H. (1976) 'Words on chronic pain.' *Pain, 2*, 73–81

Annett, M. (1970) 'A classification of hand preference of association analysis.' *Br. J. Psychol., 61*, 303–21

Bakan, P. (1975) 'Dreaming, REM sleep and the right hemisphere: a theoretical integration.' Presented at the Second International Congress of Sleep Research. Edinburgh, Scotland

Banquet, J.P. (1983) 'Inter- and intrahemispheric relationships of the EEG activity during sleep in man.' *Electroencephalogr. Clin. Neurophysiol., 55*, 51–9

Biziere, K., Guillaumin, J.M., Degenne, D., Bardos, P., Renoux, M. and Renoux, G. (1985) 'Lateralized neocortical modulation of the T-Cell lineage.' In *Neural Modulation of Immunology* (eds. R. Guillaumin, *et al.*, pp. 81–94, New York: Raven Press

Boyar, R.M. and Aiman, J. (1982) 'The 24-hour secretory pattern of LH and the response to LHRH in transsexual men.' *Arch. Sex. Behav., 11* (2), 157–69

Chalkley, A.J. and Powell, G.E. (1983) 'The clinical description of forty-eight cases of sexual fetishism.' *Br. J. Psychiatry, 142, 292*–5

Cohen, A.S., Rosen, R.C. and Goldstein, L. (1985) 'EEG hemispheric asymmetry during sexual arousal: psychophysiological patterns in responsive, unresponsive and dysfunctional males.' *J. Abnorm. Psychol., 94*, 580–90

Cohen, H.D., Rosen, R.C. and Goldstein, L. (1976) 'Electroencephalographic laterality changes during human sexual orgasm.' *Arch. Sex. Behav., 5* (3), 189–95

Coppen, A.J. (1959) 'Body-build of male homosexuals.' *Br. Med. J., 26 Dec. 1959*, 1443–52

De Clerambault, G.G. (1908–1910) 'Passion érotique de étoffes chez la femme.' In *Archives D'Anthropologie Criminelle*, Reprinted in 'La passion des etoffes chez un neuro-psychiatrie, GG. de Clerambault', Y. Papetti, F. Valier, B. De Freminville, S. Tisseron, Solin, (1980), Paris

Denenberg, V.H. (1981) 'Hemispheric laterality in animals and the effects of early experience.' *Behavioural and Brain Sciences, 4* (1), 1–49

Dörner, G., Rhode, W., Stahl, F., Krell, L. and Masiús, W. (1976) 'A neuroendocrine predisposition for homosexuality in men.' *Arch. Sex. Behav., 4*, 1–8

Evans, R.B. (1974) 'Biological factors in male homosexuality.' *Medical Aspects of Human Sexuality, 4* (8), 8–13

Everitt, B.J. (1983) 'Monoamines and the control of sexual behaviour.' *Psychol. Med., 12*, 715–20

Fedora, O., Reddon, J.R. and Yeudall, L.T. (1986) 'Stimuli eliciting sexual arousal in genital exhibitionists: a possible clinical application.' *Arch. Sex. Behav.* (in press).

Flor-Henry, P. (1976) 'Epilepsy and psychopathology.' *Recent Advances in Clinical Psychiatry* (ed. K. Granville-Grossman) Chapter 10, pp. 262–95, Edinburgh: Churchill Livingstone

—— (1980) 'Cerebral aspects of the orgasmic response: normal and deviational.' *Medical Sexology* (eds. R. Forleo and W. Pasini), pp. 256–62, Amsterdam: Elsevier-North Holland

—— (1985) 'Observations, reflections and speculations on the cerebral determinants of mood and on the bilaterally asymmetrical distributions of the major neurotransmitter systems.' In *Pharmacotherapy of Affective Disorders: Theory and Practice* (eds. W.G. Dewhurst and G.B. Baker), pp. 151–84, Beckenham: Croom Helm/New York University Press

——, Koles, Z.J. and Sussman, P.S. (1984) 'Further observations on right/left hemispheric energy oscillations in the endogenous psychoses.' *Advances in Biological Psychiatry*, *15*, 1–11

——, Koles, Z.J. and Reddon, J.R. (1985) 'EEG studies of sex differences, cognitive and age effects in normals (age range 18–60 years).' *Abstracts in Electroencephalography and Clinical Neurophysiology*, *61* (3), S161

——, Koles, Z.J., Reddon, J.R. and Baker, L. (1986a) 'Neurophysiological studies (Quantitative EEG) of exhibitionism.' In *Electrical Brain Potentials of Psychopathology* (ed. C. Shagass), Amsterdam: Elsevier Science

——, Koles, Z.J. and Reddon, J.R. (1986b) 'Age and sex related EEG configurations in normal subjects.' In *Individual Differences in Hemispheric Specialization* (ed. A. Glass), London: Plenum Press

Gaffney, G.R. and Berlin, F.S. (1984) 'Is there hypothalamic-pituitary-gonadal dysfunction in paedophilia? A pilot study.' *Br. J. Psychiatry*, *145*, 657–60

Gerendai, I. (1984) 'Lateralization of neuroendocrine control.' In *Cerebral Dominance — The Biological Foundations* (eds. N. Geschwind and A.M. Galaburda), pp. 167–78, Cambridge, Mass.; Harvard University Press

Geschwind, N. and Behan, P. (1982) 'Sinistrality, learning disability and autoimmune diseases.' In *Proc. Natl. Acad. Sci. USA*, *79*, 5097–100

Geschwind, N. and Galaburda, A.M. (1985a) 'Cerebral lateralization. Biological mechanisms, associations, and pathology: III. a hypothesis and a program for research.' *Arch. Neurol.*, *42*, 634–54

—— (1985b) 'Cerebral lateralization. Biological mechanisms, associations, and pathology: II. a hypothesis and a program for research.' *Arch. Neurol.*, *42*, 521–52

Gladue, B.A., Green, R. and Hellman, R.E. (1984) 'Neuroendocrine response to estrogen and sexual orientation.' *Science*, *225* (4669), 1496–9

Grob, C.S. (1985) 'Single case study, female exhibitionism.' *J. Nerv. Ment. Dis.*, *173* (4), 253–6

Grossman, C.J. (1985) 'Interactions between the gonadal steroids and

the immune system.' *Science*, *227* (4684), 257–61
Halliday, J.L. (1937) 'Psychological factors in rheumatism. A preliminary study.' *Br. Med. J.*, *1*, 213–17
Haslam, D.R. (1970) 'Lateral dominance in the perception of size and of pain.' *Q.J. Exp. Psychol.*, *22*, 503–7
Hirshkowitz, M., Ware, J.C., Turner, D. and Karacan, I. (1979) 'EEG amplitude asymmetry during sleep.' *Sleep Research*, *8*, 25
Howard, K.J., Rogers, L.J. and Boura, A.L.A. (1980) 'Functional lateralization of the chicken forebrain revealed by use of intracranial glutamate.' *Brain Res.*, *188*, 369–82
Karacan, I., Goodenough, D.R., Shapiro, A. and Starker, S. (1966) 'Erection cycle during sleep in relation to dream anxiety.' *Arch. Gen. Psychiatry*, *15*, 183–9
Kolarsky, A., Freund, K., Machek, J. and Polák, O. (1967) 'Male sexual deviation: association with early temporal lobe damage.' *Arch. Gen. Psychiatry*, *17*, 735–43
Langevin, R. (1983) *Sexual Strands: Understanding and Treating Sexual Anomalies in Men* Hillsdale, N.J.: Lawrence Erlbaum Associates
—— (ed.) (1985) *Erotic Preference, Gender Identity, and Aggression in Men: New Research Studies*, Hillsdale, N.J.: Lawrence Erlbaum Associates
——, Paitich, D., Ramsay, G., Anderson, C., Kamrad, J., Pope, S., Geller, G., Pearl, L. and Newman, S. (1979) 'Experimental studies of the etiology of genital exhibitionism.' *Arch. Sex. Behav.*, *8* (4), 307–31
Lesniak, R., Szymusik, A. and Chrzanowski, R. (1972) 'Multidirectional disorders of sexual drive in a case of brain tumour.' *Forensic Science*, *1*, 333–8
Lewis, S.A. and Oswald, I. (1969) 'Overdose of tricyclic antidepressants and deductions concerning their cerebral action.' *Br. J. Psychiatry*, *115*, 1403–10
MacCulloch, M.J., Snowden, P.R., Wood, P.J. and Mills, H.E. (1983) 'Sadistic fantasy, sadistic behaviour and offending.' *Br. J. Psychiatry*, *143*, 20–9
McIntosh, T.K. and Barfield, R.J. (1984a) 'Brain monoaminergic control of male reproductive behaviour. I. Serotonin and the post-ejaculatory refractory period.' *Behavioural Brain Research*, *12*, 255–65
McIntosh, T.K. and Barfield, R.J. (1984b) 'Brain monoaminergic control of male reproductive behaviour. II. Dopamine and the post-ejaculatory refractory period.' *Behavioural Brain Research*, *12*, 267–73
McIntosh, T.K. and Barfield, R.J. (1984c) 'Brain monoaminergic control of male reproductive behaviour. III. Norepinephrine and the post-ejaculatory refractory period.' *Behavioural Brain Research*, *12*, 275–81
Meyerson, B.J. (1964) 'Central nervous monoamines and hormone-induced estrous behaviour in the spayed rat.' *Acta Physiol. Scand.*, *241* (Suppl.), 1–128
Meyerson, B.J., Carrer, H. and Eliasson, M. (1974) '5-Hydroxytryp-

tamine and sexual behaviour in the female rat.' *Adv. Biochem. Psychopharmacol.*, *11*, 229–42

Morgenstern, F.S. (1970) 'Chronic pain: a study of some general features which play a role in maintaining a state of chronic pain after amputation.' *Modern Trends of Psychosomatic Medicine*, *2*, 225–45

Nordeen, E.J. and Yahr, P. (1982) 'Hemisphere asymmetries in sexual differentiation of mammalian brain.' *Science*, *218*, 391–3

Perachio, A.A., Marr, L.D. and Alexander, M. (1979) 'Sexual behaviour in male rhesus monkeys elicited by electrical stimulation of preoptic and hypothalamic areas.' *Brain Res.*, *177*, 127–44

Perkins, M.W. (1981) 'Female homosexuality and body build'. *Arch. Sex. Behav.*, *10* (4), 337–45

Purves-Stewart, J. (1924) *The Diagnosis of Nervous Diseases*, London

Remillard, G.M., Andermann, F., Testa, G.F., Gloor, P., Aube, M., Martin, J.B., Feindel, W., Guberman, A. and Simpson, C. (1983) 'Sexual ictal manifestations predominate in females with temporal lobe epilepsy: a finding suggesting sexual dimorphism in the human brain.' *Neurology, March*, 323–30

Renoux, G., Biziere, K., Renoux, M. and Guillaumin, J.M. (1983a) 'The production of T-cell-inducing factors in mice is controlled by the brain neocortex.' *Scand. J. Immunol.*, *17*, 45–50

Renoux, G., Biziere, K., Renoux, M., Guillaumin, J.M. and Degenne, D. (1983b) 'A balanced brain asymmetry modulates T Cell-mediated events.' *J. Neuroimmunol.*, *5*, 227–38

Rodriguez, M., Castro, R., Hernandez, G. and Mas, M. (1984) 'Different roles of catecholaminergic and serotoninergic neurons of the medial forebrain bundle on male rat sexual behaviour.' *Physiol. Behav.*, *33*, 5–11

Rogers, L.J. (1980) 'Functional lateralization in the chicken fore-brain revealed by cycloheximide treatment.' Proceedings of the 17th International Ornithology Congress

Sackeim, H.A., Greenberg, M.S., Weiman, A.L., Gur, R.C., Hungerbuhler, J.P. and Geschwind, N. (1982) 'Hemispheric asymmetry in the expression of positive and negative emotions: neurological evidence.' *Arch. Neurol.*, *39*, 210–18

Spengler, A. (1977) 'Manifest sadomasochism of males: results of an empirical study.' *Arch. Sex. Behav.*, *6* (6), 441–56

Szechtman, H., Caggiula, A.R. and Wulkan, D. (1978) 'Preoptic knife cuts and sexual behaviour in male rats.' *Brain Res.*, *150*, 569–91

Taylor, D.C. (1981) 'The influence of sexual differentiation on growth development and disease.' In *Scientific Foundations of Paediatrics*, Second ed., (eds. J. Davis and J. Dobbing), pp. 29–44, London: Heinemann Medical Books

Tucker, D.M. (1983) 'Asymmetries of coherence topography: structural and dynamic aspects of brain lateralization.' In *Laterality and Psychopathology* (eds. P. Flor-Henry and J. Gruzelier), pp. 349–62, Amsterdam: Elsevier Science Publishers

——, Dawson, S.L., Roth, D.L., Bair, T.B. and Sawler, B.G. (1982) 'Regional changes in power and coherence during cognition:

Longitudinal study of individuals.' Paper presented at the meeting of the International Neuropsychological Society, Pittsburgh

Ward, I.L. (1984) 'The prenatal stress syndrome: current status.' *Psychoneuroendocrinology*, *1*, 3–11

Whipple, B. and Komisaruk, B.R. (1985) 'Elevation of pain threshold by vaginal stimulation in women.' *Pain*, *21*, 357–67

Yeudall, L.T., Fedora, O., Schopflocher, D., Reddon, J.R. and Hyatt, P. (1986) 'Neuropsychological characteristics of different types of sexual offenders.' To be submitted. Department of Neuropsychology, Alberta Hospital Edmonton, Research Bulletin 125.

4

An Ethological Approach to Sexual Deviation

Glenn D. Wilson

In this chapter I will discuss the insights that may be gained by considering sexual deviation in relation to instinct and evolution theory (i.e. ethology and sociobiology). I believe this approach to be instructive because the sex drive itself has clearly evolved to promote gene survival and is deeply seated within phylogenetically ancient parts of the brain. The behavioural strategies that serve sexual instincts are therefore guided by powerful and inflexible emotions that are not readily responsive to rational persuasion or clinical modification. The ethological approach also seems to me best placed to account for the most outstanding single fact about sexual deviation: namely, that the paraphilias are predominantly (often almost exclusively) associated with male gender. Since this applies across culture, time and species, no social learning theory is adequate to explain it.

At first sight it may seem that deviant sexuality could not be explained in terms of instinct, since almost by definition it is non-reproductive and thus defies the 'reproductive imperative' of the genes. Despite this, I hope to show that the occurrence of paraphilia is predictable and explicable within the context of evolutionary theory sometimes in a manner that removes it from the realm of medical pathology. Rather, its inevitability and adaptive features are highlighted.

PARENTAL INVESTMENT

The key to understanding male and female sexuality, and especially the difference between them, is the concept of 'parental investment' (Trivers, 1972). Females produce eggs, which are large and few in number and therefore at a greater

Table 4.1: Gender differences expected on the basis of evolutionary theory and observed empirically

Males	Females
Physical	
Greater size and strength	Lesser size and strength
Capacity for short-term energy output	Capacity for endurance
Mental	
Spatial and mathematical skills	Verbal and social skills
Rationality	Empathy
Temperamental	
Sexual initiation and exploration	Sexual selectivity and relationship seeking
Aggression	Nurturance
Independence	Attachment
Courage	Anxiety
Dominance	Submission

Compiled from various sources such as Symons, 1979; Seward and Seward, 1980; Mitchell, 1981

premium than male sperm, which are small and plentiful. This basic gender difference is ultimately responsible for all the well-documented differences between men and women in body, brain and behaviour (Table 4.1).

For present purposes, it is the difference on the sexual diversification factor that is most relevant. For the male, with his almost unlimited supply of sperm, the optimal reproductive strategy (from the point of view of 'the selfish gene') is to impregnate many females simultaneously, hence his interest in multiple mates of breeding age. From the female point of view, no advantage is gained from multiple partners — only one pregnancy can occur at a time. Rather, the survival of the offspring depends upon the quality of their sire and his willingness to support them — hence female selectivity and relationship building (Symons, 1979).

After all the biological and social pressures have combined, this male-female difference emerges not as a hard-and-fast rule but as one of degree, which in the human case can be illustrated in Tables 4.2 and 4.3. Although there is much overlap between the sexes, men are markedly more inclined toward casual sex and novel partners; women are more interested in stable and loving

Table 4.2: Percentage of British men and women expressing willingness to engage in sexual intercourse at various phases of a new relationship

Phase	Age of men (%, *n*=1862)		Age of women (%, *n*=2905)	
	<30	>30	<30	>30
The first moment you can	38	32	9	9
When you have got to know them a little better	44	40	44	36
Not until there is some commitment to a steady relationship	8	8	25	28
Not outside marriage	10	18	18	22

Source: Wilson, 1981b

Table 4.3: Male versus female conceptions of the ideal sex life

	Age of men (%, *n*=1862)		Age of women (%, *n*=2905)	
	<30	>30	<30	>30
Not getting enough sex at the moment	55	56	41	41
If not enough, then ideal would be:				
(a) More sex with spouse or steady partner	37	38	62	63
(b) More exciting variations with partner	34	38	24	26
(c) More different partners	38	37	20	18

Source: Wilson, 1981b

relationships in which devoted attention is paid to them. These differences are unaltered from one generation to the next despite the recent women's movement. The exact mechanism by which the genes influence our emotions, preferences and modes of thought remains a matter of speculation (Lumsden and Wilson, 1983) but the fact appears indisputable.

MALE COMPETITION

This difference between men and women helps us to understand why paraphilia is an almost entirely male phenomenon. If males have an instinctive harem-building tendency, then it follows that successful males will monopolise more than their share of the young (reproductive) females with the result that others are bound to miss out. An extreme example is the North American grouse, in which only one in ten males gets to mate (Sparks, 1978). For a human example, take the late King Sobhuza II of Swaziland who had approximately 100 wives — this must have created a problem for 99 Swazi men. I shall discuss their alternatives later in the chapter; in the meantime, it is interesting to look at the manner in which intermale competition for breeding privileges leads to their evolutionary modification.

Darwin was among the first to note that the spectacular tail display of the peacock was probably selected because it impressed the female of the species. Experimental support for this idea comes from studies of Kenyan widow-birds in which the long tail feathers of some males are docked and used to extend those of others. Females of the species show a striking preference for those males with elongated tails, and reject those with the pruned tail. The human male has a very much larger penis than other apes, which might also have something to do with female preferences (Eberhard, 1985).

The male bower-bird of New Guinea has a different means of impressing the female. He constructs an amazing Gaudi-style garden with colourful towers and pavements, which functions to attract females, but which, not being carried on his body, makes him less vulnerable to predators. One wonders if the creativity of the human male, seen in architectural, artistic and scientific projects such as the Taj Mahal, Disneyland, Wagner's *Ring Cycle*, and the theory of relativity, might be equivalent in some way to the courtship-motivated industry of the male bower-bird. Certainly megalomania is a characteristically male trait, and nothing attracts women more than great accomplishment.

RESPONSE TO FAILURE

When two or more males compete directly for dominance within a hierarchy, biochemical changes take place following the outcome, such that the victor is prepared for sexual activity and the losers lapse into a state of relative depression (Rose, Bernstein and Gordon, 1975; McGuire, Raleigh and Johnson,

1983). Loss of libido is often noted in depressive patients, and many of the conditions that predispose to depression could be interpreted as relating to a decline in social status.

While depression is commonly regarded as an illness (and help is quite reasonably provided), it may be adaptive in some circumstances for a male who is losing a fight to withdraw from competition, at least in the short-term, so he lives to fight (and possibly reproduce) another day. The fact that men have a capacity to 'turn off' libido when faced with long periods of deprivation is evidenced by a decline in sexual fantasy in men who are imprisoned or in hospital (Wilson, 1978). This probably reflects a psychogenic decline in output of testosterone, or some other neurochemical adaptation, rather than the fabled bromide in the tea.

Clearly it is not possible for all men to be simultaneously dominant, and assuming that libido is not dissipated entirely, what other adaptations are possible? One of the most obvious is masturbation — a partial solution that is very widely employed. Women do sometimes masturbate, but for different reasons from men — usually because they are short of orgasms, not potential partners. The term 'wanker' carries the connotation that a man is inadequate to the task of obtaining women.

Masturbation provides short-term relief and may even have some advantages (as the advocates say, 'you don't have to look your best'), yet it does not provide optimal sensation and lacks the important interpersonal element. Therefore, some men elaborate with fantasy-like partial experiences such as viewing pornography, peeping at lovers in the park or women undressing in bedroom windows, flashing shoolgirls, rubbing up against women in crowds or close contact with symbolic or conditioned associations of womanhood such as high-heeled shoes and underwear.

A dominance-failure interpretation of fetishism is supported by the work of La Torre (1980), who found that ego-deflatory feedback given to male students to the effect that women found them unattractive diminished their interest in women as complete, living entities, while at the same time increasing their response to impersonal female approximations such as shoes and underwear. Also consistent with this interpretation is the work of Chris Gosselin and myself (1980) showing that most types of sexually deviant men tend towards shyness and introversion (Figure 4.1).

Figure 4.1: Location of variant and normal groups in relation to Eysenck's E and N personality factors.

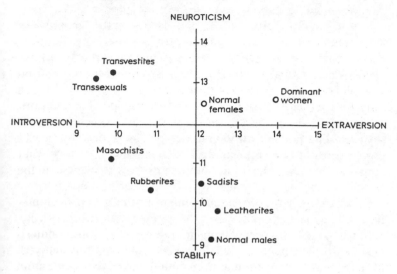

Source: Gosselin and Wilson, 1980

A high proportion of fetishistic men are sexually inexperienced. Of Chalkley and Powell's (1983) clinical sample, nearly half had never had intercourse in their lives, and there was a high frequency of socially stigmatising and debilitating conditions such as psoriasis, dermatitis, epilepsy, personality disorder, anxiety and depression. Although a clinical sample is bound to exaggerate the extent of pathological connections, it seems probable that perceived disadvantage in the mating arena is one of the predisposing factors in sexual unorthodoxy.

Paedophile men are also characterised by shyness and sensitivity (Wilson and Cox, 1983). On their own report they often prefer children because they find them 'more approachable' than adults as potential sex partners. A heightened concern with dominance and submission within their construct system is revealed in repertory grid analyses of paedophiles (Howells, 1979) and social skills training is the only treatment approach to have shown any degree of promise (Crawford, 1981).

OPTING OUT

Another possible solution to the problem of inter-male competition is to opt out and assume certain aspects of the female role. Many masochists, transvestites and trans-sexuals say they feel 'more relaxed' in assuming a submissive, feminine role (Gosselin and Eysenck, 1980), and this may represent relief from the stress of striving for masculine dominance.

There are plenty of animal models for this type of adaptation. A species of fish that lives in the coral reefs of the Pacific changes sex according to its position in the dominance hierarchy. Social groups consist of one male and a harem of females occupying an aquatic territory. The male suppresses any tendency of his females to change sex by aggressively dominating them, until he dies, whereupon the dominant female in the group promptly turns into a male and takes over the harem (Robertson, 1972).

Much of the homosexual behaviour that occurs among animals in the wild also appears to be dominance related. In one species of tree lizard, mature males maintain territories containing several females. Smaller males may copulate with the females of the harem, but if the larger male comes around they must themselves assume the female role in copulation (Trivers, 1976). Intermale battles in mountain sheep often end with the loser being mounted by the victor (Geist, 1971) and male monkeys use the female presentation position as a gesture of acquiescence to a superior male (Eibl-Eibesfeldt, 1971).

It is unlikely that all human homosexuality can be explained in these terms, but certain kinds, especially that occurring in all-male environments such as prisons, single-sex schools, ships and monasteries, often have such overtones. In the Arabian State of Oman, where women are virtually inaccessible outside of marriage, what is essentially a third gender has emerged. The *Xaniths*, as they are called, are biological males, who dress differently from both men and women, with intermediate-length hair and make-up. They work in servile occupations and assume the submissive role in sexual relations with men (Wikan, 1977). Thus is a great deal of excess male libido tapped off without female involvement.

There are a great many reasons why some men might feel unable to compete for women, and find it easier to pursue sexual outlets in the gay community. Perhaps they had unfortunate early encounters with women causing them to feel incompetent or unattractive. Perhaps they were savagely punished for heterosexual play in childhood. Perhaps they hated their mother and generalised this attitude to women at large. Perhaps they are afraid of pregnancy or commitment. For whatever reason these men decide to opt out of the heterosexual rat race and take their pleasure with others of their own gender.

From the point of view of survival of the species, it matters not that some males are removed from the breeding pool by their pursuit of non-reproductive sexual outlets. All the females can be (and usually are) fertilised by the remaining males. If women were to adopt deviant sexual practices that did not lead to impregnation there would be an irrecoverable loss of reproductive efficiency to the species. Perhaps it is partly for this reason that this does not happen to any extent. Almost any woman, however unattractive, is able to persuade some man to service or even marry her. The result is that, as with other animal species, women breed fairly evenly while men are more variable with respect to the number of children they sire.

The dominance theory may also help to explain why sadomasochistic practices such as slavery and humiliation are apparently more common within gay male circles than in the 'straight' heterosexual population (Spengler, 1977; Kamel, 1980). Assuming that some degree of social dominance is necessary for adequate performance of the male sexual role (erection and insertion) then heterosexuals have less of a problem because male dominance over females is readily assumed (whether for social or biological reasons). When two men are preparing for the sex act, the matter of their relative dominance is usually more ambiguous, and so role-playing games, such as master-slave, doctor-patient, headmaster-pupil or torturer-victim, may be contrived to assist in the turn-on. Of course, many heterosexual couples experiment with fantasies of this kind also, but they are not so frequently obsessed or dependent upon them.

Also consistent with the dominance interpretation is the discovery that fetishists, sadomasochists and transvestites share many common interests (Gosselin and Wilson, 1980). When members of clubs catering to these three male variations were surveyed with respect to their sexual fantasies and behaviour, there emerged a considerable degree of overlap among them (Figure 4.2), the outstanding common elements being enjoyment of impersonal sex objects such as clothing, instru-

Figure 4.2: The extent of overlap in the interests of three major groups of variants

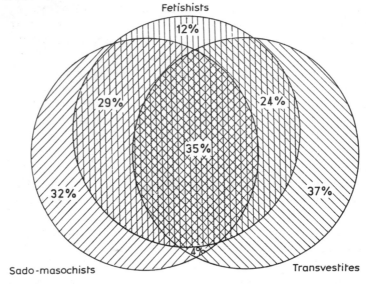

Source: Gosselin and Wilson, 1980

ments and materials (e.g. 'being excited by rubber', 'wearing clothes of the opposite sex') and a desire to take a submissive role in social and sexual encounters (e.g. 'being forced to do something', 'being tied up', 'being whipped or spanked'). It appeared that choice of membership of the particular society was to some extent arbitrary and that the sexual interest of these men was directed either towards inanimate objects (where the issue of dominance does not arise) or an unequivocal reversal of the normal dominance relationship such that they became child-like victims, abrogating any competitive struggle and thus avoiding possible rejection.

EXPLORATORY DEVIATION

Since men tend, on average, to have high libidos relative to women, their sexual interest is inclined to generalise quite widely beyond the confines of their ideal target. A certain amount of sexual behaviour sometimes classified as deviant may therefore be attributable to 'overspill' rather than substitution. Many husbands who have a good, active sex life with their wife report that they occasionally also enjoy masturbation, just for a change. Likewise, some men report having tried homosexuality or bestiality not because they expected to prefer these activities over heterosexual intercourse as a staple sexual diet, but purely in a spirit of exploration. Consistent with this 'overspill' theory is the finding that bisexual men show indications of higher libido than either exclusive homosexuals or exclusive heterosexuals (Wilson and Fulford, 1979). There is a large body of evidence in psychology to support the idea that the stronger a state of drive or deprivation becomes the greater the range of stimuli that are capable of evoking consummatory behaviour; apparently this applies also in the sexual sphere. This is another reason to expect men to be more likely to adopt deviant behaviour than women; men are presumed to have a chronically stronger sex drive. It is, however, questionable whether exploratory sexual variations should be classified as deviant at all, since the primary, preferred sexual target remains 'normal'.

GENETICS AND PARAPHILIA

To some extent the predisposition toward homosexuality appears to be genetically determined. Kallmann (1952) investigated 37 pairs of identical twins in which one member of the pair was homosexual, and found that in every case the other member of the pair was also homosexual. By contrast, a sample of non-identical twins showed only 15 per cent concordance for homosexuality. Heston and Shields (1968) reported a family of 14 children, which included three sets of identical twins. Two pairs of twins were concordant for homosexuality, while the third pair was heterosexual. Since the time of Kallmann's study, several pairs of identical twins have been reported upon who were not concordant for homosexuality, so genes do not provide a total explanation. Nevertheless, it does appear that genetic factors are involved in the origins of homosexuality (and also masochism and transvestism — Gosselin and Wilson, 1980).

From the evolutionary standpoint this is something of a puzzle. Any gene predisposing towards homosexual preference should rapidly be eliminated because homosexuals produce fewer children than heterosexuals. Yet survey evidence suggests that there is a reasonably high proportion of people in any time or culture (perhaps four or five per cent of men and one per cent of women) who are exclusively homosexual throughout their lifetime, and there is no sign of this proportion diminishing from one generation to the next (see Chapter 8).

A number of explanations of this paradox have been offered. One is that the predisposition to homosexuality is continuously supplied by mutation to produce a steady state. That is, the creation of new homosexuals by mutation may exactly equal the rate at which they are extinguished by reproductive deficiency. Such a state of affairs could also apply to a number of other genetic anomalies that are disadvantageous, such as haemophilia and colour blindness. These are both sex-linked recessive characteristics, meaning that they do not manifest themselves in all individuals carrying the genes, and appear much less often in females, since anomalies on one X chromosome are usually overriden by 'healthy' information on the other. Although it does not appear to follow simple Mendelian laws of inheritance, the genetic tendency to homosexuality could survive more readily as a recessive than a dominant trait, and sex-linkage might help to explain the male preponderance. In any case, susceptibility to a wide variety of diseases, including schizophrenia, cancer and heart disease, is known to be influenced by genetic factors, so there is no reason to assume that anything genetic is necessarily advantageous.

Hutchinson (1959) suggests that homosexual genes may produce some reproductive advantage when the individual has genes for homosexuality that are dominated by genes for heterosexuality. Such a person may be a superior breeder to the one who possesses only genes for heterosexuality. This 'heterozygote advantage' theory cannot be ruled out, and the Wilson and Fulford (1979) finding that bisexual men display greater sex drive and activity than exclusively homosexual or heterosexual men might connect with it. Perhaps the degree of discrimination with respect to sex objects is a mediating factor that accounts for the survival of homosexual genes; high generalisation of the male sex drive yielding interest in a greater variety of women, including those that are less attractive, as well as extending to male targets. The theory is testable by examining the fecundity of the relatives of homosexual people in societies that make minimal use of birth control.

Wilson (1975) suggests that homosexual members of primitive

societies may have been particularly useful to their tribe because they could adopt a third, independent sex role. Being free of the responsibilities either for hunting or child rearing, they could be particularly useful in providing assistance for either the men on the hunt or the women in the domestic situation, or occupy a new niche of their own, and this would help the group as a whole to survive. This theory implies kin selection — the idea that behaviour may be selected if it is sufficiently helpful to the group that carries many of the same genes even though it is detrimental to the individual concerned. Although this clearly does apply to insect societies with effective genetic cloning, its relevance to primates is less certain.

What seems to me a more likely hypothesis is one that admits no genes predisposing specifically and directly to homosexuality or the paraphilias. The genetic contribution could be more of a negative one, that is, an absence of whatever it takes to make a male successful in competition with other males. Those males that are successful then monopolise several females, have more offspring, and their strengths are emphasised in the following generation. Of the males who miss out, some find it comfortable and convenient to assume certain aspects of the female role, being submissive in relation to the dominant males, thus appeasing them and sharing in the protection that they offer to the females. Others, feeling a need for some kind of substitute sexual activity, find it easier to make contact with these submissive males than compete against the dominant males for females. The tendency of men to adopt homosexual behaviour as a substitute for heterosexuality in the forced absence of women, as in prison or public schools, has already been noted.

This implies that the biological basis of the paraphilias, such as it is, is much the same as the biological basis of dominance versus submission. Those men who can successfully compete for women become heterosexual; those who are less successful adopt one of several possible alternatives that we label as sexual deviations. If we are to identify any benefit to the social group as a whole, it is that reproduction is left to those men with the most vigour and strength to contribute to the species.

Whatever the causes of their anomalous sex orientation, homosexual men have proved to be of great benefit to society throughout history, particularly in the arts. Having some of the male qualities of persistence and creativity, but without the responsibilities assigned to either partner in the reproductive relationship (breadwinner or nurse), homosexual men have contributed greatly to the culture as philosophers, writers, artists and musicians. To what extent this is vital to the survival of our society, as implied by the kinship selection theory, is open to question, but gay men (and women) have certainly improved the quality of life for all of us.

Nor is this theory incompatible with the Gay Lib argument that some homosexuals choose their life style freely, on the basis of preference, rather than because of any psychological or biochemical deficiency. It is possible to identify certain benefits of the Gay life: there is no risk of pregnancy or entanglement with a person of the opposite sex who, in certain intellectual and temperamental ways, may seem like an alien being, and no risk of the radical change of life style that seems to reduce many heterosexual people to slaves of their spouse and family. Men might find other men more compatible in terms of sex drive and adventurousness, while women might find others of their gender more tender, sensitive and faithful as lovers.

It is not my intention to denigrate homosexuality or the paraphilias, but rather to point out that their appearance is inevitable given that young women are a scarce commodity. Christianity, traditional morality and some brands of feminism have tried to promote a system of universal monogamy that would ensure an equal distribution of sexual resources, and the aim is admirable, but they have to contend with an instinctive tendency towards polygyny that seems impossible to override completely. This being the case, the hope that sexual deviation can be eliminated from the whole population, like smallpox or syphilis, is forlorn.

EMBRYONIC DEVELOPMENT

Since all fetuses develop as female unless instructions to the contrary are received via the hormones, there is a sense in which male brains undergo a greater conversion process during embryonic development. Since it is the male brain that needs to be changed from the standard pattern of development, it follows that there is a greater chance that something can go wrong with the brain mechanisms involved in sexual choice. The male fetus has developed male genitalia well before this brain conversion takes place; in fact, it is the male gonads of the fetus that release hormones which modify brain development in the male direction. If the parts of the brain that are supposed to receive the masculinisation message from hormones in the blood stream fail to receive that message for some reason, they will remain female components in an otherwise male body. For several years it has been supposed that this might be an explanation of some forms of male homosexuality (Feldman and MacCulloch, 1971) and there is some experimental evidence in support of the idea (Dörner, Rohde, Stahl, Krell and Masius, 1975).

Such a theory is consistent with the fact that homosexual and trans-sexual men outnumber their female equivalents by a considerable factor. One could conceive of the reverse happening — male hormones somehow finding their way to the critical hypothalamic nuclei in a biological female — and there is some evidence that this can happen if the mother of a girl fetus is treated with male-type hormones in the latter part of her pregnancy (Reinisch, 1977). But such an event is bound to be relatively rare and therefore it is not surprising that we observe fewer disorders of sex orientation in females.

The prenatal hormone theory would also explain why sexual identity disturbances in boys who will grow up to be homosexual or trans-sexual in adulthood can be observed from the earliest years (Zuger, 1978). Equally, it explains why these individuals cannot necessarily be discriminated from normal males in terms of the amount of male hormone circulating in adulthood; if certain switches in the brain were not masculinised before birth they will not respond to circulating testosterone after puberty. Over-production of male hormones has been noted in a high proportion of female trans-sexuals (Sipova and Starka, 1977) but this might also be attributable to events occurring in the critical prenatal period. Male hormones given to a normal adult female do not alter sex orientation, however much they may enhance libido or masculinise the body.

MALE VS FEMALE HOMOSEXUALITY

Environmentalists (e.g. Griffitt and Hatfield, 1985) believe that men and women are much the same by nature but have been led by sex role learning to assume widely discrepant life styles. The opposite (evolutionary) hypothesis is that men and women are basically very different but the difference between them has been masked or minimised by the requirements of social living. Since the ideal male and female strategies are in direct conflict, the two sexes have to meet half-way in order to establish some working arrangement. Homosexual people are therefore of great theoretical interest because they provide an opportunity to look at the way in which men and women behave sexually when they have no need to compromise with the differing proclivities of the opposite sex. Furthermore, homosexuals can hardly be said to be behaving in accordance with stereotypes or social expectations since society generally deplores, or at least derides, their behaviour.

If sex role learning is of major importance, men and women should be relatively undifferentiated when it comes to homosexual contacts. In fact, the differences between men and women seem to be magnified in homosexual relationships (Harry, 1983; Chapter 8). Men tend to be promiscuous and impersonal in their encounters with other men to a quite remarkable extent. According to one estimate (Bell, 1974) they average between 100 and 1000 partners in a lifetime, most of these being fleeting contacts made at gay bars and parties, parks and public toilets. This compares with an average of about ten different female partners for the heterosexual man. While long-term affectionate relationships ('marriages') between men are not unknown, they are much less common than brief encounters. Most homosexual men have no desire to get to know their contacts before having sex or ever to see them again afterwards. The recent AIDS scare, which applies particularly to gay men, may have suppressed this promiscuity to some extent, but the proclivity is still recognised.

Lesbians behave quite differently from homosexual men. They tend to have fewer relationships, perhaps only two or three in all (which is less than heterosexual women), and these are intimate and caring — much like the relationships that heterosexual women seek with men but have such difficulty in attaining. Sexual involvement between lesbians often grows out of a deep and longstanding friendship with the partner and is seen by both partners as a natural outgrowth of that relationship.

In a survey of bisexual men and women, Blumstein and Schwartz (1976) found similar gender differences. Men were more likely to have their first homosexual contacts with strangers or male prostitutes whom they would never see again, and were more likely to run homosexual and heterosexual affairs in parallel. Women more often had sex with a close female friend, seeing this as a development of a long-standing emotional attachment, and more often alternated their orientation rather than engage in simultaneous affairs with men and women.

The interpretation that bisexuals put on their own behaviour is illuminating. Many men viewed their homosexual experience as a kind of modified masturbation, a diversion engaged in primarily because females are difficult to obtain. One of Blumstein and Schwartz's subjects explained:

> I'm straight, but I need outlets when I'm away from home and times like that, and it's easier to get them with men than with women. So I go into the park, or at a rest station on the highway and get a man to blow me. I would never stay the night with one of them, or get to know them. It's just a release. It's not like sex with my wife. It's just a way to get what you need without making it a big deal.

By contrast, women saw their bisexuality as an extension of their natural affectionate behaviour. Genital sex usually followed a period of deepening friendship and love with a person who happened to be of the same gender.

Gender differences are also apparent in the homosexuality that develops in prisons. Whereas with men the homosexuality serves purposes either of physical release or of dominance, homosexual liaisons in women's prisons seem to be connected with the development of a quasi-kinship system — the women variously adopting the roles of wife, husband, aunt and so on (Giallombardo, 1974).

Clearly, male and female homosexuality is different in character and provides impressive support for the evolutionary theory of gender differentiation. The majority of homosexuals do not adopt all aspects of the opposite sex role. Gay men remain distinctly male as regards the exploratory nature of their libido and their concern with the youth and physical attributes of their partners. Lesbians retain their feminine concern with the emotional aspects of their relationships and their long-term prospects.

SADOMASOCHISM

The practice of gaining sexual arousal from inflicting or receiving pain is perhaps the most popular sexual variation after homosexuality. At first sight this also seems extraordinary from the evolutionary point of view because pain is the guideline by which we avoid stimuli that are dangerous to us. How this comes to be connected with the very positive pleasures of sex is something of a paradox.

Again, the observation of animal behaviour is illuminating. Prior to copulation, many species (particularly mammals) engage in a kind of fight or struggle. Often the male will bite the female on the back of the neck in order to maintain a good hold on her while performing the sex act, and this no doubt inflicts a degree of pain. In some species this pain is known to be instrumental in releasing ovulation, and the fertility of the female is thus increased. This effect is presumably mediated by her emotions and endocrine system, so it is not unreasonable to suppose that the rough treatment she receives from the male is in some sense 'a turn-on'. An evolutionary advantage can also be seen in the fact that the male has to be assertive in order to pass on his genetic material, not just in competition with other males but also in gaining the cooperation of the female. By mating with males who pursue them with vigour and strength, the females ensure similar survival-related characteristics in their offspring.

Does this pattern of sex combined with brutality extend into human psychology at all? It has often been suggested that women invite and enjoy rape, usually most unfairly. Women don't usually want to be raped by the kind of man that commits actual criminal rapes that result in court convictions. However, they do frequently fantasise about being taken forcefully by an extremely dominant man (being 'swept off their feet' as the saying goes) and there is little doubt that they enjoy male assertiveness and initiative (Wilson, 1978). Feminists who advocate female assertiveness in the bedroom have not succeeded in altering the behaviour of the average woman to any great extent, despite the fact that most men say they enjoy women who are sexually aggressive. Thus, some degree of masochism seems inherent in the female psyche.

There is also some evidence that could be interpreted as indicating increased fertility in women taken by force. Apparently, women who have been raped are more likely to get pregnant than would be expected on the basis of a comparison with a similar number of consenting acts of intercourse (Parkes, 1976). This could mean that the special emotional circumstances surrounding the act of rape precipitate ovulation and thus increase the chance of pregnancy. There are, however, other possibilities. Men who rape may be particularly potent and fertile at the time of the offence because they are in a state of deprivation, or they may be generally more fertile because of high testosterone levels or some such biological trait. Alternatively, some of the girls may have classified the origins of their pregnancy as rape because it was easier thus to explain their condition to dismayed parents, husbands or boyfriends. All told, it is premature to conclude that rape promotes fertility.

If animal behaviours have any relation to adult sadomasochistic behaviour we would expect that masochism would be primarily a female predilection while sadism would more often be found in males. This appears to be the case. A general tendency for female fantasies to be passive and masochistic and male fantasies to be active and sadistic was found by Wilson and Lang (1981). When it comes to actual behaviour the difference is also apparent. Hunt (1974) asked a representative sample in the USA whether they had ever obtained sexual pleasure from inflicting or receiving pain. Although the actual numbers admitting to such practices were quite small (less than five per cent of the population), twice as many males as females reported sadistic pleasure, while twice as many women as men were masochistic. Given that replies to the questionnaire were anonymous and that the admission of such perverse sexuality is socially unacceptable anyway, it is unlikely that social pressures were responsible for the difference in these reports.

Hunt's results imply that sadomasochistic deviations are, on balance, just as common in women as in men, yet folklore and clinical impression suggest that most sadomasochists are male. Certainly, the vast majority of people joining clubs that cater to this preference and buying pornography and equipment connected with it, are male. Most of the women who do participate in such practices apparently turn it on for the benefit of men — either lovers or professional clients (Gosselin and Wilson, 1980).

How can these conflicting pictures of the sex balance be reconciled? Probably it is a question of how the sexuality comes to be classified as deviant. Many of the women who reported pleasure in receiving pain in the Hunt study may have been referring to acts taking place within the context of a loving, intimate relationship with a particular husband or boyfriend. These acts would include the receipt of playful spankings or being tied to the bed; they would also include normal intercourse taken to a painful extreme, for example, forced entry with insufficient lubrication or extended intercourse to the point of soreness. The male sadomasochism that is regarded as deviant, on the other hand, is more likely to be impersonal and involve torture equipment that is peripheral to normal sexuality, such as whips, studded and sharp objects, pincers, tongs, heated objects, or electrical equipment. Often, it has connections with homosexuality, fetishism, transvestism, bondage, or other such characteristically male variations (Spengler, 1977). The men interested in such activities may alternate the roles of sadist and masochist, but they generally prefer the masochistic experience. It is probably these facts that cause such men to be thought of as deviant. In other words, it is the impersonality and role reversal, more than the predilection for pain, that requires explanation.

Here again, we might consider an explanation in terms of the failure of some men to succeed in competition with other men for access to women. This leaves them with an adaptation problem. One solution to this problem is to engage in fantasy violence with other men in which they gain power and ascendancy, for example, chaining them to a wall and burning them with cigarettes. Or they may skip the struggle with other men and go straight to the fantasies of super-masculine power over women — hence the bondage, enslavement, spanking, etc. Again, and perhaps more commonly, they undergo a kind of role reversal — becoming submissive slaves, babies with dummies or honorary females (transvestites). Such role-playing bypasses the need to exert dominance at all, and for such men sex as a victim may become just as exciting and satisfying as sex as a victor.

THE VISUAL TARGETING NATURE OF MALE SEX DRIVE

The sex differences described above are presumably based on hormonal brain differentiation (mostly prenatal) and there is increasing evidence that hypothalamic regions are critical, at least in lower mammals such as the rat (Raisman and Field, 1973). More specifically, McEwan (1980) has found that the

Table 4.4: Main elements of anonymously reported sexual fantasies (%). Columns add to more than 100 because categories are not mutually exclusive

Fantasy	Men ($n=291$)	Women($n=409$)
Group sex	31	15
Voyeuristic/fetishistic	18	7
Steady partner incorporated	14	21
Identified people (other than partner)	8	8
Setting romantic/exotic	4	15
Rape/force	4	13
Sadomasochism	7	7
No fantasies	5	12
Everything	3	0
No answer	21	19

preoptic area of the anterior hypothalamus is the prime site for the activation of male sexual behaviour by testosterone, while ventromedial nuclei are more involved with the activation of female behaviour by oestrogen.

Although the hypothalamus, with its control of endocrine activity, shows the most obvious sex differentiation, limbic circuits lying under the temporal and frontal lobes are also important in the control of sexual behaviour (Kolb and Whishaw, 1985). In lower mammals sexual arousal is primarily dependent upon smell, which accounts for the anatomical location of the limbic system, but for primate males visual factors assume greater significance. Certainly, it appears that men are more readily aroused by visual configurations, such as buttocks and breasts, than women are by any aspect of the male form, and men are markedly more susceptible to inappropriate visual fixations of the kind that we call fetishisms. This is not because men have superior visual acuity to women; the difference appears to be in the readiness with which connections are formed between visual stimuli and sexual arousal.

The visual orientation of the human male is clearly evidenced in the sexual fantasies than men report. Apart from group sex, the most frequently occurring theme of male fantasies could be described as fetishistic or voyeuristic (Wilson, 1986: Table 4.4). This commonly involves reference to clothing such as black stockings and suspenders, high-heeled shoes, leather gear or nurse's uniforms. Other typically male fantasy elements related to the visual emphasis include details of anatomy (such as colour of pubic hair or size of breasts), reference to the age and race of the partner, and descriptions of the sexual activity engaged in. Only occasionally do women refer to the physical characteristics of their fantasy partners; the most common themes for women revolve around the identity of the partner, the amount of attention indicative of love and devotion that he is demonstrating, and the romantic, exotic and peaceful nature of the setting (islands, beaches, waterfalls, moonlight, candlelit dinners, fur rugs in front of an open fire). Clearly, men are primarily concerned with the physical form of their partners, while women are preoccupied with the context and the emotional aspects of the relationship.

INNATE RELEASING MECHANISMS AND IMPRINTING

Studies by ethologists such as Lorenz and Tinbergen, based on the observation of a variety of species from birds to primates, point to the conclusion that sexual attachments are arrived at by two major instinctual mechanisms. First, the range of potential sex objects is restricted to certain broad classes of stimuli by inborn neural circuits called *innate releasing mechanisms* (IRMs). Most animals have an innate ability to recognise and respond sexually to adult members of the opposite sex of their own species. A male chimpanzee reared in isolation from members of its own species is still sexually excited by the rearside presentation signal of the female chimpanzee (although knowing what to do about it is another matter, which does seem to require a certain amount of trial and error — Mason, 1960). Since this applies to our nearest relatives it almost certainly applies to humans too. Wickler (1967) and Morris (1971) have discussed the likelihood that the visual configuration of paired, pink hemispheres, typified by female buttocks and breasts, is an innate sexual stimulus to the human male.

The second instinctual mechanism is *imprinting* (Bateson, 1981). At certain stages of maturation, particularly in early infancy, the range of stimuli that are to become sexually exciting in adulthood is further delimited and specified. Imprinting adds detail to the blueprint for arousal that was broadly sketched by the innate mechanisms, and to some extent it depends upon the visual stimuli that are available in the environment of the animal

(Immelmann and Suomi, 1981). Thus zookeepers may become the sexual targets of a wide variety of animals in their care if these animals do not have sufficient exposure to members of their own species at the sensitive period of development. Owners of pet cats and dogs are subject to the same effect, often to their embarrassment with neighbours and guests. The importance of the environment is also apparent when it is considered that rubber fetishism was not possible before the advent of rubber.

Either of these instinctual mechanisms (IRMS or imprinting) can go wrong (as can any other finely tuned piece of neurology) so that sexual responses can be attached to classes of stimuli that appear peculiar and socially unacceptable. Sometimes the categories of arousing stimuli are left too broad. One rather bizarre sex deviation occasionally observed by clinicians is that of men who are sexually excited by other men and by certain animals (usually domestic) of either sex. They are not, however, sexually aroused by human females. The interest in animals, which may be observed as much in masturbation fantasies and wet dreams as in actual behaviour, cannot be explained simply as substitute gratification, since these patients have plenty of opportunity for contact with human males. Also, it cannot be explained away as a 'village idiot' phenomenon; among patients in this category described by Pinkava (1971) were a senior clerk, an antique expert, a surgeon, an organist and a university teacher. While one might resort to a Freudian explanation in terms of the 'castration complex' causing these men to be afraid of women, this seems less convincing when applied to similar phenomena in non-human animals. The most satisfactory theory is one of impairment in the innate releasing mechanisms that normally specify sex targets as members of the opposite sex of one's own species. The homosexual choice seems to imply an intact gender discrimination process within the 'home' species, but an inverted preference mechanism.

Other sexual deviations, again particularly in men, seem to involve an over-detailed specification of the sex object. The prototype is fetishism, in which some article or material becomes the focus for sexual arousal. These attachments commence very early in life, often being recalled as well established by the age of four. They are very resistant to any form of psychotherapy whether analytic or behavioural, and for reasons that are not yet understood, they often become more insistent in middle age (Gosselin and Wilson, 1980).

Certain characteristics of popular fetish objects make impairment of imprinting a plausible explanation. They usually have strong gender associations, are worn close to sexually arousing parts of the body (e.g. high-heeled shoes, underwear, leather belts and buckles) and have striking visual attributes that are reminiscent of genital signals (e.g. wet, shiny, black, pink or furry). Quite a high proportion of men find fetish materials erotically enhancing to some extent; what characterises the full-blown fetishist is not so much the misdirection of his imprinting, but its overspecification and exclusivity.

IMPRINTING VS CONDITIONING

The fact that fetish targets usually appear in conjunction with biologically ideal targets (women and their genitals) is often taken to support a learning or 'conditioning' theory of the acquisition of fetishisms (McGuire *et al.*, 1965). Indeed, it does seem possible to condition sexual arousal to pictures of boots by pairing them in a laboratory with pictures of nude women (Rachman and Hodgson, 1968), and McConaghy (1970) has shown that geometrical patterns with no erotic connotation can also be used as a conditioned stimulus. But the conditioning paradigm does not provide a satisfactory model for the acquisition of clinical fetishisms, for several reasons: (1) It does not explain why the true fetishist is unconcerned about whether or not his fetish object is accompanied by a female in the flesh, i.e. why the real woman ceases to be sexually arousing after the fetishism has become established. (2) It cannot easily explain why fetishisms are so resistant to extinction even though they become totally detached from the original source of arousal. Conditioned responses will normally disappear in the absence of reinforcement, as did the experimental fetishisms of Rachman and Hodgson. (3) It does not explain why some people (always men) become fetishists, while others do not. In these respects, the conditioning model of fetishisms is unconvincing.

There is another explanation of the close association between fetish object and actual female that fits the imprinting error theory. Suppose that normal imprinting upon female genitals requires that the infant male has some visual or olfactory exposure to them. If women's genitals are not accessible at the critical time for imprinting, the mechanism may seize upon the nearest sensory approximation that is actually available. Women's underwear occupy the crotch area and often take on the shape of pubis and vulva to some extent; so they are likely candidates for sexual imprinting. If pheromones are also involved in eliciting the imprinting process, underwear would be at a particular advantage since it is steeped in female odours. Shoes, especially black and high-heeled, bear some similarity in size, colour and shape to the pubic triangle, they move at the eye-level of a crawling infant and are made of leather, which is known to fix fatty acids produced by the skin that are similar to the copulins found in vaginal secretions. Belts, suspenders and fabrics such as fur and rubber may become focuses for sexual arousal for similar reasons, and if the disciplinary function of the mother is prominent during the sensitive period for sex target imprinting this might also explain masochistic practices and infantilism.

Note that this theory of the origins of fetishisms differs from both the conditioning model and the psychoanalytic theory. The conditioning model supposes that the fetishism is established by simultaneous (or near simultaneous) presentation of the fetish with a high level of sexual arousal that is originally a response to an actual woman or her genitals. By contrast, the imprinting model suggests that *unavailability* or partial masking of what, in conditioning theory, is called the 'unconditioned stimulus' is basic to the acquisition of the fetishism. Psychoanalytic theory emphasises *symbolic* associations between the fetish and female genitalia. For example, a shoe is taken as equivalent to a 'substitute penis', which the fetishist attributes to women because he cannot brook the idea of their 'castration'. Imprinting theory assumes that a direct sensory association is basic to the choice of substitute sex target — shoes share certain visual, tactile or olfactory qualities with the female pubic area. The fact that non-human primates also show fetishistic behaviour (Chapter 6) would seem to argue against the necessary involvement of high-level symbolic thinking.

Two strands of evidence support the imprinting theory of sex deviation. One is the frequently reported finding that deviant men of all kinds come from families that are sexually restrictive and do not permit nudity in the house. Sexually deviant men are also less likely to have seen pornography as children (Goldstein, Kant, Judd, Rice and Green, 1971). A popular interpretation of these facts is that early exposure to sexually explicit materials provides 'innoculation' against the potentially harmful effects of pornography in later life. But a far simpler explanation is that the sight of female genitals in early childhood is a prerequisite for appropriate sexual imprinting and development. If this theory is correct we might expect to find fewer fetishists and sexual deviates in the future, since society as a whole is becoming more and more tolerant of nudity in and outside of the home. (We have noted that the majority of men with clinical fetishisms are currently well into middle age, though there are other possible explanations for this fact, such as the possibility that fetishism augments with age.)

The second kind of evidence that supports a 'faulty wiring' view of male deviation is directly neurological. If fetishisms and other compulsive sexual interests result from impairment of neural circuits laid down before birth and shortly afterwards, we would expect them to be associated with other indications of minor brain damage occurring in infancy, and this indeed is the case. An association of temporal lobe epilepsies with fetishism and transvestism in men was observed by Epstein (1961) and a similar connection with trans-sexualism has been reported by Hoenig and Kenna (1979). There have been several clinical reports of compulsive sexual deviations that have been surgically removed along with a focal epilepsy (e.g. Mitchell, Falconer and Hill, 1954). Research by a Czechoslovakian team (Kolarsky, Freund, Machek and Polak, 1967) showed that a wide range of male deviations including homosexuality, sadomasochism and exhibitionism, as well as fetishism, were associated with minor damage to the temporal lobe, and what is most interesting, this damage only affected sexual preferences if it occurred before the age of three. Typical brain lesions associated with sexual deviation in adulthood were those due to head trauma during birth (often associated with forceps delivery) and meningitis or encephalitis contracted within the first year of life. The brain damage involved was usually very subtle and could only be detected by EEG examination or clinical symptoms relating to epilepsy. Most of the subjects were of normal intelligence and free of gross psychiatric disturbance. More recently, Langevin (1985) reported CAT-scan evidence of right temporal lobe abnormality in sadistic rapists. This raises the question of whether other indications of unusual or impaired brain wiring would also be connected with deviant male sexuality — symptoms such as stammering, tics, aphasias, amnesias, mixed dominance of the left and right hemispheres of the brain, and standardised neuropsychological tests of brain function.

Evidence for neurological involvement in sexual deviations leads to further speculation about the reasons for the male preponderance of this kind of behaviour. Male brains differ on average from female brains in the degree of specialisation of the right hemisphere — the side of the brain that deals with spatial configurations (McGlone, 1980; Levy and Gur, 1980). The importance of the right hemisphere in males may well have something to do with their visual sex orientation, while the left-hemispheric advantage of women (such as their superior verbal processing, sequential thinking and future time perspective) would seem well-suited to the support of their particular mating strategies. Minor damage such as might occur in forceps delivery or infantile meningitis may be less critical to the female brain because the second hemisphere acts as a back-up system. In the case of the male brain, the second hemisphere does not replicate function to the same extent and so damage to one temporal lobe is more likely to be manifested in peculiar behaviour. A parallel may be seen in the specialisation of the Y chromosome in males, which leaves men more susceptible to a wide variety of sex-linked recessive disorders such as colour blindness and haemophilia. This idea of male vulnerability arising out of hemispheric specialisation is speculative at present but merits further consideration as our knowledge of neurology advances.

CONCLUSION

I have focused this discussion of the origins of sex deviation around what I see as the most striking fact about the phenomenon — its male preponderance. I have sought to explain this by looking at the separate evolution of male and female sexuality and have noted two male characteristics that seem to me central to the understanding of sex deviation:

(1) Competition for access to reproductive (young/healthy) females, the uneven success in this struggle, and the problems of libido management among unsuccessful males.
(2) The target-seeking nature of male libido, which apparently results from androgen effects in the brain and which leads, via a process of imprinting overlaid upon innate releasing

109

mechanisms, to more or less rigid and sometimes inappropriate associations between sensory configurations and sexual arousal.

Women seldom become sexually deviant because they do not have to succeed in a hierarchy struggle for sexual access and because their hormones do not dictate the acquisition of simple (particularly visual) arousal blueprints. The central processes by which I believe that much of male paraphilia can be accounted for are as follows:

(1) Males (unlike females) acquire stimulus patterns or scenarios that they find sexually exciting in adulthood. These templates for arousal are established (or at least consolidated) by a process akin to imprinting. In the human case this may not be as simple as that seen in birds (visual) or lower mammals (mainly olfactory) but it nevertheless occurs at sensitive periods in infancy and is fairly inflexible thereafter, being manifested in masturbation fantasies and pornographic preferences.

(2) Sociobiological forces have dictated that, apart from female anatomical details such as genitals, breasts and buttocks, and the various indications of youth, health and reproductive fitness, certain other criteria are usually satisfied in the sexual selection process. One is the preference for anonymous, unfamiliar, novel and multiple partners, which has the dual purpose of gene proliferation and incest avoidance. The deviant extension of this tendency is the impersonal and sensation-seeking nature of many male predilections (e.g. fetishism, transvestism, rape, bestiality, group sex). It is necessary that sexual imprinting be impersonal, otherwise there would be a risk of the male child fixating upon the mother as an identity rather than a displayer of certain attributes of universal female application. (Note how this position differs from the Freudian idea of 'resolving the Oedipus complex.')

(3) Assuming that human males imprint upon certain behavioural characteristics in addition to the purely sensory (visual and olfactory) ones, then strictness/punitiveness is a strong contender since the outstanding role of the mother at the time of sexual imprinting is likely to be that of disciplinarian. The tension between fear and security, the actual tingle

of chastisement (with possible redistribution of blood supply to the genitals) and the possible sexual connotations of punishment and control (smacked buttocks, tightly wrapped nappies, or whatever) could all promote associations between pain/humiliation and whatever sexual cues are being imprinted at that critical time, thus accounting for masochism/submission as a common male sex variation. Sociobiologically, this predilection might be advantageous because it would attract men to women likely to provide firm disciplinary guidance to their children, who are therefore ardent caretakers (just like the mothers who successfully raised them). Put simply, if the boy's mother is the model for sexual imprinting then discipline may easily be incorporated in the excitement template.

(4) Effective performance of the male sex role in sexual inter-course requires a degree of dominance over other males and the female partner. If this is not present, whether for constitutional or social reasons, the likelihood of certain adaptations is increased. These include paedophilia (approaching young boys because they are less threatening than adults) transvestism, trans-sexualism and passive homosexuality (because they bypass the need for dominance), masochism (which makes a virtue out of helplessness) and fetishism (which does not involve real partners at all). The direction in which the dominance failure manifests itself will be determined mainly by hormonal factors and imprinting experiences.

Recognition of the importance of these major ethological forces is not to deny the role of genetic and hormonal factors and broader learning involving parental relationships, infantile punishment and reward, adolescent orgasmic experiences and self-esteem. However, the evolutionary/adaptive model seems to me more illuminating than the traditional medical/pathological approach.

Viewed within this ethological framework, many of the sexual predilections that have hitherto appeared as totally irrational and inexplicable may seem instead to be inevitable, almost natural. Perhaps if people better understood the origins of these practices they would be less intolerant of them. After all, they may sometimes be beneficial to society at large because of their eugenic consequences. It will also be clear that simple-minded attempts to eliminate sexual variations by conditioning methods or psychoanalysis are likely to be ineffective or even counterproductive. The biological origins and evolutionary significance of these behaviours, as well as the range of alternatives that are available to the individual, should be taken into account when attempts are made to 'treat' them.

NOTE

This chapter is an updated revision of Chapter 7 in my book *Love and Instinct* (1981) London: Temple Smith.

REFERENCES

Bateson, P. (1981) 'Control of sensitivity to the environment during development' in *Behavioral Development* (eds K. Immelmann, G.W. Barlow, L. Petrinovich and M. Main), Cambridge: Cambridge University Press

Bell, A.P. (1974) 'Homosexualities: their range and character.' In *1973 Nebraska Symposium on Motivation*, Lincoln: University of Nebraska Press

Blumstein, P.W. and Schwartz, P. (1976) 'Bisexuality: Some social psychological issues.' *Proceedings of American Sociological Association*, New York.

Chalkley, A.J. and Powell, G.E. (1983) 'The clinical description of forty-eight cases of sexual fetishism.' *Br. J. Psychiatry*, *142*, 292–5

Crawford, D.A. (1981) 'Treatment approaches with paedophiles.' In *Adult Sexual Interest in Children* (eds. M. Cook and K. Howells), New York: Academic Press

Dörner, G., Rohde, W., Stahl, F., Krell, L. and Masius, W.G. (1975) 'A neuroendocrine predisposition for homosexuality in men.' *Arch. Sex. Behav.*, *4*, 1–8

Eberhard, W.G. (1985) *Sexual Selection and Animal Genitalia*, Cambridge, Mass.: Harvard University Press

Eibl-Eibesfeldt, I. (1971) *Love and Hate: On the Natural History of Basic Behaviour Patterns*, London: Methuen

Epstein, A.W. (1961) 'Relationship of fetishism and transvestism to brain and particularly temporal lobe dysfunction.' *J. Nerv. Ment. Dis.*, *133*, 247–53

Feldman, M.P. and MacCulloch, M.J. (1971) *Homosexual Behaviour: Therapy and Assessment*, Oxford: Pergamon

Geist, V. (1971) *Mountain Sheep: A Study in Behaviour and Evolution*, Chicago: University of Chicago Press

Giallombardo, R. (1974) *The Social World of Imprisoned Girls*, New York: Wiley

Goldstein, N.J.. Kant, H.S., Judd, L.L., Rice, C.J. and Green, R. (1971) 'Exposure to pornography and sexual behaviour in deviant and normal groups.' In *Technical Report of the Commission on Obscenity and Pornography*, Vol. VII, Washington, D.C: U.S. Government Printing Office

Gosselin, C.C. and Eysenck, S.B.G. (1980) 'The transvestite double image: a preliminary report.' *Personality and Individual Differences*, *1*, 172–3

Gosselin, C.C. and Wilson, G.D. (1980) *Sexual Variations*, London: Faber & Faber

Griffitt, W. and Hatfield, E. (1985) *Human Sexual Behavior*, Glenview, Ill.: Scott-Foresman

Harry, J. (1983) 'Gay male and lesbian relationships.' In *Contemporary Families and Alternative Lifestyles* (eds. E.D. Macklin and R.G. Rubin), Beverly Hills: Sage Publications

Heston, L.L. and Shields, J. (1968) 'Homosexuality in twins: a family study and a registry study.' *Arch. Gen. Psychiatry*, *18*, 149–60

Hoenig, J. and Kenna, J.C. (1979) 'EEG abnormalities and transsexualism.' *Br. J. Psychiatry*, *134*, 293–300

Howells, K. (1979) 'Some meanings of children for paedophiles.' In *Love and Attraction: An International Conference* (eds. M. Cook and G.D. Wilson), Oxford: Pergamon

Hunt, M. (1974) *Sexual Behaviour in the 1970s*, New York: Dell

Hutchinson, G.E. (1959) 'A speculative consideration of certain possible forms of sexual selection in man.' *American Naturalist*, *93* (869), 81–91

Immelmann, K. and Suomi, S.J. (1981) 'Sensitive phases in development.' In *Behavioral Development* (eds. K. Immelmann, G.W. Barlow, L. Petrinovich and M. Main), Cambridge: Cambridge University Press

Kallman, F.J. (1952) 'Comparative twin study on the genetic aspects of male homosexuality.' *J. Nerv. Ment. Dis.*, *115*, 283–98

Kamel, G.W.L. (1980) 'Leathersex: meaningful aspects of gay sadomasochism.' *Deviant Behaviour*, *1*, 171–91

Kolarsky, A., Freund, K., Machek, J. and Polak, O. (1967) 'Male sexual deviation: association with early temporal lobe damage.' *Arch. Gen. Psychiatry*, *17*, 735–43

Kolb, B. and Whishaw, I.Q. (1985) *Fundamentals of Human Neuropsychology*, New York: W.H. Freeman

Langevin, R. (1985) *Erotic Preference, Gender Identity and Aggression in Men: New Research Studies*, New York: Erlbaum

La Torre, R.A. (1980) 'Devaluation of the human love object: Heterosexual rejection as a possible antecedent to fetishism.' *J. Abnorm. Psychol.*, *89*, 295–98

Levy, J. and Gur, R.C. (1980) 'Individual differences in psychoneurological organization.' In *Neuropsychology of Left-handedness* (ed. J. Herron), pp. 199–210, New York: Academic Press

Lumsden, C.J. and Wilson, E.O. (1983) *Promethean Fire: Reflections on the Origins of Mind*, Cambridge, Mass.: Harvard University Press

McConaghy, N. (1970) 'Penile response conditioning and its relationship to aversion therapy in homosexuals.' *Behaviour*

Therapy, *1*, 213–21

McEwan, B.S. (1980) 'Steroid hormones and the brain: Cellular mechanisms underlying neural and behavioral plasticity.' *Psychoneuroendocrinology*, *5*, 1–11

McGlone, J. (1980) 'Sex differences in human brain asymmetry: a critical survey.' *Behavioural Brain Sciences*, *3*, 215

McGuire, R.J., Carlisle, J.M. and Young, B.G. (1965) 'Sexual deviations as conditioned behaviour: A hypothesis.' *Behav. Res. Ther.*, *2*, 185–90

McGuire, M.T., Raleigh, M.J. and Johnson, C. (1983) 'Social dominance in adult male vervet monkeys: behaviour-biochemical relationships.' *Biology and Social Life*, *22*, 311–28

Mason, W.A. (1960) 'The effects of social restriction on the behaviour of Rhesus monkeys.' *International Journal of Comparative Physiology and Psychology*, *53*, 582

Mitchell, G. (1981) *Human Sex Differences*, New York: Van Nostrand Reinhold Company

Mitchell, W., Falconer, M.A. and Hill, D. (1954) 'Epilepsy with fetishism relieved by temporal lobe lobectomy.' *Lancet*, *ii*, 626–30

Morris, D. (1971) *Intimate Behaviour*, London: Cape

Parkes, A.S. (1976) *Patterns of Sexuality and Reproduction*, London: Oxford University Press

Pinkava, V. (1971) 'Logical models of sexual deviations.' *International Journal of Man-Machine Studies*, *3*, 351–74

Rachman, S.J. and Hodgson, R.J. (1968) 'Experimentally induced "sexual fetishism".' *Psychological Record*, *18*, 25–7

Raisman, G. and Field, P.M. (1973) 'Sexual dimorphism in the neuropil of the preoptic area of the rat and its dependence on neonatal androgen.' *Brain Res.*, *54*, 1–29

Reinisch, J.M. (1977) 'Prenatal exposure of human foetuses to synthetic progestin and oestrogen affects personality.' *Nature*, *266*, 561–2

Robertson, D.R. (1972) 'Social control of sex reversal in a coral reef fish.' *Science*, *177*, 1007–9

Rose, R.M., Bernstein, I.S. and Gordon, T.P. (1975) 'Consequences of social conflict on plasma testosterone levels in rhesus monkeys.' *Psychosom. Med.*, *37*, 50–61

Seward, J.P. and Seward, G.H. (1980) *Sex Differences: Mental and Tempermental*, Lexington, Mass: D.C. Heath & Company

Sipova, I. and Starka, L. (1977) 'Plasma testosterone values in transsexual women.' *Arch. Sex. Behav.*, *6*, 441–55

Sparks, J. (1978) *The Sexual Connection*, London: David & Charles

Spengler, A. (1977) 'Manifest sadomasochism in males. Results of an empirical study.' *Arch. Sex. Behav.*, *6*, 441–56

Symons, D. (1979) *The Evolution of Human Sexuality*, London: Oxford University Press

Trivers, R.L. (1972) 'Parental investment and sexual selection.' In *Sexual Selection and the Descent of Man* (ed. B. Campbell), Chicago: Aldine

Trivers, R.L. (1976) 'Sexual selection and resource-accruing abilities in Anolis garmani.' *Evolution*, *30*, 253–69

Wickler, W. (1967) 'Socio-sexual signals and their intra-specific imitation among primates.' In *Primate Ethology* (ed. D. Morris), London: Weidenfeld and Nicholson

Wikan, U. (1977) 'Man becomes woman: trans-sexualism in Oman as a key to gender roles.' *Man, 12*, 304–19

Wilson, E.O. (1975) *Sociobiology: The New Synthesis*, Cambridge, Mass.: Belknap

Wilson, G.D. (1978) *The Secrets of Sexual Fantasy*, London: Dent

Wilson, G.D. (1981a) *Love and Instinct*, London: Temple Smith

Wilson, G.D. (1981b) 'Cross-generational stability of gender differences in sexuality.' *Personality and Individual Differences, 2*, 254–7

Wilson, G.D. (1986) 'Male-female differences in sexual activity, enjoyment and fantasies.' *Personality and Individual Differences*, in press

Wilson, G.D. and Cox, D.N. (1983) *The Child-Lovers: A Study of Paedophiles in Society*, London: Peter Owen

Wilson, G.D. and Fulford, K.W.M. (1979) 'Sexual behaviour, personality and hormonal characteristics of heterosexual, homosexual and bisexual men.' In *Love and Attraction* (eds. M. Cook and G.D. Wilson, Oxford: Pergamon

Wilson, G.D. and Lang, R.J. (1981) 'Sex differences in sexual fantasy patterns.' *Personality and Individual Differences, 2*, 343–6

Zuger, B. (1978) 'Effeminate behaviour present in boys from children: Ten additional years of follow-up.' *Compr. Psychiatry, 19*, 363–9

5

Logical Models of Variant Sexuality

Václav Pinkava

It is with some hesitation that I begin this chapter. Whilst the theory to be described may appear plausible to ethologists or systems engineers, I realise that the background of many psychologists and others is somewhat incompatible with my approach. Thus I can foresee difficulties in making myself understood and find it hard to decide which approach to use in order to decrease the likelihood of this happening. It is not that the theory is so difficult to grasp: in fact, I believe it is clearer than some other theories of variant sexuality, and potentially of great interest to clinical psychologists.

To explain it properly, there are of course the logical networks as modelling tools and these do require some mathematical thinking, yet probably less than some other branches of mathematics currently applied in behavioural sciences. However, these technicalities cannot be explained in a short chapter and so the actual models will only be shown as a kind of illustration in a simplified form indicating that they really exist. Even so, difficulties may be expected. The models, although some of them do involve learning, are not behaviourist or learning-theoretical ones, and it so happens that the so-called scientific way of thinking in contemporary clinical psychology, apart from designing experiments and measuring, is largely restricted just to this approach, whilst other approaches tend to employ a kind of metaphorical and generally artistic way of reasoning.

Now, the theory in question, having features of a scientific approach, whilst not being behaviourist, is likely to puzzle some readers as it does not fit into any familiar pattern. This realisation dawned on me some time ago when I gave a talk to a gathering of probation officers. Another speaker was a well-known sociologist interested in sexology and a campaigner for the rights of sexual minorities. He opened his speech by asserting that sex has nothing to do with reproduction. Now, the hall was packed with some four or five hundred listeners, so one might have wondered how all these people actually happened. Naturally, sex is also about things other than reproduction even at subhuman level: the males of the common bedbug, *Cimex lectularius*, for instance, feed their young by copulating with them and thus inject sperm into their alimentary tract, which is then digested. Many equally bizarre instances of sex not being used for reproduction might be quoted from 'nature', and yet asserting that sex has nothing to do with reproduction is obviously nonsense.

Another remarkable thing I remember from that particular lecture was the speaker's assertion that a homosexual wasn't a homosexual, wasn't a homosexual, wasn't a homosexual. I presume he was trying to say that the fact that someone reacts sexually to persons of his own sex does not describe him exhaustively; for instance, he may be as bright as Leonardo da Vinci or as dull as ditchwater.

Yet, this academic way of thinking fills me with gloom, as it seems to violate the basic logical postulate of identity of a concept with itself. Thus the logical models of variant sexuality don't seem to me to stand much chance of being understood if this kind of mental climate prevails among people interested in the topic.

The theory to be explained in this chapter was formulated some time ago in a series of articles (Pinkava 1962, 1963, 1965a, 1965b, 1966) in Czech and German and later summarised in an English paper (Pinkava 1971). Although it uses logical nets as a modelling tool, it may easily be re-formulated in terms of computer programs. With the progress in computer graphics and image processing it might be developed further with regard to the relevant input configurations in more concrete or specific terms, so perhaps its time is now coming.

CURRENT TYPES OF THEORIES OF VARIANT SEXUALITY

There are basically three types of etiological theories of variant sexuality, not counting the one that states that it is a matter of voluntary decision and nothing else, similar, say, to the way one decides what to wear or what to drink. We shall return to this view later, probing whether it is at all tenable. The voluntary-choice theory is kind of self-explanatory, done with in one sentence (unless of course we wish to ponder over the phenomenon of will as such), so it is not even open to further discussion. Of the remaining three, one is restricted practically only to male and female homosexuality, so let us first deal with the remaining two types, which also apply to other types of variation.

One of these theories, or rather types of theories, as the general idea has many different varieties, is again basically very simple. It states that variant sexuality comes about by a kind of getting used to it or by learning of some kind. The learning or getting-used-to theories range from primitive ones to more sophisticated approaches using an armory of theoretical concepts. Just to quote one example, Krafft-Ebing, nearly a hundred years ago (1894, 1901), used to think that homosexuality came about through excessive masturbation, which caused focusing of interest on the male genitals and prevented development of interest in women. Alfred Binet (1887), better known as the pioneer of intelligence testing, was the first to open the floodgate of learning-theoretical approaches to variant sexuality: he did not as yet put it in terms of conditioning, talking only of associations of ideas, but the basic reasoning is already there. Variant sexuality comes about by means of a 'choc fortuit' in childhood, by which a strong pathological association is built between sexual arousal and some irrelevant or 'wrong' object. Bechterev (1923) put this idea into the terms of conditioning, where it remains to this very day, as one of the most widespread etiological theories of sexual variation.

Objections to this theory are two-fold. From a purely practical point of view, it does not seem to be therapeutically efficient. Of course there are claims to the contrary, but in my own experience deconditioning of homosexuals yields only fragmentary and fortuitous results, if any at all, and the same seems to apply to other deviations of which patients want to be rid. I participated in a major research program on deconditioning homosexuals (Freund, 1965) and was directly involved in the follow up, not to mention repeated attempts at deconditioning variant sexual behaviours in individual clinical situations. I also had the opportunity to check on other therapists' results, and the general impression, based on statistics and accumulated experience, is that deconditioning does not work, whatever the specific technique. If variant sexual behaviours cannot be removed by deconditioning, they are unlikely to have arisen by conditioning. The variations may still be acquired by some kind of learning: language, for instance is definitely an acquired disposition to behaviour and yet, after a certain age, with individual variations, it is impossible to acquire a new language with perfection. However, the simple conditioning model must be wrong, as variations do not come and go the way simple phobias may do — if there is learning it is probably of a different type.

The second objection is theoretical, and already involves a certain general approach, so here we are actually jumping ahead: as sexual behaviour in humans seems to be an instinct, as it is in other animals, and 'designed' by evolution (or whatever) primarily for the purpose of reproduction, it would be strange if it were left open to a chance 'choc fortuit'. The behaviourists' idea seems to be that only the pre-orgasmic and orgasmic reactions are innate, an unconditioned reflex, while everything else is acquired by associative learning. However, one feels that if this were the case, there would be many more deviations than there are in reality. Most people's sex life starts with substitutory and inadequate sexual activities and practically always there is some perception, which, if the Binet theory were correct, would lead to fetishism. Considering this, there seems to be some innate guideline, some pattern for potential behaviour, just as, for example, a cat does not learn to catch mice simply by trial and error and by associating certain movement patterns, originally produced at random, with the experience of getting food. We shall return to this idea later. On the other hand, while it is thinkable that variations like homosexuality or paedophilia have at their roots some flow in the innate programs, it does not seem possible to explain fetishism in this context. Hence it appears that the object which arouses sexual desire is influenced by learning after all.

The second group of etiological theories of sex deviation has to do with motivation. The classical and perhaps most elaborate of this group is Freud's theory. As for the classical alternatives to psychoanalysis, built along the same basic lines, Adler's doctrine does not offer any elaborate explanation of deviation, but seems to accept the basically Freudian model, with the modification that only spoiled children, who expect everything, including sexual gratification, from their parents, develop the Oedipal complex and the consequences. C.G. Jung accepts the Freudian model for one part of the neuroses, explains other neuroses according to Adler and adds his own bit: neuroses coming from not attaining mystical salvation. Thus the classical doctrines inspired by Freud accept his teaching nearly completely as far as sex variations are concerned. Basically, the teaching postulates a progressive development of the force 'libido' which goes through various stages, charging different organs, until it reaches the 'normal' genital stage. Variations arise when libido regresses again, the main reason for this being castration anxiety.

Apart from being difficult to verify by accepted scientific methods, and giving a generally far-fetched impression, the main objections against the psychoanalytic theory are of three kinds: (1) It does not explain some phenomena known from experience to the clinician and is defective where women are concerned. (2) Therapeutic results based upon it are poor. (3) There are deviations also in animals, mainly domesticated ones, and one cannot expect them to suffer from regression and suchlike.

Lately, various less elaborate and more plausible models of sexual behaviour have been developed, sometimes invented *ad hoc* in individual cases, for instance, a sadistic murderer kills little girls 'because he hates his dominant wife'. These ideas also suffer from being primitive, similar to some pre-Freudian theories, and they do not explain why another person with the same problem never develops the particular deviation. The therapeutic application is also generally disappointing.

The third type of theory, restricted to homosexuality and lesbians, postulates some kind of biological effeminacy (or virilism), which then has a psychological effect on the direction of sexual desire. The evidence is usually not convincing and the link between the biological cause and the psychological effect is vague and global. An exception is the theory of Dörner, which, however, is contested as based on insufficient experimental evidence.

So much, very briefly, on the existing types of etiological theories of sexual deviation.

AN ALTERNATIVE THEORY

I believe that the theory, of which the logical models mentioned in the heading form a part, is closer to reality than the current theories. However, it is difficult to demonstrate this in a short chapter as the necessary technicalities cannot be explained in the space allocated. Also, some of the postulates depend partly on certain beliefs or feelings, acquired during many years of clinical and research work with subjects showing deviant sexuality of various kinds. Most psychologists do not work exclusively with variants as I did for some seven years, and they tend to view patients through the prism of certain fixed preconceptions, mostly either dynamic or learning-theoretical. For instance, I am convinced that neither conditioning, deconditioning or re-learning nor dynamic or motivational psychotherapy can ever change the proclivities of a homosexual, a view I have arrived at after having seen hundreds of them, listening to their histories (including having been through various psychotherapies), and trying to influence their tendencies by various methods falling under the general heading of behaviourism or learning theory. This made me search for some other theoretical framework for this and similar psychological manifestations. Most psychologists do not seem to share my scepticism and therefore see no need to look for different approaches to the established ones. What I hope to demonstrate is that this theory has at least the same degree of rationality and plausibility as current theories of the phenomena in question.

THE DEFINITION OF VARIANT SEXUALITY

Before studying any phenomenon, we should be able to recognise it. In the present context this means that we need a definition of variant sexuality. It is sometimes believed that this task is difficult or impossible. On the contrary, I believe that it is rather easy. The only difficulty is that my approach is likely to meet with certain prejudices which prevent some people from seeing that the points of which they so strongly disapprove are by no means included in the bare and simple statements used in building up the definition, nor are they being implied in any way.

We start with the obvious, yet somehow irritating, statement that sexual behaviour is primarily about reproduction. This seems self-evident, yet owing to the emotional reactions mentioned above I had better explain further what I mean. First, perhaps, it is necessary to stress that by sexual behaviour I mean such behaviour that is generally recognised as sexual: I do not

121

consider eating or defecation as sexual behaviour as a classical Freudian might do. Further, I hasten to assure the reader that by saying 'sexual behaviour is basically about reproduction' I by no means deny that it may serve other purposes, nor do I maintain that this is the only admissable purpose of the said sexual behaviour.

We may perhaps define a kind of basic, classical or 'normal' way of sexual behaviour, which would serve us as a starting point in assessing variations. Again, I hasten to reassure the reader that this does not imply any evaluative judgement; it is a purely methodological consideration, fixing a kind of starting point. Thus we may say that basic or 'non-variant' sexual behaviour is that which, other things permitting, would lead to reproduction of the species. By 'other things' I mean the fertility of the individuals involved, absence of contraception, and the like. Obviously, two males cannot reproduce, nor does flogging bring about fertilisation. Thus we can distinguish between variations in the erotic partner or object and in the behaviour involved.

Elaborating on these ideas more systematically, and concentrating first on variations in the erotic object, we see that in the non-variant case the object is a conspecific individual of the complementary sex with signs indicating the probability of successful reproduction, this also including successful care of the young. Perhaps this statement again needs explanation. There is no mystery about what a 'non-variant' human male finds sexually attractive: our culture has been inundated with models, which are often used to advertise goods for sale and generally to attract attention. The model is a human female of reproductive age (i.e. young, yet sexually mature) with signs of general health (not too fat, not too skinny, nice hair and teeth, etc), free from deformities ('pretty' in face and body) and with signs that are likely to be associated with successful care of the infant. The attraction of long straight legs in a human female is less easy to explain: it may date back to the time when the human ancestor was a hunter in the plain and the long straight legs in a female seemed to indicate that the offspring to be sired with her would be well equipped for running after prey and away from danger. Yet, this is only conjecture. The other signs or features are much more obvious. Every non-variant male knows that it is the female's bottom and her breasts that attract him most, apart from the external genitals: the female should be able to deliver the baby, hence she should have broad hips; she must be able to nurse it, as evidenced by well-developed breasts. The recent finding that fat stored in the region of the thighs, hips and buttocks is used for conversion into milk explains the attractiveness of these parts of the body for the male. It is therefore clear that the features which attract a non-variant male to an erotic object are in direct connection with reproduction, *even if the male wants to prevent it at a non-instinctive, conscious level.*

Now, by removing various relevant characteristics from the non-variant erotic object, we arrive at variations as far as the human male and his erotic object is concerned:

First of all, the non-variant object is a living being of certain general characteristics. By removing this condition we arrive at what is sometimes called 'great' fetishism, exclusive attractiveness or erotic quality of inanimate objects, like rubber, safety pins, furs, etc.

If the object is a living being it should be conspecific. By removing this condition we arrive at zoophilia. (In many cases animals are only substitutes, but there are other cases in which the animal is positively attractive to the subject.)

The next step is that the conspecific animal or human should be of the opposite sex. Failing this we have the variation of homosexuality.

Now if the attractive object is a human female, she should be within the reproductive age range, not too young and not too old. A variation in this respect produces either heterosexual paedophilia or heterosexual gerontophilia. Perhaps we may stress that some cases, which may be classified as paedophilia in a 'social' or legal context may not be paedophilia from a biological point of view. (This statement does not imply that the age limit should be changed, as this depends on considerations of a different kind.) Nor is marital life of an elderly couple to be considered as a manifestation of gerontophilia: it is more like a substitutive sexual activity facilitated by life-long conditioning.

The next step concerns the general rule that the conspecific female of reproductive age should be free from deformities and her attractiveness should primarily have to do with those signs associated with secure reproduction. This principle is vitiated in various cases of partialism, where irrelevant parts of the body are more attractive than the general configuration, or where the attractiveness of only one relevant part, like the breasts or buttocks, outweighs the general configuration. To this we may add attractiveness of deformities such as limping, amputation,

123

and the like and the so-called 'small' fetishism. Converse to the 'great' fetishisms, in which inanimate objects assume the role of sexual partners, 'small' fetishisms consist of various inanimate objects adding to or actually determining attractiveness of live sex objects.

Adding a fetish may sway the balance in favour of a less suitable sex object and hence small fetishisms may again vitiate the principle of optimal potential reproductivity. Some small fetishisms, however, are so widespread that they may be considered 'normal' in the human male of our civilisation (things like stockings, suspender belts and the like). In this respect we have to realise that there are various definitions of the 'norm', the choice of which, in a particular context, will also influence our definition of variant sexuality.

Now, all these variations may combine in various ways, thus producing other well-known variations. For instance, if the conditions of the opposite sex and of reproductive age are violated together, we have homosexual paedophilia or gerontophilia. If the opposite sex condition is violated together with the relevant features only condition, we get homosexual fetishism, etc. This 'taxonomy' is absolutely formal, albeit meaningful, and does not imply any etiological suggestions. However, it provides a neat and logical method of approaching the description and definition of variant sexuality.

This applies as far as the *object* of erotic desire is concerned. It does not, however, exhaust the class of phenomena usually referred to as sexual variations. There are modes of variant sexuality in which the sexual object may be normal, i.e. a healthy human female of reproductive age, and yet the preferred sexual activity is not. To sort out this dimension of sexuality, we may again resort to the basic criterion of possible reproduction as the starting point. Again, we do not attach any evaluative judgement to the statement that we shall consider as normal such sexual behaviour that, other things being favourable, would lead to reproduction.

The situation here is less clear than in the case of variant objects for several reasons. First, before genital intercourse takes place, there are certain preliminary activities, which, although analogous to or identical with those of other mammals, may be considered improper or 'sinful' according to certain traditional moral codes. As it is also possible to effect reproduction without these activities, the strict logical principle of our definition is not applicable in this form. Further, humans are capable of re-directing and re-shaping their primary proclivities, for instance, in order to avoid conception. Fortunately, animal studies show that copulation is only the culmination of sexual activity (see Lorenz) and also that mammals tend to show a certain degree of uniformity in this behaviour, as far as different species are concerned. Thus, we may say that non-variant sexual behaviour is that which is likely to evoke an adequate response in a (non-variant) partner and which culminates in coition which (other things being favourable) would allow reproduction.

Variant activity, to be defined or recognised as such, has to replace or be preferred to genital coition and it must not be only a preparatory activity. For instance, sniffing and licking the vulva is a common pre-copulatory activity in male mammals; thus, however repulsive or ridiculous it may appear to the rational, detached human mind, it is actually a part of normal male sexual behaviour, provided it does not replace genital coition. If it does, and if it is not motivated by other reasons such as prevention of pregnancy or preservation of physical virginity, it has to be considered a variation. To decide this, one has to use the method of interview and analysis of clinical data, to see whether there is a craving for the suspected variant activity, which is greater than that for 'normal' genital coition. This requires certain skill in interviewing, and experience in evaluation. When deciding whether an activity is variant or not, one has to consider the nature of the sexual object, in case this is variant, and to decide what the activity would be if the object were 'normal'. Thus, most methods of intercourse between homosexuals and lesbians cannot be considered variant, although they are not 'normal', for purely anatomical reasons. A homosexual man playing an active or penetrative role in anal intercourse cannot be considered as deviant or variant in activity, as this is the nearest to vaginal penetration he can get given his partner's anatomy. As for the receptive partner, many feminine homosexual men indulge in the fantasy that they are actually women with female sex organs, so again we would not necessarily consider such a person as having an extra deviation in activity.

However, the situation here is rather complicated. For instance, there are men, albeit extremely rare, who are attracted to 'conventional' sex partners of the complementary sex, yet they want to experience penetration by a female partner. They again seem to come in two subcategories, those who view themselves as men, and those who have the fantasy of being women (a kind of lesbianism in a male body). Bearing in mind the existence of trans-sexual individuals with or without homoerotic inclinations and transvestites with or without trans-sexual tendencies, we are obviously obliged to recognise yet more dimensions of variant sexuality apart from object and activity. These seem to be the dimensions of sex identification and penetrativity versus receptivity as the preferred sexual role.

In a non-variant individual, sex identification, i.e. whether male or female, and preferred role with respect to penetrativity-receptivity (this is a better term than active-passive: a receptive individual may be very active) conform with the anatomicophysiological sex of the individual; however, these are clearly different constituents as they may be dissociated in variant cases. Again, the degree or urgency of assuming a sex role or identification (whether male or female) may differ and seems even to have a special degree of intensity in various types of variants, e.g., the 'classical' type of homosexual man, conspicuous by his feminine mannerisms and articulation mimicking a high-pitched voice (it is a matter of resonance brought about by shaping the mouth cavity in a certain way: usually homosexual men do not differ in vocal range from heterosexual men). This type prefers 'mature', (i.e. not necessarily teenage) partners, the receptive role in intercourse, and shows a mild degree of female identification, which may be satisfied by taking up 'feminine' occupations and activities, and by occasional wearing of 'drag'. Another, far less conspicuous type of homosexual man is attracted exclusively by teenagers, prefers the penetrative role and has no feminine identification at all. There are also transitional types and individuals who do not fit any of the typical categories.

Contrary to general opinion, male trans-sexuals with a very strong craving for the female role, to the extent that they are willing to undergo a sex change operation, are usually not sexually interested in other men. If they make statements to this effect it may be in order to stress their femininity. Some transvestites prefer dressing as women and then masturbating in front of a mirror to any other sexual activity. It appears that their sexual appetite is directed towards their own body viewed as being female. Thus it appears that there is yet another dimension to be considered, a kind of 'externalisation' of the sex object: if this fails the object is then the subject himself. If the non-externalised object is otherwise 'normal', we get the above mentioned type of transvestitism. If the object is homosexual, we get a variation called 'narcissism' or 'automonosexualism', frequently described by the psychiatric taxonomists of the 19th and early 20th century (Krafft-Ebing and Moll, 1924).

The dimensions of object, externalisation, identification, penetrativity/receptivity and general activity seem to cover all the variations. Naturally an individual with variant sexuality may differ in more than one respect from the norm, e.g. a homosexual fetishist or a homosexual sadist. Also, a variation in the object may include several objects at once. These cases provide an important theoretical clue as to the possible etiological mechanism. Apart from the fact that the subject may be unwilling to talk or not sufficiently aware of his tendencies, which he may rationalise away by different tactics, the issue is also frequently obscured by the fact that sexual behaviour in humans is more flexible than in nonhuman animals. For example, there may be some methods of anticonception in use in a culture that mimic variant behaviour, and the degree of feminine mannerism in homosexual men may vary in accordance with fashion. Also, as will be discussed later, the specificity of the object of an instinctive activity may vary according to the level of motivation: the higher the motivation, the less specific the object. Thus, for example, in situations where there are no specific sexual objects available, a subject may turn to less specific ones and so mimic a variant, e.g. homosexual or lesbian activities in closed unisex communities like boarding schools, convents, etc. On the other hand, in a situation of deprivation of his own specific object, a variant individual may turn to the norm, e.g. a married homosexual man who has decided to 'drop his vice'. Yet, the sexual object or activity (we may call it his sexual pattern) tends to re-emerge whenever the specific stimuli appear and is also the subject of the individual's sex fantasies and dreams when asleep. This is usually the best way of assessing whether a certain pattern is a genuine variation or only a substitutive or fortuitous activity. Another factor that can obscure the assessment of an individual sexual pattern is the fact that, in mammals, penetrative and receptive types of sex behaviour seem to exist in both sexes, even though one of them (the one that is not in accordance with the anatomicophysiological sex) is usually only refractory.

In the present chapter I shall restrict myself only to variations in the object, leaving the other dimensions aside. I hope to show

127

that a certain approach to the question of sexual behaviour, combined with some ideas derived from the theory of logical networks and finite automata, yields the outline of a theory that differs from current approaches and yet is equally consistent and explanatory, if not more so.

INSTINCTS IN ANIMALS AND HUMANS

In animals there are some modes of behaviour that are very complicated and yet are not based on any kind of learning as it is usually understood. Frequently we may observe that an organism is able to perform rather complicated tasks, yet if confronted with other problems, of the same or lesser complexity, is incapable of solving them or of dealing with them in an efficient way. These complicated behaviour patterns have to do with the animal's survival as an individual or species, they appear fixed in all organisms of the given species, which are of the same type (with respect to sex, developmental stage, 'caste', etc.) and they appear to be largely innate. We usually call these behaviour patterns (or dispositions to them) *instincts*, from the Latin verb *instinguere*, meaning to impel, to urge or to drive. This term conveys the characteristic of urgency and a certain automaton-like 'blind' quality of the instincts.

Until recently, we had no direct insight into how instincts might be brought about or how to explain their nature. With the advent of the theory of self-regulating systems, and especially its branch called 'robotics', we have acquired a much clearer view of the nature and basis of instincts. In fact, nowadays there are man-made systems in existence that we may say show instinctive behaviour: they are able to perform certain activities or tasks, some rather complicated, yet are incapable of learning any other activities of even a much lower complexity. True, some animals show patterns of instinctive behaviour that, as yet, may be difficult to emulate with man-made robots, but at least the general principles of how instinctive behaviour occurs are finally clear.

The systems that behave like animals directed by instincts are called special-purpose automata or special-purpose robots, as opposed to general-purpose systems such as computers. Their behaviour is secured by means of switching circuits or logical networks, which nowadays are realised by means of microchips.

We may infer that in organisms showing instinctive behaviour, there are also switching circuits or logic networks in the nervous system, mainly the CNS. The kinds of rigid behaviour patterns, characteristic of instincts, may be viewed as a function of 'fixed' or 'wired in' programs, which presumably evolved in the same way as complex organs such as the eye.

Some groups or classes of animals, especially insects and other invertebrates, have instincts as their main basis of behaviour and yet are a very successful group of animals with respect to survival. Whilst in insects their whole life seems to be regulated mainly by fixed innate programs or instincts, in vertebrates the acquired forms of behaviour also become rather important. Instincts are still very important in birds, but birds are already well capable of associative learning, as amply demonstrated by Skinner's pigeons. Some birds, like tits and corvids, have been shown to be capable of problem solving. In mammals, learning and problem solving are even more to the fore, yet there is evidence that they also have instincts. The patterns involved in catching prey by a cat are obviously innate; there is no way they could be acquired by trial and error in such a short time. Examples abound. Naturally, reproduction, including sexual behaviour, also has a strong instinctive base in mammals. Let me repeat that by instincts I mean innate fixed programs regulating vitally important modes of behaviour.

Humans are mammals like others, but their problem-solving capacities are perhaps the best developed of all. Just as his general anatomy and physiology conforms with those of other mammals, just as his perception is similar, but in some sensory modalities like smell and hearing less acute than in most other mammals, just as his learning and problem-solving ability obeys the same principles, with the difference that in this respect it happens to be much more developed, so it is reasonable to expect that man will also have sexual instincts or fixed programs regulating his sexual behaviour.

The existence of these relatively fixed programs is actually quite evident both from introspection and from every-day experience. Very often instinctive tendencies, especially those to do with sex, show an inclination to assert themselves 'against our better judgement', in other words, against the results of computations provided by our main problem-solving computer. Now these patterns are rigid, fixed programs, most likely 'wired in' in the form of given neuronal structures, although an arrangement

129

in the form of a Read-Only Memory (ROM) would also be technically possible. Be it one way or another the programs are basically innate, although I shall later discuss a special kind of predetermined learning that seems to operate in conjunction with instincts. The respective structures must develop the way our organs do; for instance, the way the image-processing system comes about together with central visual information processing.

Apart from the indirect evidence that there are sexual instincts in humans just as in other mammals, coupled with the insight that instincts can be nothing else but fixed programs, there is another course of reasoning that supports the present view. Arrangements in nature are demonstrably purposeful: the eye develops 'in order to see', the legs 'in order to walk', etc. Organs and behaviour patterns are usually admirably suited for a specific kind of task. Now, since sexual behaviour primarily serves the purpose of reproduction, it would be strange to leave the development of such important behaviour to chance learning. If this were the case, if indeed fetishism came about the way Binet thought, it would be almost a miracle that there are people who are not fatally hooked on some irrelevant inanimate objects. So even from this point of view it is plausible that the sexual instincts are based on fixed, wired-in programs, in the same way as the predatory behaviour of a cat.

Now we come to the core of our theory of sexual variation: in an exact analogy with innate physical 'malformations' or simply 'variations' in shape, variations in the shaping of the respective neural circuits regulating sexual behaviour (the sexual instincts) may also occur. I again hasten to stress that the theory of these different 'formations' of the 'networks' securing the programs does not necessarily imply any evaluative judgement. True, the original or 'wild' pattern will secure smooth reproduction, but if the new pattern does not, no moral censure necessarily follows logically. If you attend an exhibition of thoroughbred dogs, then, in comparison with the original, 'wild', wolf-like shape of their ancestors, the exhibits are actually monsters. Yet they are not viewed as such, and their different physical (and behavioural!) characteristics are, on the contrary, carefully preserved.

INSTINCTS VIEWED AS FINITE AUTOMATA

Students of animal behaviour have accumulated empirical evidence pertaining to the nature of instincts. The basic findings have been summarised by Tinbergen (1951). Instincts appear more-or-less invariant within a given species (taking into consideration things like age, sex, etc.), an observation implying that the underlying neural or neuro-hormonal mechanisms are inherited in the same way as other physical characteristics, morphological as well as psychological. The innate character of instinctive behaviour patterns is sometimes obscured by the fact that a specific type of learning, called 'imprinting', is also involved. This I shall discuss in a later context.

In an instinctive pattern the following general characteristics may be discerned. There is a definite repertoire of percepts releasing the behaviour so that under normal circumstances the pattern cannot be elicited by any other type of stimuli. These perceptual configurations are frequently of a rather 'schematic' character. Sometimes it is possible in an experiment to abstract the relevant features from a more complex perceptual configuration (as it actually occurs in nature) and to form a dummy comprising just the relevant characteristics, which then suffice to set the behaviour pattern in motion. This arrangement is described by the term innate releasing mechanism (IRM). The behaviour pattern elicited also appears to consist of a definite number of identifiable components. The activation of the instinctive behaviour pattern also depends on the inner states of the organism. Thus, apparently, there are internal states in play as well. It is possible to model such a behaviour pattern in terms of the theory of finite automata. For further technical details see Pinkava (1971, 1986).

Instincts may be viewed as finite automata and are presented by means of logical networks, binary or multivalued. This representation is conventional in a way as the same instinct could be represented by many possible structures, theoretically by an infinite number of them. The automaton may also be represented by other means, mathematical (e.g. by certain groupoids) or 'physical' (e.g. by computer programs). The representation by means of a chosen logical network, which may be given in a simple paper and pencil form (provided the network is not too big) serves an heuristic purpose and helps the speculation as to the way in which an automaton would have to be structurally defective in order to provide a required variation of behaviour. In this way we may obtain models of sex variations, the chosen nets and their modifications standing for whole classes of possible structures as their representatives or 'illustra-

131

tions'. Giving the more complicated models would be impossible or useless without the necessary technicalities. Instead, we are going to show the principle of modelling on a primitive model in first approximation, which does not require much mathematics.

A PRIMITIVE LOGICAL MODEL OF SOME MODES OF VARIANT SEXUALITY

In order to model sex variations or theories about them one has to know the respective dispositions to behaviour, or 'syndromes'. In humans, of whom direct observation is difficult, one has to rely mainly on the verbal communications of the subjects. Obtaining this kind of information requires certain skills that seem to be in rather short supply in contemporary clinical psychology. This has to do with the basic philosophy. If abnormal behaviour is caused by learning or by subconscious motivation, it is not important to really know that behaviour in detail. With respect to the present topic, whatever a subject may feel attracted to he has acquired this attraction via learning, so he may de-learn it again, no matter what it may be. It also has no real relevance: anything may become a conditioned stimulus. As for subconscious motivation, the 'symptom formation' is flexible anyway, the subconscious tactics may, and will, change in the course of therapy according to the theory, so again it is not terribly important to know all the details about the variation in question. Moreover, if we believe that this is simply a matter of choice, there is nothing we can do about it whether we know the details or not. Thus the skill of meticulous and patient exploration is no longer required. In the case of variation we either do not bother at all, as the subject has the free right of choice, or as soon as we have learnt the basic facts, we immediately start with either designing a therapeutic strategy for de-conditioning or start delving into the subject's childhood. Finally, people are often reluctant to talk about their sexual tendencies if they differ a lot from the norm, so gaining an accurate picture really does require some effort and skill.

Yet, from our present point of view, detailed knowledge is obviously important. If the dispositions to sexual behaviour are programs, like in a man-made robot (yet more sophisticated and capable of being modified by other 'programs') then knowing the detailed nature of a variant behaviour pattern and comparing it with 'normal' behaviour may provide us with insight into the way the program in question has been modified or 'impaired'.

Amongst a sample of 222 homosexual males studied by Kurt Freund and the present author at the Prague University Psychiatric Hospital (Psychiatrická Klinika K.U., Prague) there was a small, interesting group of patients with a rather bizarre deviation: they were homosexual with regard to human partners, but they were also attracted to animals, mostly domestic and big, of either sex. There were eight patients in all; however, three of them may be considered as dubious or not sufficiently clear cut with respect to the variation in question. One subject admitted sexual intercourse with chickens: it is not clear whether this is not just a kind of masturbation. Another subject got sexually excited when stroking dogs and cats regardless of their sex (furs had no erotic value for this subject). The third subject reported sexual excitement while throwing cats and dogs in the air and catching them again. He also indulged in sexually exciting fantasies consisting of feeding exotic animals like giraffes, camels, etc. The remaining five subjects were quite unequivocal in their appetence of men plus animals of either sex. The animals were mostly cattle, also horses, deer and dogs. Cows with big udders were especially attractive to some of them. (For details see Freund, 1965, p. 94.) I was able to enlarge the sample by two other cases. There is also a similar case described by Henry (1948).

The widespread view that such people are simply dull, find it difficult to get a more 'respectable' sex partner and therefore take to animals, is untenable with the sample in question. There was only one subject in the sample who would possibly fit the conventional image of a country simpleton, yet even he had normal IQ and his behaviour was rather cunning. The rest of the subjects were mostly members of the middle classes, some of them with definite intellectual tastes — a senior clerk, a manager of an antique shop, an optician, a surgeon, a church organist and the like. Henry's patient was a professor (of what he does not say). Apart from the country boy mentioned earlier, the man who ranked lowest in social status was a tailor, the only craftsman in this otherwise preponderantly professional group. Whilst dull and primitive people may sometimes use animals for sexual gratification, this clearly does not apply to the group in question. The animals are definitely not substitutive sex objects. In some of the cases animals had never been approached in reality, they only appeared in the subject's sex fantasies and wet dreams and evoked sexual feelings when sighted. Many of the subjects led active homosexual sex lives, yet the sexual attractiveness of animals never disappeared. Thus it is obvious that the animals are not substitutive objects in the sense of the ethological law of 'double quantification', which states that the higher the motivation the less specific a releasing stimulus (which might account for substitutive homosexual behaviour in otherwise heterosexual persons, as in boarding schools, monasteries and prisons).

Now the hypothesis of a substitutive sex object not being tenable, this particular variation seems rather puzzling. The subjects are attracted by animals, but also by human beings, thus not being human (i.e. not showing the specific features of a human) does not impede sexual appetence. Further, the subjects are attracted by both male and female animals (of certain species). They find the genitals of those animals particularly attractive. Those who are attracted by cows find the udder attractive too, apparently in analogy to the 'normal' human male, being attracted by a woman's breasts. It is therefore difficult to explain why these subjects do not feel attracted to human females: as neither the features of the Species Humana nor the features of the female sex impede sexual appetence in themselves, it seems rather incomprehensible that these features do not attract when presented together. A psychoanalyst would no doubt say that this clinical picture is due to extreme castration anxiety: the human female (basically the mother) is prohibited, hence everything else is not. However, if this were the mechanism, it ought to be rather widespread, whereas homosexual men do not usually care at all for animals. Besides, animal phobias are usually explained by psychoanalysts by saying that the dreaded animal stands for the castrating father. Why should this be so different in the subject in question? This way of extremely flexible reasoning, re-valuating everything according to purpose does not seem very scientific, to say the least. The alternative I propose is much simpler, and thus should be preferred on the basis of Occam's razor.

Let us suppose that in a normal man the class of potential sex objects is originally given by an innate IRM, as is the case in other animals. Behaviourists tend to ignore this fact, so they cannot make the logical transition to humans. This primitive class is later restricted owing to imprinting. Imprinting is a kind of learning that usually takes place at an early age in the animal and, once finished, it is irreversible. This discovery was pioneered by Lorenz (1935, 1943, 1958) and Tinbergen (1951) and has since been abundantly documented. In birds the original class is usually given in very broad terms. The future sex object is usually the type of organism (maybe a human) that the young birds perceive taking care of them. Some features of the imprinted object, however, are innate. For instance, it was found by Räber (1948) that a turkey reared in isolation from his conspecifics (the so-called Kaspar Hauser experiment), which imprinted humans as potential sex partners, reacted with hostility to women but courted men. It was discovered by experiment that he reacted with hostility to their long hair, which the innate part of his sex behaviour program interpreted as the pendulous structure hanging from the head of a turkey cock. In ducks, females recognise conspecific males on the basis of an innate program but males or drakes imprint the features of the conspecific female from their mother, i.e. the adult bird they see constantly in their surroundings (Schutz, 1963). In this way it is possible to produce 'homosexual' and 'zoophilous' drakes, but not female ducks. In mammals, it seems that the innate program depends on more features than is the case with birds. However, indirect evidence, which will be discussed later, compels us to believe that the appropriate sex object in the human male is pre-formed only in a rather schematic way and more detailed features are acquired by imprinting. Otherwise we could not explain, within the context of this theory, that zoophilous subjects are attracted by various species of animals (sometimes one subject by several). The assumption of a globally given sex object that is then specified by imprinting also allows us to incorporate fetishism into the present theory.

Now the primitive IRM or effective configuration will consist of features classing the potential sex object as human (H) and as female (F). We may speculate what these features are likely to be, but for understanding the theory such concretisation is unnecessary. So the class or set of primitive sexual objects S, is given by the equation: $S = H \cap F$ where $\cap$ is the operation of intersect, in the theory of sets. After imprinting has been completed a subclass S_1 is sorted out such that $S_1 \subset S$. A model of this kind may easily be represented by means of a computer program, especially if, for illustrative purposes, we choose some simple configurations to represent the classes H and F. However, for the sake of our simple paper and pencil models, we shall do it here by means of abstract logical networks. Considering the IRMs as most likely to be innate wired-in programs, the representation by logical networks (abstract switching circuits) also seems more realistic with respect to its probable realisation in a CNS.

Let us suppose that the IRM is represented by a binary net, realising a 'sharp' membership function for the set $S = H$ F. It is possible that in reality the IRM realises a 'fuzzy' membership function but we do not consider this possibility in our first approximation. Thus, there will be some binary features $h_1, h_2, . . ., h_n$, (the n may be considered as a rather large integer, if we consider these features as pertaining directly to the first, image recognition level) which enter a logical function $f(h_1, h_2, . . ., h_n)$ being a membership function of the set H. In other words, if $f(h_1, h_2, . . ., h_n) = 1$, the object, furnishing a particular substitute for the 'feature words': $h_1, h_2, . . ., h_n$, i.e. a particular Boolian vector, will be recognised as belonging to the set H. Similarly we may envisage another binary function $\phi(f_1, f_2 . . . f_m)$, defined on the feature words $f_1, f_2, . . ., f_m$, being the membership function of the set F. Thus the membership function of the set S may be represented by: $f(h_1, h_2, . . ., h_n)$ and $\phi(f_1, f_2, . . ., f_m)$. In terms of the formal language chosen: the subset S_1, representing the 'narrowed' class of sexual objects, acquired by imprinting may be expressed by the equation: $S_1 = H \cap F \cap L$, where L is the set ruled by or having the membership function $\psi(l_1, l_2, . . ., l_r)$, where again $l_1, l_2, . . ., l_r$ are binary features representing the imprinted characteristics. Please note that there is a *function* over the characteristics or 'feature words' $l_1, l_2, . . ., l_r$, which is *not necessarily* a simple logical multiplication or conjunction. Thus the membership function of S_1 may be given as: $f(h_1, h_2, . . ., h_n)$ and $\phi(f_1, f_2, . . ., f_m)$ and $\psi(l_1, l_2, . . ., l_r)$. We may now write the membership function in the simplified form of: h & f & l. We may presume that the feature words $l_1, l_2, . . ., l_r$ are not 'preformed' or given a 'wired-in' form, but, according to definition, are acquired by imprinting, so that they may differ in different individuals to some extent at least. At the moment we are not considering the possible impairment of the network, realising or actually generating the function $\psi(l_1, l_2, . . ., l_r)$, which, as we shall see, may account for fetishistic variations.

Instead, let us return to the hypothetical network, realising the

136

membership function of the set S, or the function h & f, as we now write it in its simplified form. Provided the network, realising the function h & f is intact (and provided the subject is exposed to a more or less 'normal' environment) the network realising the function h & f will ensure that the sexual object is a human female (with relevant additional features imprinted).

Now this model provides us with the theoretical possibility of explaining the etiology of homosexuality with bisexual zoophilia in a manner that is not only exhaustive and simple but also quite exact and concise. We postulated that the respective network, whatever its actual representation in the brain, may be considered as innate or 'wired-in'. Now owing to some 'impairment', either innate or acquired, the respective net develops or turns out in such a way that it represents a membership function with a negation. Such a possibility is again quite realistic in logical networks: for example considering a switching circuit, the primitive elements of which realise the operations NAND or NOR, it is quite easy to imagine a malformation that would effect the realisation of a function negative to the intended one. Thus instead of h & f we have $\overline{h \& f}$, which, according to the De Morgan law may also be written as $\bar{h} \lor \bar{f}$.

In informal or 'natural' language: whilst in the intact IRM the potential sexual object must have the features of being both human and female, the class or set of objects defined by the *impaired* IRM will be that of living beings that are either not human or not female. Thus the set will comprise men and animals of either sex as potential sexual objects, but not women. Supposing that the features defining 'human' and 'female' in the innate IRM are simplified or schematic, the additional features of the potential objects are acquired by imprinting. If the IRM is intact, additional (relevant) features of human females will be imprinted, if it is impaired in the way under consideration, then, owing to the negative definition of the potential objects, any animal of either sex may become imprinted. Naturally, those likely to be seen more frequently by a little child will have a greater chance of becoming sex objects. This reasoning seems to agree with empirical facts. The subjects in question are attracted to a variety of animals but mostly domestic ones. We see that the conception given above provides us with a simple and elegant theory of the strange deviation in question.

Postulating that analogous 'negational' impairments may occur also in the partial nets realising respectively h and f, as well

Table 5.1: Possible sex deviations

	η	ζ	σ	$F(h.f)^*$	Verbal description of deviation
1	0	0	0	$h.f$	norm
2	0	0	I	$\overline{h.f}=h\lor f$	homosexuality with bisexual zoophilia
3	0	I	0	$h.\overline{f}$	homosexuality
4	0	I	I	$\overline{h.\overline{f}}$	heterosexuality with bisexual zoophilia
5	I	0	0	$\overline{h}.f$	heterosexual zoophilia
6	I	0	I	$\overline{\overline{h}.f}$	bisexuality with homosexual zoophilia
7	I	I	0	$\overline{h}.\overline{f}$	homosexual zoophilia
8	I	I	I	$\overline{\overline{h}.\overline{f}}=h\lor f$	bisexuality with heterosexual zoophilia

* The functor '&' is here represented by '.'

as over the entire function, we arrive at a system of eight IRMs, including the basic or 'normal' condition and the variation already described. In Pinkava (1966, 1971) the situation has been formalised by introducing the function: $[(h\oplus \eta) \ \& \ (f \oplus \zeta)] \oplus \sigma$, where $\oplus$ means the exclusive OR or 'addition mod 2', and where the variables η, ζ, σ are propositions meaning respectively:

> η net h is impaired
> ζ net f is impaired   } in a way causing its negation.
> σ net (h & f) is impaired

The resulting simplified system of possible sex deviations in the dimensions human, female, is given in Table 5.1.

Although the system is entirely deductive, all the variations thus derived have been found to exist: as for variations 2 and 3, 2 gave rise to the present speculation and 3 is commonly known. I have observed type 4 in the Prague University Psychiatric Hospital: a heterosexual man attracted also by horses of either sex and by cows. There was no evidence of homosexuality. A case fitting type 5 is described by Kowalewsky (1887) and quoted by Moll (1914) and by Krafft-Ebing and Moll (1924). Type 6, a man bisexual with humans but attracted also by male dogs, has been observed by the present author. Several cases of type 7 are described by Kurt von Surry (1909) and again quoted by Krafft-

Ebing and Moll (1924). I have observed type 8. It is described by Freund (1965) as a case B_{15} illustrating bisexuality (with humans), yet it transpired that the subject was also attracted to cows.

Since all the variations derived from the abstract principles explained have been found to exist, it seems plausible that the present approach reflects, in simplified form, some actual facts to do with the 'programs' regulating sexual appetence.

A BRIEF NOTE ON FETISHISM

Viewed superficially, the existence of fetishism seems to defy any theory of sexual variation based on the assumption that there are innate factors involved. Fetishes are frequently man-made objects, which change with time, place, culture and fashion, and thus they cannot possibly be 'pre-formed' in any IRM. Yet the present conception allows fetishisms to be easily incorporated. As stated previously, the final class of sexual objects, S_1, originates from S by intersecting the set $H \cap F$ with the set $L: S_1 = H \cap F \cap L$. Now L has a membership function $\psi(l_1, l_2, \ldots, l_r)$, the feature words of which are acquired by learning or imprinting. We may imagine a mechanism that registers features, occurring in connection with f(h,f) and those that appear most frequently or are recognised as relevant are incorporated into the membership function. It is possible to form models of this and to impair them so that they would add 'irrelevant' features to the innate IRM. This would account for fetishisms, depending on the character and extent of the defect or malformation of the respective switching system. Thus we may obtain a compatible, concrete and demonstrable model of fetishism.

CONCLUSION

In conclusion, I would like to outline some future research perspectives: one may study the IRMs in normal and variant cases by means of a phallograph and one may use computers for modelling the principles outlined in this chapter in more detail. This may eventually break the vicious circle in which the theory of sex deviation has been running to this day.

Female variant sexuality is not included, as it is much more difficult to study. Women are usually much more reserved and secretive about their sexual feelings and it is also much more difficult for a male investigator to learn about variant female sexuality, for obvious reasons. If the pattern of homosexual men mimics that of normal women, as seems to be the case, one could easily develop an analogous system: if in Table 5.1 we replaced f by m and 'homosexuality' by 'lesbianism', we would get a system based on such assumption. However, female sexuality may also be based on a different pattern, like in some animals. One would first need more data to decide.

As for models of variations in behaviour (as opposed to variations in the sex object), these are best envisaged in terms of dynamic programs and their impairments.

REFERENCES

Bechterev, V.M. (1923) 'Die Perversitäten und Inversitäten vom Standpunkt der Reflexologie.' *Arch. Psychiat. Nervkrankh.*, *68*, 100
Binet, A. (1887) 'Le fétichisme dans l'amour.' *Rev. Phil.*, *24*, 143–52
Freund, K. (1965) 'Die Homosexualität beim Mann.' Leipzig: Hirzel Verlag
Henry, G.W. (1948) *Sex Variants*, 2nd ed. London — New York
Kowalewsky, P.S. (1887) 'Über Perversionen des Geschlechtssinnes bei Epileptikern.' *J. Psychiat. Neurol.*, *VII–3*, 289
Krafft-Ebing, R. (1894) 'Zur Eklärung der konträren Sexualempfindung.' *Jahrbücher Psychiat. Neurol.*, *12*, 338–65
Krafft-Ebing, R. (1901) 'Neue Studien auf dem Gebiete der Homosexualität.' *Jahrb. Sex Zwischenstufen*, *3*, 1–36
Krafft-Ebing, R. and Moll, A. (1924) *Psychopathia Sexualis*. Stuttgart.
Lorenz, K. (1935). 'Der Kumpan in der Umwelt des Vogels.' *J. Ornithol.*, *83*, 289
Lorenz, K. (1943) 'Die angeborenen Formen möglicher Erfahrung.' *Z. Tierpsychol.*, *5*, 235
Lorenz, K. (1958) *King Solomon's Ring*. New York: Crowell
Moll, A. (1914) 'Die Behandlung sexueller Perversionen mit besonderer Berücksichtigung der Associationstherapie.' *Z. Psychother. med Psychol.*, *3*, 3–29
Pinkava, V. (1962) 'Model stupňovité preference s psychopatologickou aplikací.' *Čs. Psychol.*, *6*. (In Czech with an English summary.)
Pinkava, V. (1963) 'K otázce koincidence homosexuality u muže s bisexuální zoofilií a k některým příbuzným otázkám.' *Čs. Psychol.*, *7*. (Czech with an English summary.)
Pinkava, V. (1965a) 'Systém sexuálních deviací ve dvou hrubých dimensích a jedna z výkladových hypothés jejich mechanismu.' *Sborník: Kybernetika a její využití*. Prague. (Czech with an English summary.)

Pinkava, V. (1965b) 'Cifrový model ražby, fetišismu a příbuzných poruch.' Čs. Psychiat., 61. (Czech with an English summary.)

Pinkava, V. (1966) 'Logické modely sexuálních deviací v objektu.' Prague (In Czech. Unpublished PhD. thesis available at Charles University Library, Clementinum, Prague.)

Pinkava, V. (1971) Logical Models of Sexual Deviations. International Journal of Man-Machine Studies, 3, 351–74

Pinkava, V. (1986) Introduction to Logic for Systems Modelling. London: Abbacus Press, in press.

Räber, H. (1948) 'Analyse des Balzverhaltens eines domestizieren Truthahns (Meleagris).' Behaviour, 1

Schutz, F. (1963) 'Über geschlechtlich unterschiedliche Objekrfixierung sexualler Reaktionen bei Enten im Zusammenhang mit dem Prachtkleid de Mänchens.' Vrh. dtsch. zool. Ges. München.

Surry, K. von. (1909) 'Die Unzucht mit Tieren.' Arch. Krim. Anthrop., 35

Tinbergen, N. (1951) The Study of Instincts. London: Oxford University Press

6

The Phylogenetics of Fetishism

Arthur W. Epstein

Phylogeny refers to the evolutionary development of a species; the history of its descent from an ancestor. This history necessarily antedates the species itself. The ancestry of the human (*Homo sapiens*) has great depth. Amongst others, *Homo sapiens* is vertebrate, mammal, and primate. He is a member of the primate order.

Primate history suggests that the hominoid superfamily and the monkeys represented two different streams diverging from the anthropoid line in the Miocene Period. From the hominoid superfamily again came two different streams, the hominids and the pongids, the latter now represented by the great apes. The tool-using hominids arose, it is believed, at the beginning of the Pleistocene. The genus *Homo* appeared in the hominid line during the first interglacial. The genus *Homo* is now only represented by one species, *Homo sapiens* (Washburn, 1960).

The human's behaviour toward external objects may well have ancient roots. Consider, for example, the behaviour of an animal, perhaps a mammal, as it moves about its territory, its attention suddenly captured by an object. Exploration ensues, then further approach or perhaps avoidance. Approach if the outcome enhances self or species survival, thus pleasure endowed; avoidance if survival is threatened, thus endowed with painful feeling-tone. Perhaps the object is simply manipulated or eaten, perhaps it is stored, perhaps if the animal is sufficiently advanced, it is used for a shelter.

Similarly, the animal's attention may be captured by another of its species. A stereotyped gesture or posture, a change in skin coloring or contour, in short, some display or signal, may be the stimulus. Again, the animal approaches or avoids, depending upon the stimulus and its own motive state.

For self and species survival, all organisms must respond to substances or objects outside their own organised selves. Indeed, a sharp dichotomy between self and external object or the 'other' is somewhat artificial. Provision must be made within the mental apparatus and therefore within the brain for the various approach (reward) and withdrawal (aversive) behaviours, vis-à-vis objects or displays emanating from the species 'other'. As primate levels are reached, the substratum for this behaviour is probably widespread, but the preponderent locus is probably in the limbic system.

With increasing complexity of brain structure, elaborations of behaviour towards objects are to be expected. This should reach its apogee in the primate order. No infra-human primate, however, has the apparatus (language) to report its introspections and therefore only careful observation, and speculation, can be employed to infer its mental workings.

Such speculation would predict that with the increased neuronal mass of the higher infra-human primates, connections are increased. A greater number of associative linkages are formed between one cognitive item and another and between a cognitive item and an affect. These linkages may be later retrieved as memories. Therefore, images of external objects perceived in past time appear as memories so that the external object is now internalised and, as internal representation, is subject to approach (pleasure) and withdrawal (pain) in a fashion similar to that initially employed toward the external. Both external object and internal representation may thus become heavily endowed with affect, including those affects, the sexual, related to species survival.

The endowing of an object with such affects has been noted in a zoo-dwelling chimpanzee (*Pan troglodytes*) who displayed sexual arousal toward one specific object, a rubber boot (Epstein, 1969). This high primate male was born in captivity. His stereotyped behaviour upon seeing a boot had been known by his keepers for some time and was observed by the author when the chimpanzee was 17 years of age.

The chimpanzee quickly approached, gazed at the boot and handled it. The penis became erect and was touched to the boot. Shortly thereafter, manual self-stimulation and ejaculation occurred. The ejaculate was then consumed. This response was said to be invariable and occurred whether the boot was worn by a keeper or simply placed in front of the cage.

How are we to explain this great ape's reaction to a boot? The object attracted him instantly, evoked contact with hands and penis, produced ready penile erection and sufficient excitation to lead to ejaculation. Is the shininess of the rubber linked to a genital display that might arise from a female chimpanzee? If this male was not actually exposed ontogenetically to a female, then was there some innate tendency? Is the boot linked to a keeper, source of food and pleasure? If so, the boot represents the keeper; becomes the symbol of the keeper. These questions cannot be satisfactorily answered. All that can be said is that the boot has great excitatory power and is the focus of other linkages. The intrinsic qualities of the boot give it the power, more so than other objects, to evoke linkages perhaps to innate displays or to significant persons or events. The boot becomes a symbol; a numinous object.

The power of this object, the boot, to evoke sexual arousal in an advanced infra-human primate is confirmed by another resident in the same zoo, a male guinea baboon (*Papio papio*). The sexual behaviour of the baboon was not personally observed by the author but was reported to him, and a photograph is available. The animal's age is estimated at 17 years; he, too, had lived in captivity since early life. Upon seeing a boot, the baboon approaches, chatters his teeth, touches and smells it. The penis erects but is not placed on the boot. Neither self stimulation nor ejaculation occur. The baboon's reaction appears more intense when the boot is worn than when placed in front of the cage.

It is almost uncanny that through correspondence with Dr Aristide H. Esser in 1977–8, it was revealed that a socially isolated male gibbon, living in the C.R. Carpenter Primate Centre at Hall's Island, Bermuda, showed attachment to a man's boots, 'grabbing and sniffing them at infrequent subsequent visits'. An overt sexual response was not noted. The man had rescued the ape from drowning and applied artificial respiration before the animal revived. In this case, the boot is clearly linked to a person, the linkage apparently established during a catastrophic event. Such an event may produce specific mnemonic qualities — that is to say, the circumstances of initial engramming may endow the trace with unique subsequent power.

Behaviour of affective intensity toward a boot has thus been noted in two great apes and in a third high primate, the baboon. Does identical behaviour occur in *Homo sapiens*? The answer of course is in the affirmative, and indeed the behaviour occupies a position in psychiatric nosology under the term fetishism.

Boot fetishism is well known and, as is true of all fetish objects, the boot exerts an 'imperative' pull, when perceived externally or via its internalised brain trace (image). Sexual arousal is quickly evoked. *Homo sapiens*, as fetishist, also contacts the boot with hands, mouth or erect penis and ejaculates spontaneously or by self-stimulation. Associated with arousal and intense pleasure, the fetish object may be sought out restlessly, or its image may be summoned through fantasy. Its affective intensity is such that the image may appear involuntarily and may then, because of its intrusive and demanding nature, have a painful quality.

In the human, not only may fetishistic behaviour be observed but introspections can be gathered, the latter not possible in all other primates, devoid of speech. These reported introspections indicate the dominance of the fetish object in the mind, its frequent voluntary and involuntary appearance. There is often an early event in ontogeny, cited by the fetishist, which appears significant in the encoding of the object; for example, a boot fetishist reported a sense of pleasure and childish admiration while observing his grandfather in boots (Epstein, 1969). He played with his grandfather's boots, experiencing excitement when handling and putting them on. Once so encoded, the memory trace is active and may appear in dreams. In the same individual (Epstein, 1969), the following dream, cited to show identity with the chimpanzee, was reported: 'I grabbed a boot and rubbed it on my penis. I naturally had a wet dream.'

One is dealing with a trace, early encoded, endowed with strong feeling tone, primarily pleasurable, leading to sexual arousal and consummatory behaviour. Avoiding pitfalls of naive cerebral over-localisation, nevertheless such memory and visceral activity is considered a limbic function, and therefore one is not surprised that fetish objects may become associated with temporo-limbic seizures (Epstein, 1961), in some instances precipitating them (Krafft-Ebing, 1931; Mitchell, Falconer and Hill, 1954), and, in two instances, the 'imperative' pull of the objects abolished by left anterior temporal lobectomy (Mitchell, *et al.*, 1954; Hunter, Logue and McMenemy, 1963). It is likely that the crucial brain substratum for fetishism is temporo-limbic, an area the origins of which are believed to antedate the neo-cortical.

Primate interest in external objects is of ancient vintage. Tools are associated with the earliest hominids, indeed with the pongids as well (Goodall, 1964: Kollar, 1972). Since both hominids and pongids stem from the hominoid line, an even more ancient hominoid association is likely. Therefore, from the very beginnings of *Homo* in the first interglacial, there must have been interest in external objects, particularly evaluation of them for their value as tools. The capacity to be attracted to external objects would seem inherent because of its adaptive value for species survival. Certain objects may exert more attraction than others because of their glistening or other unique surfaces or because of their textures or unusual shapes. This attraction would evoke states of pleasure, perhaps coupled with wonder or with erotic stirring. It is the dawn of aesthetics!

What are the fundamental responses of a member of *Homo sapiens* to an object exciting intense attraction? Here, information is provided by human behaviour towards the fetish object, behaviour assumed to arise from deep sources in human phylogenetic history. As noted, an object exerting attraction produces an approach reaction. There is a wish for physical contact with the exciting object. Just as did the chimpanzee, the human takes the object in his hands or even rubs it with his penis. Contact of this type indicates a possession of the object. The use of the hands may involve repetitive actions as in the instance of the 'wet canvas shoe' fetishist (Epstein, 1975), who wet, scrubbed and dried the shoe. Repetitive and prolonged manipulation enhances the sense of possession. A more complete possession requires attaching the object to the body. To satisfy this need, for example, the boot fetishist puts his foot inside the boot; the 'wet canvas shoe' fetishist puts his foot inside the shoe. Object and organism become one. This is a fusion, an assimilation. Assimilation makes possession complete. The individual wishes to take the admired object into the body, into the self. The term incorporation may be used in this context. It may be mentioned that ejaculation itself has a relation to magical feelings of possession.

These fundamental modes of behaviour towards a fetish object become more elaborate in the human with the development, past infancy, of the neo-cortical association areas and their related language capability. The object becomes enriched in meaning as its associative linkages increase. The fetish object develops into a powerful focus in the mind with widespread connections. The fetish object may be evoked by a word; rituals revolving about the fetish object may increase in complexity; the object becomes more magical, more of a mystery. In both human and infra-human primates, the fetish object may 'stand for' a significant person, but the associative power of the object would appear greater in the human.

The prolonged dependency of the human, in the early years, is a species characteristic. It is ensured by powerful mechanisms of attachment present in both members of the mother-child dyad. Fear of rupture of this attachment and the need for clinging by the infant or child to the mother may be assuaged by an object that 'stands for' the mother — or, it might be added, for another significant nurturing or admired figure. The attachment to this object may become joined to pleasurable arousal and to genital excitation, thus leading to its endowment with fetish power.

As noted, there is a not inconsiderable number of cases in which fetishism is associated with temporo-limbic epilepsy. Indeed, the involuntary and affect-laden appearance of the fetish image in consciousness, even in the absence of conventional epileptic manifestations, suggests that it is a product of a discharging neural substratum. This is a neural substratum that forms an active and dominant focus, so to speak; is the centre of many linkages with a capacity for ready activation. It is a behavioural chain, and it may be permissible to characterise it further as a limbic reflex chain with epileptoid properties.

Since fetishistic behaviour has been observed in infra-human primates and is well known in human history, there must be transmission of this active neural chain. What is transmitted? Perhaps nothing more than a particular type of response to an attractive object. Can it be more specific? It is likely that objects with particular qualities are preferred (Marks, 1972). Therefore, excitation by objects with these qualities and the stereotyped contact or assimilative response to such objects may be transmitted. Reference here is made to a biological transmission through genetic mechanisms. In this context, it should be noted that fetishism has been described in identical twins (Gorman, 1964).

In conclusion, the phylogenetics of fetishism may be summarised as follows:

(1) Fetishistic behaviour, well known in the human, has also been described in infra-human primates.
(2) Fetishistic behaviour may thus represent a high primate

behavioural automatism evoked by an exciting object. The object is sexually arousing and, likely, must contain certain specific qualities.

(3) The substratum for the fetishistic automatism seems to have a temporo-limbic component. The substratum is envisioned as a complex chain, highly excitable.

(4) This complex chain may represent a mechanism essential for reproductive behaviour, that is for species survival. Therefore, the chain may be inherent in the high primate brain, transmitted by a genetic mechanism. The chain is normally subject to inhibition in the maturing human but is released in several contexts including cerebral pathophysiology.

(5) Fetishistic behaviour may be the resultant of forces beside the sexual. Other likely forces are the strong human interest in external objects, stemming from tool use, and the attachment mechanisms arising from the child-mother bond. In the human, the fetish object may be related to fundamental levels of aesthetic appreciation. Through neocortical development, it also, as a symbol, may condense multiple meanings.

NOTES

The chimpanzee was observed at the Bernstein Park Zoo in Monroe, Louisiana in 1966. I am particularly indebted to Dan Knox, then Assistant Director at the zoo, for his interest and active participation.

REFERENCES

Epstein, A.W. (1961) 'Relationship of fetishism and transvestism to brain and particularly to temporal lobe dysfunction.' *J. Nerv. Ment. Dis.*, *133*, 247–53

Epstein, A.W. (1969) 'Fetishism: a comprehensive view. In *Science and Psychoanalysis*, Vol. *15* (ed. J.H. Masserman) pp. 81–7, New York; Grune and Stratton

Epstein, A.W. (1975) 'The fetish object: phylogenetic considerations.' *Arch. Sex. Behav.*, *4*, 303–8

Goodall, J. (1964) 'Tool-using and aimed throwing in a community of free-living chimpanzees.' *Nature*, *201*, 1264–6

Gorman, G.F. (1964) 'Fetishism occurring in identical twins.' *Br. J. Psychiatry*, *110*, 255–6

Hunter, R., Logue, V., and McMenemy, W.H. (1963) 'Temporal lobe epilepsy supervening on longstanding transvestism and fetishism.' *Epilepsia*, *4*, 60–5

Kollar, E.J. (1972) 'Object relations and the origin of tools.' *Arch. Gen. Psychiatry*, *26*, 23–7

Krafft-Ebing, R. von (1931) *Psychopathia Sexualis*, New York: Physicians and Surgeons Book Co.

Marks, I.M. (1972) 'Phylogenesis and learning in the acquisition of fetishism.' *Danish Med. Bull.*, *19*, 307–10

Mitchell, W., Falconer, M.A. and Hill, D. (1954) 'Epilepsy with fetishism relieved by temporal lobectomy.' *Lancet*, *ii*, 626–30

Washburn, S.L. (1960) 'Tools and human evolution.' *Sci. Am.*, *203*, 63–75

7

Sexual Deviation: Psychoanalytic Research and Theory

Paul Kline

In this chapter I shall first set out the psychoanalytic theory of sexual deviance concentrating upon the work of Freud rather than upon the more fantastical analysts such as Reich or Sadger (merely examples from an extensive pantheon). I shall then examine the problems involved in putting these theories to the scientific test and in the light of this discussion I shall scrutinise the pertinent research. Finally I shall evaluate the scientific status of this aspect of Freudian theory.

Much of the psychoanalytic theory of sexual deviance is set out in *Three Essays On Sexuality* (Freud, 1905) and I shall attempt here to give the essence of his case. Where necessary, of course, I shall incorporate later revisions or additions.

The first point to consider concerns what Freud meant by the term sexual deviance or aberration. It becomes clear from the early sections of the *Three Essays* that Freud has a normative concept of deviance. Sexual deviance has two aspects: one relates to the aims of the sexual behaviour, the other to the object. For example in bestiality the object is deviant, an animal rather than a human being. In heterosexual fellatio, on the other hand, it is the aim that is deviant, in that the end of the behaviour is not heterosexual intercourse. Thus for Freud any sexual activity that was not part of a series of behaviours intended to eventuate in heterosexual intercourse was deviant. He writes 'the normal sexual aim is regarded as being the union of the genitals in the act known as copulation. . .'. Furthermore, that he believes heterosexuality is the norm is confirmed by his citation of the Aristophanean argument that sexual intercourse was the joining together of two bodies that once had been sundered by the Gods. He also claims (and we must remember that this was 1905, not 1985, and AIDS was as yet undiagnosed) that it comes as a surprise to find that the sexual object of some men is men and of some women, women.

Freud, of course, knew enough about normal sexual behaviour to realise that oral genital contact, just for example, between partners, was not uncommon. However, by the definition given above, this is not deviant provided that it is a part of foreplay leading to sexual intercourse. Only when this becomes an end in itself would it be considered deviant. Sometimes, if for instance the lovemaking were interrupted, it could be the case that the act was not consummated in copulation. However if the intention was present deviation could not be classified. To some extent, therefore, the categorisation is not entirely objective but generally with Freud's definition of deviance there is no problem in deciding whether sexual behaviour is deviant or not.

There is one further point to note concerning this definition of deviance. The assumption that heterosexual intercourse is the norm would now be regarded as an outstanding example of the way that Freud was blinkered by his zeitgeist. In *Speculum de L'Autre Femme*, Irigaray (1974) has argued that Freud's ideas of female sexuality, which were part and parcel of his ideas on sexual deviance, were simply a patriarchal symptom of a particular social and cultural economy, views that can be traced back to the Ancient Greeks. It is held by feminist writers such as Irigaray that such cultural assumptions must necessarily render such views false. However such arguments are not powerful since all opinions occur within a cultural context, Irigaray's no less than Freud's. Indeed Irigaray would seem to be more typical of her age, influenced clearly by feminism and Lacan, than was Freud of his. Thus the fact that Freud was indubitably a product of his time is only relevant if it can be shown that such influences have led to scientific error. In fact, Freud's categorisation of deviance, culturally determined or not, is satisfactory in that it allows the phenomenon to be studied objectively. In the light of modern knowledge it could be the case that other categorisations are better. It cannot, however, be dismissed merely because it is eighty years old.

MALE HOMOSEXUALITY

In the *Three Essays*, especially the later editions, Freud made it clear that humans are essentially bisexual: that is, it is possible for any individual to become homosexual, although usually in our culture, at least until recent times, he or she does not. The question of homosexuality then becomes one of uncovering the determinants of the homosexual object choice.

In psychoanalytic theory the role of biological constitutional factors is admitted but is regarded as relatively unimportant. As Fenichel (1945) argues, hormonal factors and increased sensitivity of the anal mucosa play a part in the aetiology of male homosexuality. However their importance lies in their interaction with the psychological factors regarded as aetiologic in psychoanalytic theory.

As might be expected, over the years Freud, as he developed psychoanalytic theory in the light of his findings and those of his colleagues, proposed that a large number of mechanisms were implicated in determining male homosexuality. In this chapter I shall describe the most important.

According to Fenichel (1945), whose succinct summaries of Freudian theory are invaluable for research, the rejection of women by homosexual men is genital. Many homosexual men like and respect women: it is the prospect of genital contact which they find repellent or frightening. In brief, they are in the grip of the castration complex. 'For them', Fenichel writes, 'the sight of a being without a penis is so terrifying that they avoid it by rejecting any sexual relationship with such a partner.' The homosexual man is so determined on the existence of a penis and on the denial of its lack that it has to be present in his sex partner. It should be noted here that this aspect of Freudian theory can be put to the empirical test. Are homosexual men afraid of female genitals?

Associated with the castration complex are some other fairly clear hypotheses that can also be tested: the aversion to female genitals arises from castration anxiety; the vagina is seen as a castrating or biting instrument — the vagina dentata. Some of the claims made by Fenichel are frankly contradictory, thus making objective investigation difficult. For example, it is claimed that some homosexual men still like and are sexually aroused by girls. However, fearing their genitals, as described above, these men seek out feminine, delicate boys. On the other hand, some homosexual men, for the same reason, seek out masculine men (the rough trade) one presumes because anything even remotely feminine reminds them of the feared vagina.

Although the implication of the castration complex in the

determination of male homosexuality is one of the most important of the Freudian claims, there are others. One concerns the narcissism of the homosexual, often stereotypically noted in the descriptions of the literary, artistic and theatrical worlds. Oscar Wilde would be a clear example. This kind of homosexual man is particularly fixated on his mother. He identifies with her, thus taking the same sex objects that she had. He chooses, therefore, young men and boys who are like himself and he lavishes on them the love that he had desired from his mother. 'While he acts', Fenichel writes, 'as if he were his mother, emotionally he is centered in his love object, and thus enjoys being loved by himself.' Such individuals are usually tender towards their adolescent lovers although sometimes they act sadistically towards them, a complication that again renders objective research difficult. These men actively seek younger persons as objects and are labelled 'subject homoerotic' by Fenichel (1945).

There is a further type of homosexual in whom identification with the mother is followed by anal fixation. In him, sexual desire for the mother becomes transformed into the wish to enjoy the same kind of sexual gratification as does the mother, thus resulting in a passive-receptive love of the father. This leads to development of the femininity typical of a certain type of homosexual man. According to Fenichel, this group of homosexuals, the object-homoerotics, being feminine and anally fixated are most likely to enjoy being buggered.

Mention should be made of accidental homosexuals, those who when denied women, as in prisons or on board ships, turn to men as their sex objects. This accidental homosexuality Freud regarded as evidence for the universal bisexuality of man.

In summary, therefore, male homosexuality may be seen as dependent on the castration complex, identification with the mother and anal fixation. Narcissism is also important. Finally it should be noted that Freud argued that motherless boys reared by men, as in Ancient Greece, and having enjoyed pregenital pleasure at the hands of men were also disposed to homosexuality.

FEMALE HOMOSEXUALITY

In some homosexual women the castration complex is significant in the development of their homosexuality. The sight of a penis may create a fear of an impending violation. More often it excites a complex of emotions related to the anatomical difference that interferes with sexual pleasure to such an extent that pleasure becomes possible only in the absence of a penis (Fenichel, 1945). Two points are worthy of note here. First, such homosexual women are clearly similar to their male counterparts whom we discussed in the previous section. Secondly, this hypothesised aetiology would appear to fit well with the feminist position about heterosexual activity, at least as this is portrayed by Irigaray (1977).

However, according to Fenichel, there is a further basis to female homosexuality — regression to love of the mother, the first object attachment of all. Thus there are two factors in female homosexuality, mother fixation and the castration complex. While mother fixation was important in the male case, its origins were different, not resulting from regression.

Essentially, therefore, there are similar but not identical factors involved in the development of male and female homosexuality: as Fenichel argues, the aim of homosexual object choice is the avoidance of emotions around the castration complex that disturb sexual pleasure and create a more general anxiety.

OTHER PERVERSIONS

In the *Three Essays*, Freud (1905) argued that the sexual aims of perverts are identical with those of children in that pregenital components for perverts become more important than adult, genital sexuality. This means, of course, that there is no qualitative difference between perverts and normal persons and that anybody has the potential to become a pervert, for pregenital erotism is a component of normal genital sexuality: a phenomenon stemming from the fact that all men were infants. Perverts, in brief, are sexually infantile due to fixation or regression. The essential question, therefore, regarding the perversions concerns the origins of these fixations and regressions and the differentiation between perversions and neurosis. Actually, as Fenichel points out, Freud (1916–1917) in the *Introductory Lectures* made a simple distinction: perverts respond to sexual frustration by regression. Neurotics utilise other defences instead of or after the regression. Although perhaps too clear cut, this is essentially the psychoanalytic position.

FETISHISM

Fetishism, Freud (1905) argues, is the replacement of a sex object, often related to early impressions, by another which by normal standards is unsatisfactory. Some part of the body, in many cases the foot or hair, or something belonging to the person whom it replaces, is substituted. Such objects resemble the fetishes of savages, which embody their Gods.

Fenichel (1945) claims that the pre-psychoanalytic writers who attributed great importance in fetishism to some determining childhood experience, regarding it as establishing some kind of conditioned reflex, were wrong. They were there concerned only with screen memories. For example, Freud (1917) discusses a case of foot fetishism in which the patient remembered being sexually excited as a child by a glimpse of his governess's foot. O tempora, O mores, one shudders to think what part would have to be exposed today for a comparable effect. The question that needs to be asked, in psychoanalytic theory, is this: why was the patient so excited by a foot? For Fenichel the answer is clear — the symbolic equation of foot and penis is the key. In the unconscious, the glimpse of the foot means, to quote Fenichel: '"I saw the penis of my governess" or "I saw that my governess has a penis".' In other words we are back with the castration complex. Freud (1905) pointed out that most fetishes are in fact sexual symbols: shoes, long hair, earrings. Fur symbolises the pubic hair. Sometimes, inevitably, a fetish may fail to fit this description. Even here it can be shown that the object has acquired the significance of a female penis. In brief the fetish is an attempt to deny the lack of a penis.

This explanation of fetishism supports the feminist criticism of Freudian theory that it is phallocentric in that it could hardly apply to a woman who is constantly reminded of her lack of a penis. This is accepted by Fenichel and indeed female fetishists are exceedingly rare. Nevertheless in the few cases which have been studied this equation of penis and fetish does seem to hold.

TRANSVESTISM

Fenichel (1945) argues that the male transvestite combines the homosexual's identification with his mother and the fetishist's denial that a woman has no penis. This is done simultaneously and results in tranvestism. In addition, the clothes themselves may represent the penis.

In the case of the female, the denial entailed in wearing men's clothes cannot succeed, other than in the truly psychotic. It attempts to create the illusion, however, that the spectators believe in the penis and it has the significance of playing being a man. In the unconscious, female transvestism equates with playing father and making believe that one possesses a penis. Female transvestism indeed is the displacement of penis envy to envy of the masculine appearance.

EXHIBITIONISM

Fenichel claims that, as with so many of the perversions, exhibitionism is an attempt at denial of castration. I can do no better than quote the text that brilliantly catches the flavour of the psychoanalytic theory. '1. He [the exhibitionist] unconsciously says to his audience: "Reassure me that I have a penis by reacting to the sight of it." Inner doubt impels the individual to call upon witnesses. 2. He unconsciously says to his audience: Reassure me that you are afraid of my penis, that is, that you fear me; then I do not need to be afraid myself". . .' This second reason accounts for the fact that exhibitionists like to perform to little girls who would be more likely to show fear and would not fail to be impressed by the size of the penis (a fear with an adult audience). In addition to this, as was pointed out by Freud in the *Three Essays*, there is a magical gesture in the act of exhibitionism. It means, to quote Fenichel again, 'I show you what I wish you could show me.'

Again, as was the case with transvestism, a different explanation is required for women since exhibitionism will not work as a denial of castration. Fenichel claims that genital exhibitionism, as a perversion, does not exist in women. However, exposure of other parts of the body as foreplay is more common than in men. It should be noted, however, that this is not a perversion by the Freudian definition of that term. This sex difference has been explained in terms of the sex differences in the castration complex. Thus women feel their lack of penis as a narcissistic hurt and thus tend to expose all other parts of their bodies than their genitals. This displaced exhibitionism cannot serve to reduce castration anxiety and thus it never develops into a perversion.

VOYEURISM

In the unconscious of voyeurs are found similar tendencies to those of exhibitionists. The castration complex is of paramount importance. Usually, according to the invaluable Fenichel, voyeurs are fixated on experiences that aroused their castration anxiety, either primal scenes or the sight of adult genitals. Voyeurism results from the patient's attempts to deny the fright by repeating the frightening scenes, albeit with subtle changes. These changes are such that there is no danger in what is observed, although the whole event closely resembles the original.

Of course, no amount of looking can reduce the anxiety. This means that 'they have to look again and again, and to see more and more, with an ever increasing intensity — or they displace their interest . . . to scenes that may better serve as reassurances than does actual genital observation.' (Fenichel, 1945)

In female voyeurs, for whom the idea that a girl has a penis could not serve as a reassurance against the castration complex, peeping may be a substitute for sadistic acting. Indeed some voyeurs displace their interest in castration to looking itself and Fenichel claims that curiosity in women is sometimes overtly in catastrophies, accidents and operations, exemplifying this displacement.

ORAL PERVERSIONS

In the full sense of the term perversion, oral perversions, either fellatio or cunnilingus, are rare. Nevertheless when these do become the main mode of sexual expression, oral erotism, fixation at the oral level, is implicated as is castration fear (Fenichel, 1945). Fellatio is found to be a denial of or an equivalent to biting off the penis.

SADISM

From all that has been written so far on the theoretical basis of the various forms of sexual deviance it should be clear that there is running through them a common theme. They represent attempts to deal with castration anxiety. They can be differentiated from each other by the manner in which the attempt is made. For example tranvestism involves identification with the mother, while fetishism involves denial.

Sadism, too, involves the castration complex. As Fenichel argues, if anxiety is disturbing, sexual pleasure identification with the aggressor could be an effective defence. When a person does to others what he fears may be done to him, this is a relief from fear. Consequently, anything that increases a person's power or prestige can reassure against anxiety. Indeed, the idea that "before I can enjoy sexuality I must convince myself that I am powerful" is the starting point of sadistic development that ends up as "I get sexual pleasure from torturing others".

Thus the braid cutter (a figure much discussed in psychoanalytic literature although less common now) enjoys the powerlessness of his partner because he no longer has to fear her, thus allowing him sexual pleasure. This type of sadist, by threatening his object, shows, according to Fenichel, that he himself is threatened.

Another kind of sadist not only fears the castration of the sexual act but is also afraid of his own excitement. This latter fear they deal with by arousing it in others. In addition to this they are fighting certain self-destructive tendencies in themselves by turning them outwards against others.

Fenichel further argues that sadists not only fight castration by castrating but do so by pseudocastrating. That is, by symbolically castrating they reassure themselves that the fate they feared is not so dreadful after all. However, while some sadistic acts may have this element of playfulness about them, there is little doubt that this is not always the case. In many cases (those that are most publicised) sadistic injuries are serious, even fatal.

If it is accepted that the sadist is defending against his castration anxiety, the question that arises is why sadism? This depends upon the history of the component instinct of sadism. In some individuals the instinct is constitutionally strong. Sadistic fixations can occur, just as other fixations — through excessive indulgence or frustration. Sadism is connected more to the pregenital than to genital aims and, in addition, there are other forms. Fenichel mentions manual sadism, which is connected with muscular eroticism, skin sadism, the source of pleasure in beating, and a sadism derived from the destructive tendencies of the oral phase.

MASOCHISM

Masochism is interesting in that it appears to run contrary to the pleasure principle. Nevertheless Fenichel attempts to show that masochism too can be explained as a defence against castration anxiety, the general formula that accounts for perversions.

The argument runs thus: Masochism occurs if the following conditions are satisfied, each or together. If, through experience, pain has been connected with sexual pleasure such that suffering has become a requisite of it, clearly masochism is likely. Masochism may represent a sacrifice to appease the Gods: by suffering a lesser pain the more terrible threat of castration is warded off. In support of this argument in *The Economic Problem of Masochism*, Freud (1924) pointed out that masochists were willing to accept pain and injury anywhere other than the genitals. Just as some sadists denied their fears of torture by torturing others, so some masochists arrange for their torture to avoid something worse or unexpected. Some masochists again, by their helplessness, aim to appeal to the mercy of the Gods.

These four mechanisms are, however, according to Fenichel, insufficient to explain masochism. They account for the fact that patients have to undergo a certain amount of suffering before they can feel pleasure. They do not account for the fact that some masochists appear to find pleasure in the pain itself. This simultaneity of pleasure and pain is explicable by the fact that pain can become erogenised, a source of sexual excitement, as Freud argued in his paper *A Child is Being Beaten* (Freud, 1919), and as is strongly suggested by biographical accounts of masochists, of whom Swinburne is an outstanding example.

According to Fenichel the sexual excitation of beating arises from the fact that it is an intense excitation of the erogenous skin of the buttocks and the muscles below the skin. He also argues that this is due to the displacement of anal erotism to the skin. Thus, masochists should be anal and have strong castration complexes.

Freud did write more about masochism, but his 1924 paper is somewhat speculative and metaphysical, departing far from clinical data, which makes its relevance to research doubtful. Furthermore, the claims there are somewhat different from those made earlier. As the final part of this section on masochism I shall briefly mention other points not so far discussed.

In the *Three Essays* it was argued by Freud that masochism was sadism turned upon the self. Furthermore, this change brought with it a change from active to passive. Freud claimed that a basic dimension of sexual life was activity – passivity and that sadism versus masochism was an example of this writ large. Passivity was, of course, an attribute of feminine sexuality. In addition, sadism and masochism, as might be expected from this formulation are 'habitually found to occur together in the same individual . . .' (Freud, 1905). Freud again stresses that masochism is not found as a primary instinct. It is only in the later 1924 paper, when Freud was concerned with the death instinct, that masochism was conceived of as an impulse in its own right, an emanation of Thanatos.

In summary, the Freudian position on masochism is that it is an attempt to ward off the castration complex. It involves the idea of appeasement by suffering, the eroginisation of the skin, the turning of sadism against the self and a heightened passivity and femininity. Only in his later formulation did Freud link masochism to the death instinct.

COPROPHILIA AND NECROPHILIA

I do not intend to say much about these perversions, which are relatively rare. Coprophilia is obviously linked to anal erotism and Fenichel argues that again it is an instance of a defence against the castration complex. The emphasis on anality minimises the differences between the sexual organs. In addition, the unconscious equation of penis and faeces, discussed by Freud (1917) in his paper on anal erotism, helps out the defence against castration anxiety. Coprolalia, hardly a perversion by the definition in this chapter, is a combination of coprophilia, exhibitionism and sadism (Fenichel, 1945).

Necrophilia, to which I can find little reference in Freud, is regarded by Fromm (1974) as symptomatic of the death instinct. The necrophilous character is considered by Fromm to be a malign form of the anal character, an emanation of Thanatos and a personality syndrome involved in necrophilia. Such are the psychoanalytic theories of sexual deviance. I have tried to set them out as clearly as possible, thus enabling them to be evaluated in the light of empirical research. In the remainder of this chapter I shall discuss how these theories can be tested, I shall scrutinise the results of such testing and finally I shall attempt to evaluate their scientific validity.

THE SCIENTIFIC STUDY OF FREUDIAN THEORY

The approach to the study of the psychoanalytic theory of deviance that I have set out in the first section of this chapter is that advocated by Popper (1959) and Farrell (1961). This involves the statement of the theory in terms of empirically falsifiable hypotheses and the evaluation of the research bearing on these hypotheses. As Farrell has argued, this approach does not regard Freudian theory as a unified entity but as a collection of hypotheses. The task of a rational man who intends to examine the validity of psychoanalytic theory is to search through these hypotheses in order to discover which are true.

However, despite the theoretical simplicity of this approach it yielded considerable disagreement and a few points require clarification before we come to consider the relevant research. Popper (1959), Eysenck and Wilson (1973), and Eysenck (1985) have all claimed that Freudian theory is unscientific and wrong. Kline (1972, 1981) and Fisher and Greenberg (1977) have also looked at the evidence that was scrutinised in Eysenck's publications and come to different conclusions. Grunbaum (1984) has examined the philosophical basis of the theory of repression and found it wanting and thus argued that psychoanalytic theory as a whole is baseless. In addition, he claims that the experimental evidence for that aspect of the theory is also poor, a claim that has been challenged (Kline, 1986). How then can these differences be accounted for?

Eysenck (e.g. 1985) has argued that the research cited by those in support of Freudian theory is of poor quality or can be explained without recourse to Freudian theory. In this way he has attempted to dispose of the work of Kline and of Fisher and Greenberg. Unfortunately, as has been argued by Kline (1985), this will not do. Certainly it is true that Fisher and Greenberg regard as objective, scientific evidence studies using, for

161

example, the Rorschach test, which is manifestly unsatisfactory in the role of a scientific instrument. Kline, however, has largely tried to confine himself to research that has a statistical and evidential basis satisfactory to a reasonable experimental psychologist. These studies Eysenck has reinterpreted by developing *ad hoc* hypotheses to explain the results. However, when a number of such studies is considered together, the resulting collection of *ad hoc* hypotheses becomes far from impressive and begins to offend Occam's razor. This considerably diminishes the force of Eysenck's rejection of the empirical work in support of Freudian theory. In other words, the disagreement is a justifiable one in terms of the interpretation of results. The case that Freudian theory is wrong in its entirety is far from made — at least on the basis of evidence falsifying the hypotheses.

Grunbaum's point, that Freud never made the case for repression, that the arguments that he marshalled are ultimately incoherent (given that we accept the validity of Freud's clinical data) and that, consequently, there is no reason to accept the theory or any of Freud's theorising that depends upon repression, is, indeed, hard to refute. This is particularly serious given that many other important psychoanalytic claims depend upon repression, described by Freud, as the cornerstone of the theory. Nevertheless, and this is why Grunbaum's work is discussed here, to have demonstrated this is *not* to have demonstrated the falsity of psychoanalytic theory as a whole as Grunbaum concludes. Many other hypotheses remain untouched by this philosophical demolition and these include those implicated in the analysis of sexual deviance.

One further point needs to be made about the foundations of psychoanalysis. Grunbaum claims there that there is no satisfactory evidence for the Freudian theory of repression. However, as I have pointed out elsewhere (Kline, 1986), for Grunbaum, a philosopher, to assert that experimental evidence is required is one thing. It is quite another, however, to assert that such evidence is unsatisfactory. This is a matter of psychology and while it is perfectly possible for a philosopher to master the necessary technical demands of the field so that he is able to evaluate the research, for a philosopher to make unsupported psychological assertions is not satisfactory. Without the detailed argument there is no reason to take Grunbaum's strictures on the quality of this research seriously.

In summary, it is argued that despite the strident attacks on the scientific validity of Freudian theory, a wholly convincing case against it has not been made. From this it does not follow that the whole of Freudian theory is true. On the contrary, what follows is the requirement carefully and rationally to sift through the objective evidence relevant (in this chapter) to sexual deviance.

THE NATURE OF THE EVIDENCE

In evaluating the research on the psychoanalytic theory of sexual deviance I shall consider only those studies that meet the normal demands of satisfactory research design. This means, *inter alia*, the following: where groups are used the samples must properly reflect their populations and must be of sufficient size to make statistical comparisons and generalisation sensible. When research design indicates the need for a control group then a matched control group must be used. This may sound so obvious as to be banal. However, in the study of the effect of psychotherapy the absence of control groups where required is common (the majority of researches) and is a savage commentary on the scientific standing of clinical psychology. In adequate researches the hypotheses must be clearly stated and their precise relevance to Freudian theory should be made clear. All tests and measures should be of known reliability and validity and certainly the reliability should not fall below 0.7. The statistical analyses should be relevant to the questions asked and suited to the data. For example, factor analyses on samples of less than 20 are not powerful and if the number of variables exceeds the number of subjects they are meaningless. Further to this technique it is essential that simple structure be reached or that confirmatory analysis be significant. All interpretations of the statistical analyses should be apposite. Now all these points are so obvious that they should not have to be stated. However in my previous studies of Freudian theory in general (Kline, 1972, 1981) I found large numbers of studies that failed one or more of these simple criteria. Fisher and Greenberg (1977), as has been pointed out, are similarly far too uncritical in their acceptance of research findings that are clearly flawed in design.

THE EXPERIMENTAL EVIDENCE

The experimental evidence that bears upon psychoanalytic theories of sexual deviance is of two kinds. One set of researches is concerned with the basic psychoanalytic concepts that are used in the explanation of deviance. Examples of these are the castration complex and fixation. The other relates to the specific hypotheses of sexual deviance. Of these an example is the claim that homosexual men, or at least a sizeable group of them, are afraid of the female genitals.

I shall discuss these two kinds of evidence separately. I would concentrate upon the findings in the second group since these are clearly the most relevant to the theme of this chapter, but there are hardly any such studies. Nevertheless, evidence concerning the more general concepts is important and needs to be examined first. After all, if none of the general concepts can be supported the specific theories that use them must be false. The converse, however, is not necessarily true. It could well be the case that the castration complex was confirmed by empirical evidence yet was uninvolved in the aetiology of homosexuality, to give but one example.

Evidence for the general concepts

As was seen in our discussion of the psychoanalytic theories of sexual deviance, the castration complex was central in their aetiology. Which deviation was developed depended upon the way castration anxiety was dealt with. The first question to be asked therefore concerns the empirical status of the castration complex.

I do not intend in this chapter to detail all the objective evidence relevant to the castration complex. This would not only render this chapter far too long but, further, it has already been done, by Fisher and Greenberg (1977) and by myself (Kline, 1981). Instead I shall describe sufficient critical experiments to demonstrate that the castration complex has some objective, experimental support.

The work of Stephens (1961) confirms the notion of the castration complex (and incidentally of the Oedipus complex) with findings that are difficult to account for other than by psychoanalytic theory. Stephens used the hologeistic method, pioneered by Whiting and Child (1953), in their classic investigation of child-rearing. This hologeistic method entails searching through anthropological and ethnographical reports for descriptions of, *inter alia*, child-rearing methods and associated attitudes of both children and parents, and adult behaviour in a large sample of societies. These reports are then rated by independent observers for whatever variables the investigation is concerned with, for example, modesty training or aggression. Correlations are then computed between all the variables. This method is excellent in putting to the test any theory (not only psychoanalysis) that hypothesises relations between environmental variables and behaviour.

Before discussing the results obtained by Stephens, a few comments about the hologeistic method, which has been extensively examined by Campbell and Narroll (1972), will be helpful. A number of objections have been aimed at this approach, of which the most important concern the accuracy of the ethnographic reports. It must be admitted that many anthropological accounts of societies are dubious in the extreme. Some of these are little more than the anecdotes of expatriate colonials and have no sound observational base. In a previous study of Freudian theory (Kline, 1984) I cited some examples which make the point so clearly that I shall use them again. In one study of ego development in Africa, the information was derived from a colonial planter. In an investigation of gambling among the Chinese, a sample of 17 Chinese waiters from the Chinese quarter of San Francisco was used (Muensterberger, 1969), this purportedly reflecting a population of one billion on the mainland.

These examples are perhaps extreme. Nevertheless it must be remembered that even work as well known as that of Margaret Mead in Samoa has recently been challenged on this very point of data accuracy (Freeman, 1984) so that there can be no doubt that this is a real problem. Fortunately, as regards the hologeistic method, this well-founded objection is not as serious as might first be thought. This is because all the errors in the reports would drastically lower correlations between variables. Thus any positive support for the theory is made, if anything, more meaningful. All this assumes, of course, that these errors are random.

However we must now consider the possibility that the errors are not random, in which case any findings would have to be

165

regarded as highly dubious. Fortunately the chances of such positive bias (non-random error) in favour of psychoanalytic theory are so small that they can be dismissed. The source of any such bias would have to have arisen from the beliefs of the anthropologists writing the reports. For example, an anthropologist who believed in the psychosexual aetiology of the anal character might well, if he perceived his adult subjects as obsessional, distort his observations of pot-training, and I am not talking about deliberate falsification. The hologeistic method, however, samples so wide a variety of societies, who have been observed by so many anthropologists, that systematic error of this kind is hardly possible. In brief the difficulties with the observations cannot be said to reduce the value of any positive findings.

The hologeistic method is extremely powerful as a test of psychoanalytic theory for two principal reasons. First, it provides evidence relevant to the objection to Freudian theory that it attempts to draw universal conclusions from a highly homogeneous sample. Secondly, it enables much purer tests of psychoanalytic theory to be made than do conventional experimental methods. An example will clarify this point. If we are attempting to examine orality and require samples of mothers who have breast-fed their children for a long time, say five years, and a group who weaned them onto solid food very early, it might be possible to find such groups in Great Britain. However, such samples would almost certainly differ from normal in many other respects than their style of child-rearing and any differences in their children would be difficult to interpret. In societies where such child-rearing methods are the norm this confounding does not occur. In brief, it is argued that the hologeistic method is powerful in testing Freudian hypotheses.

Stephens argued from Freudian theory that the menstrual taboo was related to castration anxiety: the more intense within any society was castration anxiety the longer the menstrual taboo (on sexual intercourse) would be expected to be. In the anthropological reports, not unexpectedly, there were no direct measures of castration anxiety, a feature, incidentally, that virtually rules out bias from psychoanalytically inclined anthropologists. Consequently, Stephens evaluated the extent of castration anxiety in his sample of societies by investigating those child-rearing procedures that would be expected, from Freudian theory, to create it. Stephens used 10 measures: diffusion of nurturance; post-partum sex taboo; severity of masturbation punishment; severity of sex training; pressure for obedience; severity of aggression training; severity of punishment for disobedience; strictness of fathers' obedience commands; whether or not father is the main disciplinarian; importance of physical punishment as a discipline; and, finally, a total score derived from the previous ten variables. The anthropological reports of 72 societies that had been divided at the median into two groups — societies with long menstrual taboos and those with shorter ones — were examined. Chi-square analysis of the relation between these variables and the length of taboo indicated that five of the measures had significant associations and that all but one (pressure for obedience) were stronger in the expected group. The total score based upon all the variables was related to the taboo scale at a very high level of significance.

In that predictions from the Freudian theory of the castration complex were confirmed, this investigation may be regarded as being objective evidence for, if not a universal, then at least a far-flung castration complex. Of course, any convincing alternative explanation of the results would considerably lessen the evidential force of this investigation as support for psychoanalytic ideas. Some have tried to argue that the ten measures simply reflect the general strictness of a society and that in strict societies there are, naturally, restrictions on sexual activity. Such an explanation will, I fear, simply not do. First, if this were so then it is difficult to account for the fact that the pressure of obedience variable failed. Secondly, and this is far more important, this alternative is not an explanation at all, merely a restatement of the findings, a description. It fails to account for the fact that strict societies impose rules about menstruation and sexual intercourse.

In brief, this study by Stephens provides strong support for the castration complex. Since, as we saw in our description of the psychoanalytic theory of sexual deviance, the castration complex is central to understanding deviance, this investigation on its own means that it is worthwhile to pursue more detailed studies of the specific theories.

In *Fact and Fantasy in Freudian Theory* (Kline, 1981), I discussed a number of other investigations that I considered also provided evidence for the castration complex. There is no need to discuss these in any detail here since for our purposes all that is required is one investigation — to show that the castration complex is not a concept so far divorced from reality that to invoke it in any explanation is thereby to render such an explanation worthless. Nevertheless, one point needs to be examined, namely that many of the studies that provided some confirmation of the castration complex used projective tests. Eysenck (1972) strongly objected to my use of studies with projective tests as support for Freudian theory on the elementary psychometric grounds that such tests are almost always of low reliability and very poor validity. Thus, he argues, they can demonstrate nothing. Of course I am in complete agreement with Eysenck on this point: in general it is true. However there can be specific cases where this general point is not relevant. I shall give two examples of this.

First it is possible to develop entirely objective and highly reliable scoring procedures for projective tests. Hampson and Kline (1977) did this in a study of criminals and were able to show significant and meaningful differences between different groups of offenders on a variety of projective tests. Secondly, as was the case with the studies of the castration complex, the scoring, though not objective, is reliable and the interpretations are themselves a test of the Freudian theory. The work of Hammer (1953) exemplifies this point. Hammer administered the HTP test to a group of prisoners who had been sterilised for sexual offences and to some surgical controls. The HTP test is a projective measure that requires subjects to draw a house, a tree and a person. The features of these drawings are then interpreted by the testers. The manual to this test (Buck, 1948) is a fantastical example of the projective testers' art although some of the more astonishing assertions were indeed supported in the study of criminals to which I have referred.

In his work on the castration complex Hammer argued that the drawings of penile symbols would be distorted in those suffering from a castration complex — those in the sterilised sample. In fact, compared with the control group there were significantly more distortions of chimneys and of branches of trees in the prisoners. This is as predicted from Freudian theory. Now my reason for arguing that this study is support for the castration complex does not lie in any mystical belief concerning the validity of the HTP test or indeed of any projective test. In fact, the reasoning is as follows. If we discount the notion of the castration complex, how is it possible to make sense of the differences in drawing chimneys and branches in these two groups? It is exceedingly difficult to think of any convincing account that is not entirely *post hoc* and even this latter takes a vivid imagination.

I do not want to say any more about general studies of the castration complex. I think it is reasonable to argue that there is some supporting, objective evidence for the concept, certainly sufficient to use it as an explanatory concept in other aspects of the theory.

SPECIFIC STUDIES

I shall begin with the work on male homosexuality. Here, immediately, there is a problem. In my studies of the objective evidence relevant to Freudian theory I have been forced to conclude that only the work of Silverman, Kwawer, Wohtzaly and Coron (1973) could be regarded as support for psychoanalysis. However, Fisher and Greenberg (1977), who surveyed much of the same evidence and whose conclusions are usually in close accord with mine, disagree on this issue. They consider that my review of the evidence is woefully unsatisfactory and misses out much of the confirmatory evidence.

However, as I have argued elsewhere (Kline, 1981), the reasons for this disagreement lie in the nature of the evidence that Fisher and Greenberg are prepared to accept as confirming Freudian theory.

Before examining the work of Silverman on the psychoanalytic theory of male homosexuality one further point needs to be made about this research method. Almost all the investigations have been carried out by Silverman, colleagues and students in New York. There has been little replication elsewhere. I think this is necessary, not because I question the veracity of this work, but simply because there is the possibility in research stemming from one laboratory that artefacts of the procedures could account for the results. I do not think this is likely but the possibility cannot be ignored.

Silverman *et al.* (1973), using the dynamic activation method, investigated the role of the mother in the determination of male homosexuality. Thirty-six homosexual men were compared with the same number of heterosexuals and each of the subjects was seen in three sessions — an incest session, a symbiotic session and a control session. In every session baseline measures were compared with scores after the dynamic activation.

In the incest session the subliminal stimulus of 'Fuck Mommy' together with a nude man and woman in a sexually suggestive position was shown. In the symbiotic session the subliminal stimulus was 'Mommy and I are one' with a picture of a man and woman merged together as are siamese twins. In the control session, the subliminal stimulus was 'person thinking' with a bland picture of a man. In addition to this three baseline stimuli were used — 'person looking, person walking and person talking' each again with its bland male figure.

The tests employed in this study were rating scales and projective tests. Three Rorschach pictures were used: Rorschach 1, Harrower 2 and Zulliger 8. The assessment of sexual feelings was carried out by having subjects rate ten pictures of males and ten of females on a scale of sexual attractiveness. Homosexual men increased their scores on the homosexual attraction measure after the incest-conflict stimulation session. This was not so for the heterosexuals or for the control session. These results are held by Silverman to support the Freudian claim that relations with the mother are an important determinant of male homosexuality.

Clearly, in the light of our strictures concerning the evidence admitted by Fisher and Greenberg, it is first necessary to scrutinise the tests used in this investigation. The results from the Rorschach testing have been ignored. Until there is clear evidence for the validity of this test anything else would be inadmissible. The finding that we reported was derived from the ratings of the male and female pictures. Certainly such a measure has face validity. Furthermore, since the results were predicted from the theory it is necessary to give some other account of the findings if we want to discount them as confirming the Freudian story.

One possibility is to impugn the validity of the rating scale of sexual attraction. However the question then arises as to what it does measure. Here there is no obvious alternative. Furthermore there appears to be no alternative explanation of the pattern of results in the different conditions and in the two groups. For all these reasons, despite the doubts concerning the rating scales, it is argued that this work by Silverman does support the implication of Oedipal conflicts in homosexual feelings. When the unconscious Oedipal conflict was activated by the subliminal stimulation then homosexual attraction scores increased.

I do not intend to discuss any of the other studies of male

homosexuality, neither those discussed in Kline (1972) nor those in Fisher and Greenberg (1977), because they were all flawed methodologically (in my view). Readers must be referred to these books for details of these investigations.

This research by Silverman *et al.* (1973), which cannot be regarded as definitive support for psychoanalytic theory although it is a modest confirmation, is regrettably the only study that I have been able to find which meets any of the criteria for research to be seriously considered as objective evidence for any part of the Freudian theory of sexual deviance. In brief, the only position that can be maintained as regards this aspect of Freudian theory is that there is virtually no sound, objective evidence in its favour. Equally, there is little sound evidence against it. The fact is, there is almost no good relevant research.

Since sexuality lies at the heart of Freudian theory it might appear strange that its theories of sexual deviance lie essentially untested, almost fifty years after the death of Freud. I think there are two reasons for this empirical neglect and I shall conclude this chapter by examining them.

A basic cause of this lack of research lies in the epistemology of psychoanalysis itself, as Gellner (1985) has cogently argued. Grossly oversimplified, the point is that psychoanalytic theory assumes that accurate perception of one's inner world and that of others is possible if the distorting veil of one's own unconscious conflicts and defences is removed. Of course, this is done by and can only be done by the training analysis that all psychoanalysts have had to undergo (except, of course, in the case of the Master). With this epistemic base no empirical testing is required. Thus psychoanalysts themselves feel no need to research the theory by using any other methods of investigation. This means, essentially, that all research must spring from non-analysts.

This brings us to the second major reason why there is a dearth of adequate empirical research. Unfortunately, those most highly trained in research in the area of Freudian psychology — psychologists — are also taught that Freud is unscientific and that his theories are untestable. Hence the majority of them would consider such research a waste of time. This is largely true of academic psychologists both here and in America. Indeed, most of the empirical work into Freudian theory is carried out by psychiatrists and clinical psychologists. This accounts for the preponderance in this work of tests and methods, such as the

Rorschach, that do not meet the standards of scientific research.

This leads on to a further difficulty with research into the Freudian theory of sexual deviance. In fact, it is exceedingly difficult to carry out good research. It is easy to criticise the work of others, but far more difficult to design investigations that can put the theory to the test. In the final section of this chapter I shall rush in where only fools will go and suggest some possible research which would provide the relevant scientific evidence.

One approach that would appear hopeful is to utilise the dynamic activation method of Silverman but with all the different deviant groups. For example, it is claimed, as was seen earlier in this chapter, that narcissism and the castration complex were both important in exhibitionists. It should be possible to develop suitable subliminal stimuli to put this assertion to the test. The same is true of the other deviant groups. Fear of excitement is supposed to fire the sadist. In this instance, therefore, this could be portrayed in the subliminal stimulus. As was argued, a weakness of this method lies in the measurement. It would seem sensible to abandon Rorschach testing and other similar techniques and to use instead objective methods. Possible measures include changes in penile size and in intra-vaginal temperature, methods that might well prove valuable.

Percept-genetics provides a number of techniques that are not essentially different from those of Silverman. The best known of these, which are fully described by Kragh and Smith (1970), is the Defence Mechanism Test (Kragh, 1955, 1969). This, as the name suggests, purports to measure defence mechanisms, which it does by the serial exposure of stimuli at gradually increasing levels of illumination, beginning well below even a subliminal threshold and ending such that veridical description is possible. The theory of percept-genetics, which is a largely Scandinavian undertaking, has been fully described by Kragh and Smith (1970). However its relevance to this chapter lies in the fact that the authors claim, and there is a considerable amount of supporting evidence, that the development of the percept as each subject draws what he sees during the series of exposures reveals defences and thus the workings of the unconscious. Cooper and Kline (1985) have obtained some objective evidence for these claims and Kline (1985) has argued that subjects' protocols can be regarded as public data of the same kind as are obtained in the psychoanalytic session. These thus have the advantage that they can be scrutinised and the interpretations can be put onto a rational basis.

Again, as was the case with the dynamic activation technique, it seems possible to use the percept-genetic method (serial presentation of subliminal stimuli) to probe the unconscious of the various deviant groups. Again special stimuli would have to be prepared but there seems to be no special difficulty here. Kline and Cooper (1977) did this in a study of defences against orality when a picture of a suckling pig was used. Thus I would certainly like to see a variety of percept genetic methods used with sexually deviant samples.

In conclusion, it is disappointing to find that the often elaborate and fantastical psychoanalytic theories of sexual deviance are so lacking in objective support. This is particularly so when it is remembered that one of the major explanatory concepts, the castration complex, has some objective confirmation. Although I have described in brief two experimental approaches that may well be capable of putting these theories to the test, it would be quite wrong to argue that Freudian theories are supported. On the other hand, it would be equally wrong to argue that they have been refuted. The position is that there is no satisfactory objective evidence and what is required is high quality research into these hypotheses. Now, when psychoanalytic theories have reached a low ebb (see Eysenck, 1985; Gellner, 1985 and Masson, 1984, just for example) there seems little prospect of this research being carried out. However, good ideas usually survive ephemeral prejudice and it is my hope that they will survive to be put to the scientific test.

REFERENCES

Buck, J. (1948) 'The HTP test.' *J. Clin. Psychol.*, *4*, 151–9
Campbell, P.T. and Narroll, R. (1972) In *Psychological Anthropology* (ed. E.L.K. Hsu), Cambridge Mass.: Schenkman
Cooper C. and Kline, P. (1986) 'An evaluation of the Defence Mechanism Test.' *Br. J. Psychol.*, *77*, 19–31
Eysenck, H.J. (1972) 'The experimental study of Freudian concepts.' *Bulletin of the British Psychological Society*, *25*, 261–7
Eysenck, H.J. (1985) *Decline and Fall of the Freudian Empire*. Harmondsworth: Pelican
—— and Wilson, G.D. (1973) *The Experimental Study of Freudian Theories*. London: Methuen
Farrell, B.A. (1961) 'Can psychoanalysis be refuted?' *Inquiry*, *4* (1), 16–36

Fenichel, O. (1945) *The Psychoanalytic Theory of Neurosis*. New York: Norton

Fisher, S. and Greenberg, P.R. (1977) *The Scientific Credibility of Freud's Theories and Therapy*. Hassocks, Sussex: Harvester Press

Freeman, D. (1984) *Margaret Mead and Samoa: The Making and Unmaking of the Paradise Island Myth*. Harmondsworth: Penguin.

Freud, S. (1905) *Three Essays on Sexuality*. In Freud, S. (1966), vol. 7, 135.

—— (1916–1917) *Introductory Lectures on Psychoanalysis*. In Freud, S. (1966) vols. 15 and 16.

—— (1917) *On the Transformation of Instincts with Special Reference to Anal Erotism*. In Freud, S. (1966), vol. 17, 127.

—— (1919) *A Child is Being Beaten*. In Freud, S. (1966), vol. 17, 195.

—— (1924) *Economic Problems of Masochism*. In Freud, S. (1966), vol. 19, 157.

—— (1966) *Standard Edition of the Complete Psychological Works of Sigmund Freud*. London: Hogarth Press and The Institute for Psychoanalysis

Fromm, E. (1974) *The Anatomy of Human Destructiveness*. London: Jonathan Cape.

Gellner, E. (1985) *The Psychoanalytic Movement*. London: Paladin

Grunbaum, A. (1984) *Philosophical Foundations of Psychoanalysis: a Philosophical Critique*. California: University of California Press

Hammer, E.F. (1953) 'An investigation of sexual symbolism: a study of HTPs of eugenically sterilized subjects.' *Journal of Projective Techniques*, *17*, 401–15

Hampson, S. and Kline, P. (1977) 'Personality dimensions differentiating certain groups of abnormal offenders from non-offenders.' *British Journal of Criminology*, *17*, 310–31

Irigaray, L. (1974) *Speculum, de l'autre femme*. Paris: Editions de Minuit.

—— (1977) 'Women's exile: interview with Luce Irigaray.' *Ideology and Consciousness*, *1*, 24–39

Kline, P. (1972) *Fact and Fantasy in Freudian Theory*. London: Methuen

—— (1981) *Fact and Fantasy in Freudian Theory* (2nd edn). London, Methuen

—— (1984) *Psychology and Freudian Theory*. London: Methuen

—— (1985) *The Scientific Study of Freudian Theory*. Paper read at Symposium on Science and Psychoanalysis. University of St Andrews, St Andrews

—— (1986) Philosophy, psychology and psychoanalysis. *British Journal of the Philosophy of Science*, (in press)

—— and Cooper, C. (1977) 'A percept-genetic study of some defence mechanisms in the Test P.N.' *Scand. J. Psychol.*, *18*, 148–52

Kragh, U. (1955) *The Actual-Genetic Model of Perception-Personality*. Lund: Gleerup

Kragh, U. (1969) *The Defence Mechanism Test*. Stockholm: Testförlaget

—— and Smith, G. (1970) *Percept-Genetic Analysis*. Lund: Gleerup
Masson, J.M. (1984) *The Assault on the Truth*. Harmondsworth: Penguin
Muensterberger, W. (ed.) (1969) *Man and Culture*. London: Rapp & Whiting
Popper, K. (1959) *The Logic of Scientific Discovery*. New York: Basic Books
Silverman, L.H., Kwawer, J.S., Wohtzaly, C. and Coron, M. (1973) 'An experimental study of aspects of the psychoanalytic theory of male homosexuality.' *J. Abnorm. Psychol.*, *82*, 178–88
Stephens, W.N. (1961) 'A cross-cultural study of menstrual taboos.' *Genet. Psychol. Monogr.*, *64*, 385–416
Whiting, J.W.M. and Child, I.L. (1953) *Child Training and Personality*. New Haven, Conn.: Yale University Press

8

A Cross-Cultural Perspective on Homosexuality, Transvestism and Trans-sexualism

Frederick L. Whitam

Homosexuality, transvestism and trans-sexualism have been widely studied by social scientists, often in clinical settings. Despite such attention an adequate understanding of these behaviours cannot be achieved without consideration of their cross-cultural aspects in nonclinical contexts. Cross-cultural analysis, along with historical, hormonal and primate evidence, is important for an understanding of the origins of variant sexuality. If homosexuals, transvestites and trans-sexuals appear in all human societies and their behaviour manifests itself similarly in both childhood and adulthood in different cultural settings, then a biological basis for these aspects of variant sexuality is suggested. While social scientists are likely to invoke the 'cultural diffusion' concept to explain similarities in the behaviour of homosexuals, transvestites and trans-sexuals, the predictable appearance of these persons with similar behavioural components in widely varying cultural settings stretches beyond reason the credibility of the cultural diffusion explanation. Although all people in all societies with rare exceptions are socialised to be heterosexual, the predictable, universal appearance of homosexual persons, despite socialisation into heterosexual patterns of behaviour suggests not only that homosexual orientation is biologically based but that sexual orientation itself is also biologically derived. Thus, the study of variant sexuality has important implications not only for the origins of variant sexuality — a question interesting in its own right — but for the origins of nonvariant sexuality as well.

This analysis is based primarily upon a ten-year study of male and female homosexuality in several societies. While the main focus of this research project is homosexuality, certain manifestations of transvestism and trans-sexualism, as will be seen, are integral parts of homosexuality. It is impossible to enter and observe homosexual subcultures without encountering transvestites and trans-sexuals of homosexual orientation. In most societies these persons regard themselves as homosexuals and are regarded by more masculine homosexuals as a natural part of the homosexual world. It is mainly in the United States and Western Europe, where partly through psychiatric classification and partly through the tendency of masculine homosexuals to dissociate themselves from transvestic homosexuals and trans-sexuals, that rigid distinctions are made among homosexuals, transvestites and trans-sexuals of homosexual orientation. Not all transvestites and trans-sexuals are homosexual, however, and there is a significant group of transvestites and trans-sexuals of heterosexual or bisexual orientation. Attention also will be paid to these persons in an attempt to distinguish among these several complex groupings.

The analysis presented here is based upon a large body of material — both questionnaire data and ethnographic observation — derived from both homosexual and heterosexual respondents in several societies and cultural groups: Brazil, Guatemala, Mexico, the Philippines, Thailand, the United States and native-born Hawaiians. Tabular material and conclusions pertaining to male homosexuality already have been published (Whitam, 1980; Whitam and Zent, 1984; Whitam and Mathy, 1986). The analysis of female homosexuality is not yet complete and the present analysis will present a tentative sketch of what this material suggests about lesbianism cross-culturally. Questionnaire data on lesbians and heterosexual women so far have been obtained from the United States, the Philippines and Brazil. Plans presently call for additional field work to be done on lesbians in Peru in 1986. All field work so far was done by the author between 1975 and 1985. Apart from this work on homosexuals, observation and interviews were conducted with, and questionnaire data were collected from, a group of heterosexual transvestites and trans-sexuals in Phoenix, Arizona, from 1980 to 1985. The present analysis is an attempt to sketch out pertinent aspects of homosexuality, transvestism and trans-sexualism and to delineate the implications of this research for the origins of these manifestations of variant sexuality.

MALE HOMOSEXUALS

All societies appear to produce a continuum of persons of homosexual orientation (Whitam and Mathy, 1986). If we consider men who are Kinsey 5s (predominantly homosexual with incidental heterosexual interests) and Kinsey 6s (exclusively homosexual), and examine in detail the behaviour of such persons, we find significant similarities among such persons in different societies. There is, of course, significant individual variation in behaviour among homosexuals — all persons regardless of sex or sexual orientation are in a sense unique in their gender behaviour and sexual make-up. However, when examined cross-culturally homosexuals as a group manifest certain behavioural characteristics that are strikingly similar, despite differing cultural contexts. One of the most remarkable aspects of entering and observing homosexual subcultures in various countries is the distinctive sensation that one is seeing and hearing the same behaviour enacted in different cultural settings. For example, homosexual men in all societies talk a great deal about men, especially handsome masculine men, and much conversation concerns sex, men's bodies and penises. Another favourite topic of conversation in all male homosexual subcultures is the arts, dance, the theatre, and related entertainment forms. Male homosexual subcultures produce remarkably similar entertainment forms, such as female impersonation shows. While many social scientists assume that such behaviour results from cultural transmission, these behaviours seem to appear spontaneously, predictably, and indigenously in different societies. Philippine homosexual men, except perhaps for the very wealthy, do not know that drag shows exist in the United States. American homosexual men do not know that Thais are performing female impersonation shows in the nightclubs of the resort town of Pattaya. Brazilian homosexual men do not know that Philippine homosexual men produce drag beauty contests in all parts of the Philippines, including small towns and cities. Americans and Western Europeans often regard any behaviour similar to their own as a result of cultural transmission *from* the United States and Western Europe *to* other societies. Actually, all large societies appear to have long-standing indigenous homosexual subcultures. Early reports by Spanish priests (Blair and Robertson, 1903–1909; San Antonio, 1977) attest to this in the Philippines. In his investigations of the archives of the Portuguese and Brazilian inquisitions, the Brazilian anthropologist Luiz Mott (personal communication, 1984) has uncovered evidence suggesting that transvestic homosexuals have lived continuously for four hundred years in the same street (Rua da Ajuda) in the colonial capital of Salvador, Brazil.

Another important piece of evidence that argues against cultural transmission theory is the early appearance in all societies of elements of the homosexual subculture in childhood, long before exposure to that subculture. Interest in women's clothes, dancing, and acting often appear as important elements in childhood experiences of male homosexuals and appear much less frequently in the childhood experience of heterosexuals. The early appearance of behavioural elements that later are transmuted into the homosexual subculture have been documented by both retrospective studies (Whitam and Dizon, 1979; Bell, Weinberg, and Hammersmith, 1981; Harry, 1982; Whitam and Mathy, 1986) and observational studies of children (Green and Money, 1966; Stoller, 1968; Green, 1974; Zucker, Bradley, Corter, Doering and Finegan, 1980; Zucker, Doering, Bradley and Finegan, 1982). The most thorough recent review of literature on cross-gendered children is that by Zucker (1985).

Because of the similarity of homosexual subcultures in various societies it is sometimes difficult to know whether the general culture or the homosexual subculture is the more powerful influence on the behaviour of homosexuals. Actually both general culture and homosexual subculture operate simultaneously to shape homosexual behaviour. In all societies there is a core of nonsexual behaviour (gender behaviour) that appears regardless of culture; there is a core of sexual behaviour (genital activity) that appears regardless of culture; and there are components of the general culture that may modify these core elements and determine the specific outward form that these core elements take. For example, cross-gender behaviour is a core element of gender behaviour that manifests itself from very early childhood through adulthood and even into old age in the lives of many homosexuals and in all societies and forms a cornerstone for many elements of homosexual subcultures. Childhood cross-gender behaviour on the part of boys consists of doll-playing, cross-dressing, being regarded as a sissy, preference for playing with girls, preference for the company of women and other related behaviours more typical of girls than boys. On the part of girls it consists of liking to play with boys' toys, cross-dressing, tomboy behaviour, preference for playing with boys, preference for the company of men, and other behaviours more typical of boys than girls. For example, Philippine mothers tend to be tolerant of cross-gender behaviour when it appears in pre-homosexual children. In that country cross-dressed homosexuals walk openly in public places, some even teach with make-up, and drag shows have become a popular form of entertainment, regarded as appropriate for public festivals, neighbourhood entertainments and civic club programs. Thus, benign attitudes toward both childhood and adult manifestations of cross-gender behaviour are pervasive in that society.

Philippine society does not create the cross-gender phenomenon. It reacts to this core behaviour that appears apart from socialisation and social structural factors, amplifying the core gender behaviour and determining through its cultural traditions the specific forms that the core behaviour takes. On the other hand, the strong stigma attached to cross-dressing in North America and Western Europe probably serves to minimise the enactment of cross-gender behaviour in both childhood and adulthood.

Core components of gender behaviour in homosexual men

The most conspicuous core components of gender behaviour (behaviour not specifically sexual but nevertheless linked to sexual orientation) for homosexual men are: (1) patterns of overt femininity/masculinity different from those of male heterosexuals, (2) the cross-gender phenomenon, and (3) heightened interest in entertainment and the arts, particularly dance and theatre, and concomitant low levels of interest in sports and related aggressive activities. Culture may impinge on these core components but it neither creates them nor has the power to eliminate them. It is through these components of behaviour that we may understand the continuum of homosexuality that probably appears in all societies with sufficiently large populations. When Kinsey 5s and 6s are subjected to close scrutiny they form a complex and colourful spectrum of human behaviour.

The male homosexual continuum

It should be emphasised that among Kinsey 5s and 6s there is considerable diversity with regard to gender behaviour. While, strictly speaking, such behaviour falls along a continuum of nearly infinite gradations, several major subgroups appear in all societies, given sufficiently large populations. The more overtly feminine the individual the more likely he is to have been highly cross-gendered as a child and to manifest cross-gender interests as an adult. The more overtly feminine the individual, the greater is his interest in entertainment and the arts, and the more feminine, the lower is the level of interest in sports and other aggressive activities. There is a group — perhaps 10 per cent — of very masculine homosexual men who are Kinsey 5s and 6s. One such clique of eight very masculine homosexual men was identified and observed in Phoenix. As children they appear to have been indistinguishable from heterosexual boys with respect to childhood behaviour and interests. They have little or no childhood cross-gendering and little interest in entertainment and the arts. Their level of interest in sports corresponds to that of heterosexual men of the same age. Nearly all the masculine homosexuals in this clique spend considerable time running, swimming, working out with weights, and playing tennis and racquetball. Several of these men regularly participate in marathons and other running events. They all have traditionally masculine occupations such as engineer, mechanic or agronomist. These men have strong genital interests that are directed exclusively to other masculine men.

The largest group in the homosexual continuum is a group (perhaps 65 per cent in the United States) of men of average masculinity who as children were cross-gendered to varying degrees, including some who were highly cross-gendered. These men tend to have heightened interest in entertainment and the arts and low levels of interest in athletic and related activities. The size of this group is probably maximised in societies such as the United States and Great Britain, which strongly repress the cross-gender behaviour of pre-homosexual boys. At puberty there occurs a masculinising influence and these children, because of biological factors associated with puberty and increased social pressures, abandon many of their cross-gender activities.

In societies such as the Philippines or traditional Hawaii,

Table 8.1: As a child, did you ever feel that you had been born the wrong sex?

	Men			
	Heterosexual		Homosexual	
	n	%	n	%
Brazil				
Frequently	0	0	1	4
Occasionally	1	6	3	13
Never	15	94	19	83
Totals	16	100	23	100

$$\chi^2 = 1.255$$
$$DF = 2$$
$$P = 0.5340$$

	Heterosexual		Homosexual	
	n	%	n	%
Philippines				
Frequently	0	0	5	17
Occasionally	1	3	15	50
Never	33	97	10	33
Totals	34	100	30	100

$$\chi^2 = 29.417$$
$$DF = 2$$
$$P = 0.000$$

	Heterosexual		Homosexual	
	n	%	n	%
United States				
Frequently	0	0	2	6
Occasionally	4	7	6	17
Never	54	93	28	78
Totals	58	100	36	101

$$\chi^2 = 5.813$$
$$DF = 2$$
$$P = 0.0547$$

which are tolerant of cross-gender behaviour, the size of this group of men of average masculinity may become attenuated and the third group — transvestic homosexuals (perhaps 25 per cent in the United States) — will become enlarged. Transvestic homosexuals were usually effeminate, cross-gendered children and remain somewhat the same as adults — cross-dressing, joking with cross-gendered pronouns, referring to each other as 'she' instead of he, and conferring female names in jest. Effeminate homosexuals have strong interests in entertainment and the arts and are more likely than more masculine groups to be engaged in occupations such as hairdresser or dressmaking. For example, in Cebu City, Philippines, most of the hairdressers and dressmakers are effeminate homosexuals.

A small subgroup of transvestic homosexuals are near-trans-sexuals and trans-sexuals. As children they were highly effeminate and exhibited very strong cross-gender behaviour. Homosexual trans-sexuals are the most highly cross-gendered segement of the transvestic homosexuals, comprising probably less than one per cent of the total number of Kinsey 5s and 6s. The term homosexual trans-sexual is used here to refer to highly cross-gendered individuals of homosexual orientation who live much of the time as women and would prefer to be women regardless of whether sex-reassignment surgery is sought. Such people are probably found in all societies and are reported upon from various historical epochs predating the relatively recent use of sex-reassignment surgery. It should be noted that feeling that one has been born the wrong sex is not limited to trans-sexuals. Some views hold that the critical distinction between trans-sexuals and homosexuals is that the former feel that they were born the wrong sex. Table 8.1 suggests that while heterosexual individuals may occasionally have fleeting thoughts that they were born the wrong sex, many homosexuals as children had such thoughts. As many as 23 per cent of American homosexual men, 17 per cent of the Brazilian homosexual men, and 67 per cent of the Filipino homosexual men as children frequently or occasionally felt they had been born the wrong sex. This is consistent with the findings of Saghir and Robins (1973, p. 21) who observe:

> Among the homosexual males, a high proportion reported a repetitive desire to become a girl or a woman before the adult years. Specifically 27 per cent of the homosexual males and 3 per cent of the heterosexual controls reported the desire to become a member of the opposite sex early in their lives.

In the Filipino sample only one of the respondents is trans-sexual in the sense of seriously thinking about sex reassignment surgery.

Genital activities of homosexual men

Much has been made of the high level of genital activity of homosexual men. It is interesting to note that, despite significant cross-gender patterns occurring cross-culturally in populations of homosexual men, levels of genital interests are not cross-gendered and resemble those of heterosexual men rather than

Table 8.2: Do you regard yourself as strongly interested in sex; that is, do you spend a good bit of time thinking about, seeking and engaging in sexual relations?

	Men				
	Heterosexual			Homosexual	
	n	%		n	%
Brazil					
Yes	6	38		15	65
Somewhat	7	44		6	26
No	3	19		2	9
Totals	16	101		23	100
		$\chi^2=2.973$			
		DF=2			
		P=0.2261			
Philippines					
Yes	16	47		17	57
Somewhat	17	50		10	33
No	1	3		3	10
Totals	34	100		30	100
		$\chi^2=2.605$			
		DF=2			
		P=0.2718			
United States					
Yes	25	43		17	47
Somewhat	28	48		12	33
No	5	9		7	19
Totals	58	100		36	99
		$\chi^2=3.288$			
		DF=2			
		P=0.1932			

women. The level of genital interest among homosexual men is quite high, resembling that of heterosexual men in its intensity. Women, the preferred outlet of heterosexual men, tend to be a restraining factor on the sexual activities of heterosexual men. We do not know for certain whether the high level of genital activities of homosexual men is identical physiologically to that of heterosexual men, or whether the level of genital interest is a function of the lack of the restraining influence of women in the homosexual world. Bell and Weinberg (1978, p. 308) report that 75 per cent of white homosexual men in San Francisco had had 100 or more partners in their lifetimes. Twenty-eight per cent of the white homosexual men had had 1000 partners. On the other hand, only two per cent of white lesbians had had 100 or more sex partners. Table 8.2 shows similar levels of self-reported interest in sex by homosexual and heterosexual men in three societies.

The level of genital interest on the part of homosexual men does not seem to vary with cross-gendering or the masculine-feminine component. Very masculine homosexuals, ordinary homosexuals, transvestic homosexuals and homosexual trans-sexuals all seem to manifest strong genital interests, though the specific ways this genital interest is directed varies according to place on the homosexual continuum. For example, transvestic homosexuals and homosexual trans-sexuals sometimes cross-dress and prostitute themselves. I have observed this phenomenon in the Hotel Street area of Honolulu, Van Buren Street in Phoenix, Rua da Ajuda in Salvador, Brazil, the Silom Road district in Bangkok, Thailand; it is widely reported on by gay travel magazines and guides. Stamford (1980, p. 7) reports that Bugis Street in Singapore and Taman Lawang, under the bridge of Setiabudi in Jakarta are places of assignation for trans-vestites. The sex partners of transvestic homosexuals and homosexual trans-sexuals — whether in the context of prostitution or in more quotidian circumstances — tend to be bisexual and heterosexual men. A not uncommon relationship is that between transvestic homosexuals and bisexual male prosti-tutes who hustle for money but maintain an affectional or live-in relationship with transvestic homosexuals.

The study of homosexuals cross-culturally offers insight into the nature of paraphilic behaviour. Interest in paraphilic behaviour on the part of homosexual men seems highly developed only in Western Europe, the United States, Canada and Australia. Sexual activities associated with sexual sadism and masochism, bondage and discipline, the wearing of leather, etc. seem to occur in areas where homosexual men are affluent and financially independent enough to live alone or with other homosexual men. Thus, in cities with large affluent homosexual populations such as San Francisco and Hamburg, paraphilic behaviour, which initially is largely male activity rather than female, is subject to expansion through male-male sexual contact and exploration. In a sexual atmosphere that is free of both women and familial constraints, paraphilic behaviour tends to become highly developed. It is not highly developed in the third world where most single people, including homosexuals, tend to live with their families. Even in São Paulo, for example, which as a city of some 14 million has an enormous homosexual population, there is little interest in or conversation about paraphilic behaviour. While there probably is a limited amount of paraphilic interest that is universal and appears spontaneously in any large population, it seems likely that paraphilic interest, unlike sexual orientation itself, is subject to considerable shaping by culture and social structure.

LESBIANS

Lesbians, like homosexual men, appear in all societies. *Gaia's Guide* (1983), a travel guide for lesbians, lists 51 countries in which there are meeting places and organisations for lesbians. This guide is far from complete. For example, neither Guatemala nor the Philippines, where I have observed the presence of lesbians, is listed. While far less research has been done on lesbians than homosexual men, lesbian behaviour is no less theoretically significant. Virtually no cross-cultural work on lesbianism is available. In fact, so little cross-cultural work has been done on lesbianism that many social scientists have only the vaguest ideas about lesbians or even doubt their existence in other societies, although when one is working in other societies, such as in the Philippines and Brazil, it quickly becomes apparent that lesbians are everywhere in these countries in much the same sense as are homosexual men. Their existence is common knowledge to Filipinos and Brazilians, for example, and is taken for granted with little or no moral repugnance toward them. The Filipinos are particularly tolerant toward lesbians in much the same way as they are of homosexual men.

The lesbian continuum

While lesbian behaviour varies in significant respects from that of homosexual men, the lesbian continuum in a general way tends to resemble that of homosexual men. There appears to be a small group of very feminine lesbians, a much larger group of women who are very ordinary in appearance and mannerisms and a small group of women who are obviously masculine. Within this group of masculine lesbians there appears to be a group of highly cross-gendered lesbians called by Katz (1976, p. 210) 'lesbian transvestites'. These lesbians frequently cross-dress, sometimes live out their lives as men, adopt men's names, and engage in traditionally masculine occupations. Katz has documented numerous cases of such lesbians in the United States from 1782 to 1920. Green (1974, pp. 692–7) has described lesbian (female-to-male) trans-sexuals in contemporary American life. Such lesbians appear to correspond to the near-trans-sexuals and trans-sexuals in the male homosexual world. Nowhere, however, do they seem to give performances as do transvestic homosexuals. Dancing and performance appear to be intrinsically female behaviour and are connected with male homosexual behaviour through the cross-gendering process. Lesbians appear to be far more private in both their gender-related behaviour and in their genital behaviour, resembling heterosexual women in this respect.

Core components of lesbian gender behaviour

Core components of lesbian gender behaviour consist of (1) patterns of overt masculinity/femininity different from female heterosexuals; (2) the cross-gender phenomenon, and (3) heightened interest in athletics and concomitant low levels of interest in entertainment and the arts. While the gender aspects of male homosexual behaviour have been extensively researched, little work has been done on the cross-gendering of lesbians.

In contrast to the findings of Saghir and Robins, childhood cross-dressing seems quite common among lesbians and occurs in the three societies for which data are available. Saghir and Robins (1973, p. 196) state that cross-dressing among homosexual women is a generally infrequent phenomenon, writing:

> True cross-dressing was very rare among female homosexuals. Both females who cross-dressed in the preadult years were also tomboys. However, because of its rarity among female homosexuals, cross-dressing does not appear to be a helpful measure for cross-gender identification.

In a much larger sample, Bell *et al.* (1981, p. 147) found that 71 per cent of the white homosexual women enjoyed typical boys' activities such as baseball and football in contrast to 28 per cent of the white heterosexual women. They also found that about half

Table 8.3: As a child, were you interested in cars, soldiers, balls and other kinds of boys' toys and hobbies?

	Heterosexual		Women	Homosexual	
	n	%		n	%
Brazil					
Yes	9	37.5		24	83
No	15	62.5		5	17
Totals	24	100		29	100
			$\chi^2c=10.1260$ DF=1 P=0.0013		
Philippines					
Yes	8	24		27	84
No	25	76		5	16
Totals	33	100		32	100
			$\chi^2c=21.2801$ DF=1 P=0.0000		
United States					
Yes	25	58		35	87.5
No	18	42		5	12.5
Totals	43	100		40	100
			$\chi^2c=7.5123$ DF=1 P=0.0058		

of the homosexual women but very few of the heterosexual women liked to cross-dress in boys' clothing. It is apparent from examination of Tables 8.3 and 8.4 that considerable cross-gendering occurs with respect to the childhood behaviour of lesbians and that this behaviour occurs cross-culturally. As may be seen from Table 8.3, some pre-heterosexual girls — especially Americans — like playing with boy's toys and games as well as with girl's toys and games. On the other hand, lesbians prefer boys' toys and games almost exclusively and tend to shun girl's toys and games. Such patterns of behaviour are corroborated by interviews with lesbians. One American lesbian, for example, states:

My parents gave me frilly toys to play with. I couldn't stand them. I wanted the same toys that they gave my brother. They

Table 8.4: As a child did you like to dress up in adult men's clothing, shoes, hats, or play with men's things, such as pipes, shaving cream, etc. for pretending?

	Women				
	Heterosexual			Homosexual	
	n	%		n	%
Brazil					
Yes	2	8		12	41
No	22	92		17	59
Totals	24	100		29	100

$$\chi^2c=5.7757$$
$$DF=1$$
$$P=0.0160$$

	Heterosexual			Homosexual	
	n	%		n	%
Philippines					
Yes	4	12		23	72
No	29	88		9	28
Totals	33	100		32	100

$$\chi^2c=21.4897$$
$$DF=1$$
$$P=0.0000$$

	Heterosexual			Homosexual	
	n	%		n	%
United States					
Yes	7	16		20	50
No	36	84		20	50
Totals	43	100		40	100

$$\chi^2c=10.7360$$
$$DF=1$$
$$P=0.0009$$

gave me dolls which I hated. They furnished my bedroom with French provincial furniture. I hated it. I wanted bunkhouse beds and rough-looking furniture like my brother had. I wanted a drum set for Christmas one year but my parents gave me tap dance lessons instead. I hated them. Even though I am grown now my parents still do this to me. Last Christmas I wanted a circular saw but my mother gave me a sewing machine. They have always tried to push me into feminine things.

With regard to cross-dressing (Table 8.4) it may be seen that while many lesbians as children were not interested in cross-dressing, as many as 50 per cent of the American, 41 per cent of the Brazilian, and 72 per cent of the Filipino lesbians cross-dressed as children while few of the heterosexual women in the three societies reported childhood cross-dressing. One American lesbian stated: 'As a child my favourite playthings were a policeman's shirt and my Dad's old navy uniform.' Another reported: 'I didn't know I wasn't a cowboy until I was 14. As a child I always thought of myself as a cowboy. I had cowboy clothes, guns, and hats. I wanted to be out riding and herding and always thought I would be a cowboy when I grew up.'

In Cebu City, in the Philippines, pre-homosexual girls frequently wear 'short pants.' Shorts or short pants are regarded as exclusively masculine attire. Philippine lesbians frequently report that as children they wore 'short pants', for which they were punished or criticised. In the cases of more masculine pre-homosexual girls, family and neighbours, tired of trying to feminise them, would say, 'Oh, she's a "tomboy" (lesbian) let her wear short pants.'

As may be seen from Tables 8.5 and 8.6, lesbian respondents in the three societies report similar patterns of athletic interests both as children and adults. They are much more likely than heterosexual women and homosexual men to report strong interests in sports as children as may be seen from Table 8.5. In their childhood athletic interests lesbians seem to resemble heterosexual men. Much the same may be said for the athletic interests of lesbians as adults. As may be seen from Table 8.6, when asked to respond to a forced choice question about which type of sport they preferred, they overchose body contact, team sports. Their choices of sports are quite different from those of heterosexual women and homosexual men, tending to resemble the choices of heterosexual men more than other sex orientation categories. It is probable that these choices of body contact team sports do not always, for social and cultural reasons, materialise in the actual behaviour of lesbians. Nonetheless, the strong athletic interests of lesbians are widely and openly discussed within lesbian communities in the three societies studied. One lesbian respondent, a former professional golfer, estimated that 50 per cent of the professional female golfers in the United States are lesbian. Jokes about the large number of physical education teachers who are lesbian are common in both Brazil and the United States. Two American respondents who are career military personnel estimate the overall percentage of lesbians among female military personnel to be about 35 per cent for new

Table 8.5: As a child did you participate in sports?

| | Men | | | | Women | | | |
| | Hetero-sexual | | Homo-sexual | | Hetero-sexual | | Homo-sexual | |
	n	%	n	%	n	%	n	%
Brazil								
Yes, very much	9	56	7	30	1	4	13	45
Somewhat	7	44	6	26	8	33	6	21
No	0	—	10	44	15	63	10	34
Total	16	100	23	100	24	100	29	100

$\chi^2=9.37245$
DF=2
P =0.0092

$\chi^2=11.199$
DF=2
P =0.0037

| | Men | | | | Women | | | |
| | Hetero-sexual | | Homo-sexual | | Hetero-sexual | | Homo-sexual | |
	n	%	n	%	n	%	n	%
Philippines								
Yes, very much	25	74	8	27	7	21	20	62
Somewhat	8	24	15	50	22	67	7	22
No	1	3	7	23	4	12	5	16
Total	34	101	30	100	33	100	32	100

$\chi^2=15.19737$
DF=2
P =0.0005

$\chi^2=14.11694$
DF=2
P =0.0009

| | Men | | | | Women | | | |
| | Hetero-sexual | | Homo-sexual | | Hetero-sexual | | Homo-sexual | |
	n	%	n	%	n	%	n	%
United States								
Yes, very much	39	67	9	25	26	58	32	82
Somewhat	14	24	21	58	16	36	7	18
No	5	9	6	17	3	7	0	—
Total	58	100	36	100	45	101	39	100

$\chi^2=15.96654$
DF=2
P =0.0003

$\chi^2=6.74829$
DF=2
P =0.0342

recruits, 50 per cent for 'female permanent party personnel' (career military personnel) and 80 per cent for female drill sergeants. Moreover the lesbian presence in the military is well-known and is reportedly a topic of common gossip among both lesbian and non-lesbian female military personnel.

When asked to state their choice of 'ideal occupation', that most frequently mentioned by Filipino lesbians is 'police work.' Of 25 Filipino lesbians for whom data on this question are available, seven (or 28 per cent) chose 'police work'. Such occupational choices seem to appear quite early, before there is contact with a lesbian subculture. Six of the seven Filipino lesbians choosing police work reported that they made this choice before

Table 8.6: If you were forced to participate in one of the following sports, which would you choose?

| | Men | | | | Women | | | |
| | Hetero-sexual | | Homo-sexual | | Hetero-sexual | | Homo-sexual | |
	n	%	n	%	n	%	n	%
Brazil								
Football	7	44	6	26	0	0	6	21
Baseball	1	6	0	—	0	0	0	0
Basketball	1	6	2	9	1	4	6	21
Wrestling	0	—	0	—	0	0	3	10
Gymnastics	0	—	1	4	13	54	6	21
Swimming	7	44	14	61	10	42	8	28
Total	16	100	23	100	24	100	29	101

$\chi^2=3.60326$ $\chi^2=15.035$
DF=5   DF=5
P =0.4624   P =0.0047

| | Men | | | | Women | | | |
| | Hetero-sexual | | Homo-sexual | | Hetero-sexual | | Homo-sexual | |
	n	%	n	%	n	%	n	%
Philippines								
Football	3	9	3	10	2	6	2	6
Baseball	3	9	2	7	1	3	6	19
Basketball	24	71	4	13	1	3	15	48
Wrestling	0	—	0	—	0	—	1	3
Gymnastics	0	—	15	50	9	27	1	3
Swimming	4	12	6	20	20	61	6	19
Total	34	101	30	100	33	100	31	98

$\chi^2=29.75193$ $\chi^2=30.72739$
DF=5   DF=5
P =0.0000   P =0.0000

| | Men | | | | Women | | | |
| | Hetero-sexual | | Homo-sexual | | Hetero-sexual | | Homo-sexual | |
	n	%	n	%	n	%	n	%
United States								
Football	14	24	0	—	6	13	2	5
Baseball	14	24	3	8	8	18	17	44
Basketball	17	29	2	6	6	13	6	15
Wrestling	1	2	2	6	0	—	2	5
Gymnastics	6	10	12	33	10	22	2	5
Swimming	6	10	17	47	15	33	10	26
Total	58	99	36	100	45	99	39	100

$\chi^2=37.45674$ $\chi^2=13.21216$
DF=5   DF=5
P =0.0000   P =0.0215

puberty and in five cases this choice was made by age six. Most other choices of 'ideal occupation' by Filipino lesbians tended to be traditional male occupations such as engineer or business manager. Choices of 'ideal occupation' by Filipino heterosexual women tended to be far more traditionally female in nature, such as nurse and nutritionist — none chose police work. As with heterosexual men, athletic, military and police institutions tend to be linked. Homosexual men, in contrast to lesbians, overchose the arts and entertainment when asked to choose their 'ideal occupation'. Some 40 to 50 per cent of homosexual males in the three societies for which data are available (Brazil, the Philippines and the United States) chose an occupation related to entertainment and the arts.

Genital interests

The levels of genital interests of lesbians in three societies studied do not appear to be cross-gendered, resembling those of heterosexual women rather than homosexual or heterosexual men. The genital activity and courtship patterns of lesbians in Brazil, Guatemala, and the United States are similar. Lesbians often meet partners through friendship networks or at work rather than in bars or other specifically homosexual places. Long courtships often precede sexual relationships or decisions to live together, and fidelity is common. Filipino lesbians, for example, report that they frequently court neighbourhood girls, sending them love letters and small presents to the amusement of, and teasing by, the admired one's family and friends. Filipino lesbians may court heterosexual women as well as other 'tomboys'. Heterosexual girls are usually flattered by these attentions even if they are not responsive, and friends and family regard it as normal for 'tomboys' to court heterosexual girls.

The genital interests of lesbians in Brazil, the Philippines and the United States seem to be somewhat lower than that of the homosexual men in these societies, corroborating the observation of Bell and Weinberg (1978, p. 72):

> The fact that homosexual men tended to be more sexually active than lesbians deserves special notice. It may be that males in general tend to be more sexually active than females and that, all else being equal, there will be more sexual activity in relationships involving only males. Perhaps this is due to an innate biological difference.

Of the three groups, Filipino lesbians seem to have especially low

Table 8.7: Do you regard yourself as strongly interested in sex; that is, do you spend a good bit of time thinking about, seeking and engaging in sexual relations?

	Heterosexual		Women	Homosexual	
	n	%		n	%
Brazil					
Yes	11	46		13	45
Somewhat	10	42		16	55
No	3	13		0	0
Totals	24	101		29	100
		$\chi^2=4.116$ DF=2 $P =0.1277$			
Philippines					
Yes	3	9		2	6
Somewhat	22	67		19	60
No	8	24		11	34
Totals	33	100		32	100
		$\chi^2=0.878$ DF=2 $P =0.6447$			
United States					
Yes	15	34		11	27.5
Somewhat	12	27		16	40
No	17	39		13	32.5
Totals	44	100		40	100
		$\chi^2=1.533$ DF=2 $P =0.4646$			

levels of sexual activity. This may be due to their lack of privacy. Many of the Filipino lesbians — even those with partners — live in extended families with many family members sharing small houses or apartments. The levels of genital interest of lesbians, as may be observed in Table 8.7, tend to be similar to those of heterosexual women in the three societies for which data are available.

HETEROSEXUAL TRANSVESTITES AND TRANS-SEXUALS

The preceding sections have dealt with homosexuals, transvestic homosexuals and homosexual trans-sexuals. There is another important group of transvestites and trans-sexuals who are primarily heterosexual or bisexual in orientation. Steiner, Blanchard and Zucker (1985, p. 4) have cited five researchers who, despite somewhat different terminology, have made the critical distinction between transvestic homosexuals and homosexual trans-sexuals on the one hand and heterosexual transvestites and trans-sexuals on the other. These two groups seem to come from two different sources and are not part of the same continuum. As Freund (1985) has suggested these groups comprise two separate *spectra*, not one as some observers contend.

Not only are these groups different with respect to sexual orientation but there are several behavioural differences between them. As with homosexuals, differences between heterosexual transvestites and heterosexual trans-sexuals are subtle and represent places on a continuum rather than distinct categories. Heterosexual trans-sexuals are behaviourally similar to heterosexual transvestites except that the former have a much stronger sense of being female and sometimes desire sex-reassignment surgery. Both the sexual orientation and gender behaviour of these two heterosexual groups are similar. While these two categories of persons may be designated 'heterosexual transvestites' and 'heterosexual trans-sexuals', there seems to be a higher incidence of bisexuality among these groups than might be expected by chance, though most are Kinsey 0s, 1s and 2s. In writing about heterosexual transvestites, Benjamin (1966, p. 13), for example, observes:

> The majority of transvestites are overtly heterosexual, but many may be latent bisexuals. They 'feel' as men and know that they are men, marry, and often raise families. A few of them, however, especially when they are 'dressed,' can as part of their female role react homosexually to the attentions of an unsuspecting normal man.

Certainly, Pomeroy's contention that 'transvestites, as a group, are more heterosexual than the general population' (Pomeroy, 1968, p. 378) cannot be substantiated by observation of heterosexual transvestites and trans-sexuals. Our knowledge of these groups is limited almost exclusively to men. There is virtually no mention in the literature of female heterosexual transvestites and trans-sexuals. While the author hears occasional reports of such persons, they are either quite rare or live a lifestyle that renders them virtually invisible.

The literature on male heterosexual transvestites and trans-sexuals is based largely on reports from Western European and North American societies. This may well be a function of the fact that most of the research on these groups has been done mainly in these countries. Both homosexual and heterosexual Filipino and Brazilian respondents are surprised when told that there are heterosexual cross-dressers in the United States and Western Europe. When asked whether such persons exist in their own countries they are dubious, usually affirming that all cross-dressed males are homosexual. Whether there are groups of women equivalent to heterosexual transvestites and trans-sexuals and whether heterosexual transvestites and trans-sexuals exist in non-Western and third world countries are important questions that need research. The existence of similar patterns of heterosexual transvestic and trans-sexual behaviour, occurring in widely different societies, impinges on the important question of the origins of these forms of variant sexuality. At present there is little evidence and little consensus about their origins. Whether this behaviour is biological or social in nature is very much an open question.

Most of our knowledge of the behaviour of heterosexual transvestites and trans-sexuals comes from clinical observations and tests. The following brief description and comparisons are based on ethnographic observation of a social network of some 30 heterosexual transvestites and 10 heterosexual trans-sexuals in the Phoenix area between 1980 and 1985. Extensive interviews were conducted with a few respondents and some questionnaire data were obtained. The small size of the sample of questionnaire data obtained thus far does not lend itself to quantitative analysis.

Overt appearance and behaviour

When not cross-dressed, heterosexual transvestites and trans-sexuals tend to appear as very ordinary heterosexual men in behaviour and mannerisms. If such a group were sitting in a restaurant, for example, it would be almost impossible for a casual observer to know that these men have an atypical gender identity. Many transvestic homosexuals and homosexual trans-sexuals, on the other hand, would appear as effeminate men even when not cross-dressed. When cross-dressed, most heterosexual transvestites and trans-sexuals do not seem to change their mannerisms. Unlike transvestic homosexuals, they do not imitate feminine speech patterns and gestures. As a consequence, some heterosexual transvestites and trans-sexuals might appear to the casual observer to be masculine men dressed as women. While homosexual transvestites and trans-sexuals often dress exotically with heavy make-up and elaborate coiffures, heterosexual transvestites and trans-sexuals are likely to strive to dress like ordinary women in the everyday world. Some succeed in this effort while others remain obviously cross-dressed, because of their size or inadequate attention to details of their costume. In reality neither group really cross-dresses in exactly the way that ordinary women dress and there is rivalry between the two groups on this point. Heterosexual transvestites and trans-sexuals sometimes state that transvestic homosexuals and homosexual trans-sexuals cross-dress for superficial reasons (to perform or attract men) while they (the heterosexuals) are the true transvestites.

Sense of gender

The sense of gender in heterosexuals and homosexuals appears to be different. Many heterosexual transvestites and trans-sexuals seem to have *only* a sense of gender discordant with their biological sex with little concomitant feminine behaviour. Heterosexual trans-sexuals desire sex-reassignment surgery but do not have behavioural characteristics that are often linked to being female. In addition to having a heterosexual sex orientation they are often highly athletic, and unlike transvestic homosexuals they are not given to dancing and performances and are not usually facile with make-up, costuming, and coiffures. Tillie, a black homosexual male-to-female post-operative trans-sexual reports that as a child (an effeminate boy) she was very adept at make-up and coiffures and by the age of 12 was advising her girlfriends on their make-up, doing their hair, and dressing them for parties. She reports that she was more precocious than her heterosexual girlfriends in such matters. Ina, a highly transvestic native American trans-sexual has an extensive wardrobe of some 200 elaborate gowns that she designed and made herself. Such behaviour is unusual in heterosexual transvestites and trans-sexuals, many of whom report difficulties in learning to apply make-up correctly and in selecting appropriate clothing.

Heterosexual transvestites and trans-sexuals tend to have traditionally masculine occupations such as engineer, mechanic, salesman, or produce manager. The occupations of transvestic homosexuals and trans-sexuals, on the other hand, are frequently related to hairdressing, costuming, make-up, or entertainment. Heterosexuals do not usually give performances, dances, and female impersonations in public as do homosexuals. Dancing and performance seem to be intrinsically female behaviour which enters homosexual behaviour through the cross-gendering process. The more highly effeminate transvestic homosexuals and trans-sexuals have the most pronounced tendency toward dancing and entertaining. Many American homosexual trans-sexuals perform in Las Vegas shows. There are several hundred Brazilian transvestic homosexuals and trans-sexuals who perform in nightclubs in Paris and other European capitals. Six of seventeen homosexual trans-sexuals studied by Kandok (1973, p. 25) were working as actresses and dancers and others aspired to such occupations.

Heterosexual transvestites have a highly developed sense of feminine gender and a strong desire to cross-dress. Heterosexual trans-sexuals have a strong sense of being female. Transvestic homosexuals and homosexual trans-sexuals not only have these psychological characteristics but their everyday behaviour is much more feminised than that of heterosexual transvestites and trans-sexuals. It is somewhat paradoxical that most of the research and writing on transvestism and trans-sexualism in the past two decades has been directed toward heterosexual transvestites and trans-sexuals. Among many sex researchers the term 'transvestite' has been used to refer to heterosexual cross-dressers exclusively. Yet transvestic homosexuals and homosexual trans-sexuals appear to be considerably more cross-gendered behaviourally than do heterosexual transvestites and trans-sexuals.

CONCLUSIONS

Homosexual men and lesbians probably appear in all or nearly all societies. Their appearance does not seem dependent upon social structural conditions, and societal attitudes towards these persons are highly variable. A core of related behavioural elements appears in all male homosexual and lesbian groups regardless of culture. For homosexual men these elements consist of more significant feminisation than occurs in male heterosexual groups, cross-gender behaviour in childhood and adulthood, and heightened interest in dance and entertainment accompanied by low levels of interest in athletics and related behaviour. For lesbians, the core elements consist of significant masculinisation, cross-gender behaviour in childhood and adulthood, heightened interest in athletics and low levels of interest in dance and entertainment. Both male homosexual and lesbian groups in all societies, in addition to persons of ordinary appearance, contain transvestites and trans-sexuals. The genital interests of homosexual men resemble those of heterosexual men while the genital interests of lesbians resemble those of heterosexual women. Social structure may modify some specific details of the manifestation of these core elements, but it does not create them nor does it have the power to eliminate them.

An examination of homosexuals cross-culturally in non-clinical settings suggests that the spectrum of human sexual behaviour is far more complex than is often thought and that homosexual orientation as well as certain elements of gender behaviour may well be biologically derived. Heterosexual transvestites and trans-sexuals seem to come from a different source than do homosexuals and their origins are much less well understood than those of homosexual groups. So little cross-cultural research thus far has been done on these heterosexual groups that it is impossible to draw inferences about the origins of this aspect of variant sexuality from a cross-cultural perspective. If heterosexual transvestites and trans-sexuals emerge in all societies in much the same form, this evidence would support the view that there is a biological basis for such behaviour.

NOTE

This work was supported in part by Arizona State University through a grant from the Faculty Grant-in-Aid Program during the summer of 1979, a sabbatical leave in the fall of 1979, and a travel grant in the summer of 1984. Robin M. Mathy, my graduate assistant, provided valuable assistance in the analysis of data and reading of the manuscript.

REFERENCES

Bell, A.P. and Weinberg, M.S. (1978) *Homosexualities: A Study of Diversity Among Men and Women*, New York: Simon and Schuster.

Bell, A.P., Weinberg, M.S., and Hammersmith, S.K. (1981) *Sexual Preference: Its Development in Men and Women*, Bloomington: Indiana University Press

Benjamin, H. (1966) *The Trans-sexual Phenomenon*, New York: The Julian Press

Blair, E.H. and Robertson, J.A. (eds) (1903–1909) *The Philippine Islands: 1493–1898*, Cleveland: Arthur H. Clark

Freund, K. (1985) 'Cross-gender identity in a broader context.' In *Gender Dysphoria* (ed. B. Steiner), pp. 259–324, New York: Plenum Press

Gaia's Guide (1983), New York: Sandy Horn Publisher

Green, R. (1974) *Sexual Identity Conflict in Children and Adults*, New York: Basic Books

Green, R. (1978) 'Sexual identity of 37 children raised by homosexual or transsexual parents.' *Am. J. Psychiatry*, *135*, 692–97

Green, R. and Money, J. (1966) 'Stage acting, role-taking and effeminate impersonation during boyhood.' *Arch. Gen. Psychiatry*, *15*, 535–8

Harry, J. (1982) *Gay Children Grown Up*, New York: Praeger

Kandok, T. (1973) *Sex Change*, Springfield, Ill.: Charles C. Thomas

Katz, J. (1976) *Gay American History*, New York: Thomas Crowell

Pomeroy, W. (1968) 'Homosexuality, transvestism, and trans-sexualism.' In *Human Sexuality in Medical Education and Practice* (ed. C. Vincent), Springfield, Ill.: C.C. Thomas

Saghir, M.T. and Robins, E. (1973) *Male and Female Homosexuality*, Baltimore: Williams and Wilkins

San Antonio, J.F. de (1977) *The Philippine Chronicles of Fray San Antonio*, Manila: Historical Conservation Society

Stamford, J. (1980) *Spartacus Holiday Help Portfolio: Indonesia*, Amsterdam: Spartacus

Steiner, B.W., Blanchard, R., and Zucker, K. (1985) 'Introduction.' In *Gender Dysphoria* (ed. B.W. Steiner), pp. 1–10, New York: Plenum Press

Stoller, R. (1968) *Sex and Gender*, New York: Aronson

Whitam, F. (1980) 'The prehomosexual male child in three societies: the United States, Guatemala, Brazil.' *Arch. Sex. Behav.*, *9*, 87–99

Whitam, F.L. and Dizon, M.J. (1979) 'Occupational choice and sexual orientation in cross-cultural perspective.' *International Review of Modern Sociology*, *9*, 137–49

Whitam, F. and Mathy, R. (1986) *Male Homosexuality in Four Societies: Brazil, Guatemala, the Philippines, and the United States*, New York: Praeger

Whitam, F. and Zent, M. (1984) 'A cross-cultural assessment of early cross-gender behaviour and familial factors in male homosexuality.' *Arch. Sex. Behav.*, *13*, 427–39

Zucker, K.J. (1985) 'Cross-gender-identified children.' In *Gender Dysphoria* (ed. B. Steiner), pp. 75–174, New York: Plenum Press

Zucker, K.J., Bradley, S.J., Corter, C.M., Doering, R.W., and Finegan, J.K. (1980) 'Cross-gender behaviour in very young boys.' In *Childhood and Sexuality* (ed. J. Samson), Montreal: Editions Etudes Vivantes

Zucker, K.J., Doering, R.W., Bradley, S.J., and Finegan, J.K. (1982) 'Sex-typed play in gender-disturbed children: a comparison to sibling and psychiatric controls.' *Arch. Sex. Behav.*, *11*, 309–21

9

The Courtship Disorders

Ron Langevin and Reuben A. Lang

The term 'courtship disorders' was originally used by Freund, Scher and Hucker (1983, 1984) as a collective label for voyeurism, exhibitionism, obscene calls, toucheurism and rape. These sexual behaviours are frequently associated in clinical reports (Freud in Jones 1953; Macdonald, 1973; Rickles, 1950) and Freund *et al.* suggested that the behaviours have a common underlying aetiology.

They conceptualised normal human courtship as involving four progressive stages (Table 9.1): searching for a partner; pretactile interaction, which is largely verbal; 'getting to know one's prospective sex partner'; tactile interaction, which includes petting and foreplay; and last, genital union or intercourse. The model was borrowed from ethology and equally well describes the courtship rituals of birds. The sexual anomalies represent distortions of the normal courtship sequence. Within this theoretical framework, the voyeur is overaroused or he expends his sexual energy at the searching stage and the exhibitionist does so at the pretactile stage; he simply displays himself and masturbates to climax. Obscene calls can also be conceptualised as an abortive or hyperarousing pretactile stage since the caller talks and masturbates. The toucheur progresses to the tactile stage but

Table 9.1: Courtship stages and the courtship disorders

Stage	Disorder
1. Search for a partner	Voyeurism
2. Pretactile interaction	Exhibitionism; obscene telephone calling
3. Tactile interaction	Toucheurism; frotteurism
4. Genital union	Rape

he too expends sexual energy before appropriate genital union. The rapist short-circuits all stages and immediately attempts intercourse. For each anomaly, most stages of courtship are omitted entirely or appear only in a vestigial way. The theory has intuitive appeal since it relates, in an orderly way, animal and human behaviour and conventional heterosexual behaviour to sexual anomalies. Testing the theory is surprisingly more complex.

Humans are extremely interested in sex and they may engage in non-conventional outlets for a variety of reasons — curiosity, deprivation or unavailability of suitable partners (surrogate activity) amongst others. Sexually anomalous men may be even more open to varied sexual experiences than are conventional heterosexuals. Thus one must ask of the courtship disorders: Do voyeurism, exhibitionism, obscene calls, toucheurism and rape co-occur more often than they do with fetishism, transvestism, homosexuality or other sexual anomalies not considered courtship disorders?

Scoptophilia, the pleasure in looking, is often used to link voyeurism to the exhibitionistic act. The voyeur obtains vicarious gratification by viewing the genitals of the other person, usually covertly or publicly by attending strip shows or by watching censored erotica. Clinical studies of exhibitionists confirm that anywhere from 17 per cent (Rooth, 1973) to 100 per cent of exposers (Smukler and Schiebel, 1975) had peeped before starting to exhibit. Our own work (Lang, Langevin, Checkley and Pugh, 1986) showed that 24 of 34 exhibitionists (71 per cent) had also peeped at solitary females disrobing. The association of peeping and exposing would seem to be a close one, as noted elsewhere (Langevin, Paitich, Hucker, Newman, Ramsay, Pope, Geller and Anderson, 1979). Some men have also interpreted pornographic pictures of females as exposing. They may not enjoy the stripper or Playboy centrefold solely for their body shape or as a fancied sex partner. So, for the exhibitionist, it may be nicer if she enjoyed exposing too. Hence some exhibitionists may hold the fancied belief that the female is 'exposing' for his benefit and with similar desires.

In clinical observation of 139 courtship disorders, Freund *et al.* (1983) found that 44.6 per cent engaged in at least one other anomalous courtship behaviour. Unfortunately they did not report the incidence of other sexually anomalous behaviour. The factor analytic studies of Paitich, Langevin, Freeman, Mann and

203

Handy (1977), using the Clarke Sex History Questionnaire (cf. Langevin, Handy, Paitich and Russon, 1985b), showed some clustering of the expected courtship anomalies but to some extent this was by default. Anomalous heterosexual behaviours, including exhibiting and heterosexual paedophilia, tended *not* to occur with homosexual behaviour, and they polarised from each other in the factor analysis. More recent studies (Langevin, Paitich and Russon, 1985a,c; Lang *et al.*, 1986) suggest that (1) exhibiting and peeping are common among sexually anomalous men in general, (2) rapists engage in homosexual acts, paedophilia and transvestism as much as they do in exhibiting, toucheurism and obscene calls, and (3) exhibitionists may engage in transvestism more than in the courtship cluster, exhibiting excepted. (4) There is some evidence to suggest an overlap between classes of stimuli that the exhibitionist and the paedophile find potentially erotic. In Rooth's (1973) sample of 30 persistent exhibitionists, 25 per cent admitted to a previous paedophilic or hebephilic experience.

The results of the foregoing studies raise doubts that there is a 'courtship disorders' cluster unless more stringent criteria are employed. Phallometric studies employing the measurement of penile volume offer a direct measure of the degree of erection elicited by courtship behaviours. This provides one accepted index of erotic *preference* patterns and brings order to what may seem random sexual behaviour. In several studies by Freund and his colleagues (Freund *et al.*, 1983, 1984a; Freund, Scher, Racansky, Campbell and Heasman, 1984), penile tumescence to audiodescriptions of exhibiting, voyeurism, toucheurism and rape were compared in subgroups of rapists, exhibitionists, toucheurs, and voyeurs. For example Freund *et al.* (1984a) compared 17 patients and 20 sexually normal controls on penile responses to audiodescriptions of voyeurism, exposing, toucheurism as well as on intercourse and neutral situations. The predominantly exhibitionistic groups of patients reacted significantly to voyeurism and, in a further experiment with the groups, more to toucheurism than did controls. These studies still beg the question whether men with courtship disorders would be reactive to a wide range of erotic stimuli. Work on university students and community volunteers (Langevin *et al.*, 1979; Quinsey, Chaplin and Varney, 1981; Malamuth, 1981) suggests that, under proper instructions, sexually normal men can react erotically to a wide range of sexually unusual stimuli. Whether they would *actually* engage in the sexual behaviours in real life is doubtful. Perhaps a more useful criterion for the importance of a sexual behaviour is its frequency and the number of times it results in orgasm. Many sexual behaviours are common but non-orgasmic or, at the very least, non-preferred. Thus Kinsey, Pomeroy and Martin (1948) noted that orgasmic homosexual behaviours occur in 37 per cent of the male population but only 4 per cent are exclusively so, and likely have a same-sex erotic preference. Similarly Langevin *et al.* (1985c) required 10 incidences of peeping as a criterion to separate sex offenders from noncriminal community research volunteers. Thus one must evaluate sexual preferences.

Sexual preference is indicated first by the association of persons or behaviours with sexual climax (Stimulus Preferences, cf. Langevin, 1983) and second, it is the preferred way of attaining sexual release (Response Preference). With some effort, sets of stimuli can be found to phallometrically differentiate sexually anomalous and sexually conventional men in fantasy but it would remain to be shown that such stimuli would reflect actual sexual behaviour. In contrast, a history of orgasmic responses associated with each of the courtship disorders would provide an *in vivo* test of the hypothesis that they are interrelated as more than curiosities or surrogate acts.

Lang *et al.* (1986) used orgasm as a criterion to examine 34 exhibitionists and found that about half engaged in orgasmic voyeurism but less than 6 per cent were orgasmic in relation to frottage, toucheurism or rape. Almost 30 per cent climaxed while making obscene calls but even more, 43 per cent, engaged in orgasmic transvestism. Even 29 per cent were involved in paedophilic behaviour. Thus the original linking of voyeurism, exhibitionism, toucheurism and rape *per se* now seems tenuous. By and large, each courtship anomaly seems to have more uniqueness than communality with the others in our work over the past ten years. So each courtship disorder now will be considered separately.

VOYEURISM

Voyeurism or scoptophilia, according to Freud (1953), becomes a sexual disorder when the pleasure of looking replaces the act of intercourse. Sexual excitement depends on observing a woman disrobe or a couple in intercourse seen from a hidden vantage point, usually through a window (Tollison and Adams, 1979). Most voyeurs are heterosexual; few, if any, are homosexual (Money, 1981). Psychoanalysts see voyeuristic activity as a function of sexual curiosity, shyness, or fear of strangers (women), enacted to give the observer a sense of power over the unsuspecting women they watch.

Fenichel (1943) has described the sadistic component of the voyeuristic act as the equation of 'looking at' and 'to devour'. In what sounds allegorical, the voyeur's eye 'takes in' the female victim, as if with his penis. Thus there is mixed opinion on whether voyeurism is attributable to regression/fixation at the oral or phallic stage of development (Rosen, 1979, pp. 153–155). However impressive, there is no substantive evidence to support any such notion. On the other hand, behaviourists contend that conditioning occurs when the act of peeping becomes associated with sexual arousal and climax; that is, when the subject masturbates or fantasises at the sight of a woman or couple undressing or engaging in sexual activity. Orgasm, then, even if vicariously achieved, reinforces the voyeur's aberrant sexual needs.

Psychoanalytic theories of all sexual anomalies embody the notion that Oedipal conflicts and castration anxiety underlie the fear of retribution for masturbatory acts or the erotic fantasies that accompany it. Evident in the psychoanalytic theory of voyeurism is the presence of castration anxiety, resulting from the primal fear that, anatomically, just like one's mother, sister or female child or seeing the parents during intercourse, one's penis may be cut off as punishment for engaging in a forbidden act, real or fantasised. The voyeuristic act serves to alleviate anxiety and assure the individual he has a penis. He may vicariously identify with the male as father cohabitating with the female as mother. In turn, some voyeurs also display a preference for observing women masturbate (Gebhard, Gagnon, Pomeroy and Christenson, 1965). Watching men or women masturbate may assuage masturbation anxiety and serve to help the voyeur master conflicts involving fear or guilt.

Smith (1976) has linked voyeurism to troilism. In the latter, one identifies with his wife, sex partner or prostitute as she is performing sexually with another male. Some troilists passively observe this scenario while masturbating; others feel compelled to share the sex partner, either during or after sexual intercourse. However, this anomaly is seldom encountered in clinical practice and is based on theory difficult empirically to confirm.

Contrary to the commonly held view that voyeurism is a nuisance or minor criminal offence, Yalom (1960) contends that voyeurism and exhibiting are linked to rape but also to burglary, assault and homicide. These acts may be seen as sadistic since the victim is injured or humiliated, but there is also the erotic excitement from the risk of being caught in a forbidden act and this presumably helps the voyeur to assert his masculinity (masculine protest). Rosen (1967) noted that a sadistic element may be present in voyeurs who prefer viewing women in toilets as a way of degrading them. Even so, voyeurs are not generally depicted as potentially dangerous unless they enter the premises to view a subject or draw attention to themselves while watching a victim (Smith, 1976).

Karpman (1957) claimed that the notion of voyeurism as a precursor of assaultive behaviour was wholly without foundation. Both Smith (1976) and Yalom (1960) have also challenged the inclusion in voyeurism of an interest in filth, faeces and urine (mysophilia, coprophilia and urophilia, respectively). Undoubtedly these anomalies are rare and poorly understood and, apart from the systematic studies of Gebhard and his colleagues (1965) and Langevin et al. (1985c), there are not even uncontrolled group data to link voyeurism to other criminal acts. Strictly speaking, voyeurism appears to be associated with a wide range of anomalous erotic preferences. In fact, few cases of 'pure' voyeurism were detected in a sample of over 600 sexually anomalous men (Langevin et al., 1985c). Other explanations of voyeurism are unsubstantiated and, at present, it is best to reserve judgement on classification.

Summary of voyeurism

As a preference in itself, voyeurism seems rare. On the basis of frequency alone, Langevin and his associates (1985c) were forced to use ten or more incidents of peeping as a criterion to distinguish sexually conventional men from 'voyeurs', although one incident of orgasmic peeping was sufficient to distinguish the groups. Nevertheless, voyeurism co-occurred with practically every major sexual anomaly, suggesting that, in general, voyeurism serves as a surrogate outlet for a more preferred activity. In itself, voyeurism as a pure anomaly has yet to be

Table 9.2: Summary of evidence for theories of voyeurism

Author	Motives/theory	Experimental evidence
Freud, 1953; Fenichel, 1943	Voyeurism and exhibitionism are linked	Supported but link is weak
Freund, 1976; Freund et al., 1983	Voyeurism, exhibitionism, toucheurism and rape co-occur as courtship disorders	Supported, but it is related to most sexual anomalies. Apparently a chance relation except for connection to exhibiting
Gebhard et al., 1965; Smith, 1976; Langevin et al., 1985c	Voyeurs lack satisfactory courtship skills with females	Negative. If anything they have more experience
Langevin et al., 1985c	The more habitual the peeping, the less adequate the voyeur's sex life	Negative
Yalom, 1960	Voyeurism is associated with murder, arson and burglary	Inconsistent and weak support
Fenichel, 1943	Voyeurism is sadistic	Not tested
Karpman, 1957; Yalom, 1960; Kutchinsky, 1976; Langevin et al., 1985c	Voyeurs are uninterested in strip shows; it is the forbiddenness of peeping and being undetected that is exciting	Negative
Langevin et al., 1985c	Voyeurism is a defense against aggression	They show more manifest hostility
Langevin et al., 1985c; Money, 1981	Voyeurs have a higher incidence of homosexual acts than non-voyeurs	Negative
Yalom, 1960; Smith, 1976	Voyeurs also have an interest in filth, faeces and urine (mysophilia, coprophilia, and urophilia)	Not tested
Yalom, 1960; Langevin et al., 1985c	Voyeurs have an unusual lack of curiosity	Negative. They seem normal
Langevin et al., 1985c	Voyeurism is an exclusive anomaly	Negative. Very rarely so

established. Its rarity as a primary anomaly may explain the dearth of empirical research on the subject. Overall, most of the hypotheses about voyeurism remain unsubstantiated in an empirical test (see Table 9.2) and the existence of voyeurism as a discrete clinical entity remains inconclusive.

EXHIBITIONISM

Exhibitionism is viewed as an almost exclusively male disorder; some authors underline its rarity in women (Hollender, Brown and Roback, 1977; Grob, 1985). Exhibitionism may be briefly defined as an act involving exposure of the male genitals to an unsuspecting female in public, with the intent of obtaining sexual stimulation. By definition, also, the exposer's or 'flasher's' behaviour has a driving quality to it, as conventional sexual behaviour does. Although involving no direct contact with the victim, sexual arousal is often dependent on some response from the victim.

As a sexual anomaly, exhibitionism was first described by Lasègue (1877; cited in Evans, 1970) and, even today, continues to be classified as one of the commonest sexual offences. Surveys by Rooth (1971, 1972, 1973) suggest that acts of genital exposure account for up to one-third of all sex offence convictions in Europe, Canada and the United States. To date, a multiplicity of motives has been attributed to the genital exhibitionist: narcissism; perceived inferiority; heterosocial immaturity; Oedipal attachments; castration anxiety; a hatred of women; the urge to humiliate, shock or frighten; latent homosexuality; body-image anxiety; fear of intercourse, or, conversely, desire for intercourse; and hypersexuality, amongst others. Thus far, remarkably little research has validated theory, or linked theory to any type of treatment, whether behavioural, analytic or biological. In addressing the issue of aetiology, available empirical studies will be reviewed. Most relevant literature stems from the post–1950 period, though some reference will be made to earlier studies as well.

Both the exhibitionist and the paedophile may act out with children. Unlike the paedophile, the exhibitionist may not desire physical contact, only wishing to be seen semi-naked. One may also ask why exhibitionists choose female children when they are most erotically attracted to mature females' bodies (Langevin *et al.*, 1979). Perhaps they have a greater openness to exploratory sexual activity, as noted earlier. Alternatively, the real problem may be one of impulse control. Though physically mature females are, in general, preferred, genital exposure to pubescents or even younger girls may elicit the response some exhibitionists prefer, and children may be less likely to report the incident to the police. For example, young girls may give admiring glances, the interest or surprise reactions (e.g. childlike giggle, laugh, smile) that may satisfy narcissistic needs. One 44-year-old repeat exhibitionist prone to expose to prepubescent or younger girls acknowledged that he did so because they were more naive, and less likely to recall his facial features or record his car licence. Thus younger children or pubescent girls may serve as a secondary outlet for more wary sex offenders fearful of possible arrest. If indeed so, then two suggestive answers emerge: avoiding getting caught and getting the reaction, or at least some form of attention that he wants. Older females may be unreactive or disdainful.

Several typologies of exhibitionists have been proposed, based on dynamics of the act or on personality variables. Rosen (1979) proposed, the 'simple regressive' or 'phobic-impulsive' type and Rooth (1971), the 'inhibited young male' who exposes with a flaccid penis versus the 'sexually excited person' who has an erect penis and masturbates during the act without any accompanying shame. Forgac and Michaels (1982) proposed a personality typology based on the 'pure' exhibitionist who simply exposes his genitals, and the criminal exhibitionist with a history of greater pathology and sociopathy. Given the variety of patterns and personality profiles reported in the descriptive literature (cf. Blair and Lanyon, 1981), it has proven difficult to establish the exhibitionist's motives, sexual identity or family dynamics. In clinical practice, the typologies only have restricted usefulness and generally lack validation.

Five decades ago, Christoffel (1936) proposed 'colpophobia', fear of the female genitals, as the basic fear underlying exhibitionism. Recently Kolarsky and his colleagues (Kolarsky and Madlafousek, 1978; Kolarsky, Madlafousek and Novotna, 1983) have postulated that female courtship behaviour inhibits exhibitionists sexually but her non-courtship activity does not. This may be opposite to the normal pattern. Implicit in this view is that a usual courtship sequence leading to genital union is avoided by exposing. This hypothesis that the exhibitionist, like the voyeur, is afraid of women generally, or of intercourse in particular, is commonly held despite little systematic verification. The fear shown, as Taylor (1947) noted, is of not being able to assert one's masculinity, of failing and of being impotent. Paradoxically, however, in some cases, exposers may reveal a 'divided commitment', to flashing, or masturbating to erotica, and to the consummatory sexual acts with women. Other exhibitionists may simply express a disinterest in copulatory behaviour. Our previous studies (Langevin et al., 1979; Lang et al., 1986) confirmed that, even if the female was receptive to sex relations, only about half of the exhibitionists sampled would be willing to oblige. This may represent fear or lack of interest. If Freud is correct, the exhibiting (scoptophilia) replaces the act of genital union, and one may expect marital, especially sexual, discord in the marriages of exhibitionists. However, the typical exhibitionist, in the controlled studies reviewed by Langevin (1983), had a normal dating and heterosocial/sexual experience profile. Many are married and appear to enjoy intercourse. The exhibitionist does not seem to be afraid of conventional sexual intercourse either. Freund et al. (1983) compared exhibitionists and sexually conventional men on penile reactions to the four stages of courtship. There were no group differences including reactions to conventional intercourse. It appears that some other motivation is operative in the exhibitionists' behaviour.

Narcissism

From another theoretical perspective, Karpman (1957) put forward the claim that exhibitionism is narcissistic since (1) it has elements of autoeroticism because the exhibitionist derives pleasure from seeing himself in the nude, (2) he sees himself as conferring a service or kindness in exposing, and (3) he wishes to be envied for the possession of a penis. The first point is highlighted in males with homoerotic preferences who, at times, engage in the practice of 'outdoor masturbation with no one around' (Paitich et al., 1977; Langevin et al., 1979), masturbate in front of a mirror or, in rare cases, attempt to fellate themselves. However, Langevin et al. (1979) found that exhibitionists did not especially react to their own bodies, and their narcissism was more typically interpersonal.

Characteristically, the exhibitionist desires that the females become 'turned on' or 'get a thrill' out of seeing his genitals. When asked, many exhibitionists are under the impression that the female, however old, actually enjoyed the experience. An

211

exhibitionist in therapy blatantly stated, 'Only one in twenty women ever reported it, so the rest must have enjoyed seeing my penis'.

Wishing to be envied for possession of a penis derives from the psychoanalytic theory of the unresolved Oedipal conflict and its ensuing castration anxiety that surfaces as feelings of personal (or organ) inferiority which can manifest themselves in many forms. Some focal feelings of inferiority about the penis are noteworthy. Some exhibitionists expose only with an erect penis; others appear overly concerned about penis size. In this view, exposers presumably have a strong mother fixation when, in fact, their victims are often pubescent or immature girls who do not qualify as 'mother images'. Quite possibly, some other facet of the victim may provoke memories of the mother. Both Rickles (1950) and Karpman (1957) blame the heightened sense of narcissism on mother's excessive attention to the boy's body and his genitals. Perhaps a punitive response toward masturbatory acts is desired or, alternatively, an admiring glance, reminiscent of the tender-hearted or forgiving mother, is the desired goal. Despite its appeal, Langevin et al. (1979) found little evidence for 'organ inferiority' as a motive among exhibitionists.

When the desire to be seen and the desire for intercourse are compared, the former related more to masturbation frequency during exposing and to the total frequency of exposing (Langevin et al., 1979; Lang et al., 1986). In the same studies, narcissistic needs outranked desire for coitus. In the study of Langevin et al. (1979), about half the cases said they hoped the females to whom they were exposing (usually 16 to 30 years old) would enjoy seeing the penis and about 30 per cent hoped the female would be impressed by its size. Adding corroboration, 94 per cent of exposers studied by Lang et al. (1986) hoped the female would enjoy the experience, while 80 per cent hoped the female would be impressed by penis size. The desire for intercourse was not related to total exposure frequency and was poorly related to orgasmic behaviour during exposing in repeat exhibitionists.

Exposing and Violence

Exhibitionism has been described as a substitute act of a sadistic kind by several authors (East, 1924; Allen, 1949; Harwich, 1959). The exhibitionist's attempt to induce fear or awe in the victim assigns to this anomaly a close link to sadism. As noted by Stoller (1975), this hostility reveals itself in an uncontested superiority over the victim. In its nonbrutal form, it may be expressed generally as an attempt to shock, exploit, enslave, frustrate or humiliate another person, in most cases a female. The fact itself takes place against the will of the victim. To many women, it is 'an attack, surprise, assault or violation of their dignity'. To illustrate, one exhibitionist, with prior convictions for rape and sexual assault, reflected on how he would entrap single women in bus shelters, blocking their exit while he masturbated to orgasm. In therapy, he confided that he enjoyed their look of fear and helplessness stating, 'She has no choice but to watch. I am in total control'. This may serve to build self-esteem at the victim's expense. Such behaviours may progress to take on even more punishing qualities in blatant sadism or bondage with nonconsenting partners. In two samples of exposers studied, 20 per cent of them had committed one or more violent assaults in the past (cf. Rooth, 1973; Lang et al., 1986). The blending of exposing and rape would be such an instance, illustrated by a minority of exhibitionists (Mohr, Turner and Jerry, 1964; Turner, 1964). In general, exhibitionists are non-violent but some are; and all cases should be examined for history of violence.

Almost as an antithesis, the exhibitionist has been reported to be shy, unassertive and passive, as far as relationships with females are concerned (cf. Mohr et al., 1964; McCreary, 1975). Personality theorists proffer that he is afraid of intercourse, and although he is masculine identified he cannot act in the normal fashion because of feelings of inferiority (Arieff and Rotman, 1952; McCawley, 1965; Smukler and Schiebel, 1975). The inferiority focuses on his sexuality and in particular on his penis (Witzig, 1968). Hackett (1971) found 'sexual inhibition' common with exposers who had few heterosexual contacts. Both Mohr et al. (1964) and Rooth (1973) reported that exhibitionists were timid and had difficulty in relating in a warm and genuine way. Behind this lack of assertiveness, so the theory claims, there is unexpressed anger towards women (cf. Mohr et al., 1964). All perversions, according to Stoller (1975), embody hostility as their basis.

The exhibitionist who exposes to an unwilling female may be regressing to an adolescent stage (Witzig, 1968). It proves he is aggressive and it protects him from the fact that he may be impotent in actual vaginal penetration with a female. This is why, perhaps, exposing occurs in a public place where direct sexual contact is not possible. This does not mean that the man involved may not desire intercourse, no matter how unrealistic it may seem. To illustrate, several exposers in treatment indicated they

Table 9.3: Summary of evidence for theories of exhibitionism

Author	Motives/theory	Experimental evidence
Mohr et al.,1964; Langevin et al., 1979	Paedophiliac attraction to children	Victim age range sometimes includes children, but no body contact. No inordinate penile reactions to pubescents or children
Karpman, 1957; Rickles, 1950, 1955	Exhibiting as latent homosexuality	Negative
Freud (in Jones, 1953); Macdonald, 1973; Rickles, 1950	Associated with voyeurism	A weak but positive link
Krafft-Ebing (cf. Harwich, 1959); Langevin et al., 1979	Autoeroticism	Negative
Freund et al. 1983	Exposing as a court ship disorder (fixated 'pre-tactile phase')	Weak support, but more work needed
Christoffel, 1936; Kolarsky et al., 1978, 1979	Fear of females and of intercourse	Negative
Karpman, 1957	Interpersonal narcissism (seeking admiration from females)	Mixed support
Krafft-Ebing (cf. Harwich, 1959); Allen, 1949; Langevin et al., 1979	Exposing as a sadistic act	Negative. In the rare case it is, but another erotic preference is evident
East, 1924; Langevin et al., 1979	Hypersexuality (elevated serum testosterone levels)	Negative; biochemical studies needed
McCawley, 1965; McCreary, 1975; Smukler and Schiebel, 1975; Witzig, 1968	Shyness; feelings of inferiority; passivity	Negative
Langevin et al., 1979	Feelings of inferiority about the penis	Negative

Langevin et al., 1979	They are sexually aroused by physically mature females	Positive. Similar to normal controls
Lang et al., 1986; Rooth, 1973	Gender identity disturbance	Negative, but many engage in transvestism with orgasm
Gebhard et al., 1965; Mohr et al., 1962	Marital sexual mal-adjustment	Inconclusive. Exhibiting may result from dissatisfaction and anxiety aroused by intercourse rather than a lack of sex relations
Bastani, 1976	Marriage is a prophylaxis against exposing	Negative; little systematic data to support this view

would use dirty talk (e.g. 'Do you want to fuck?') but would run off or drive away if the female made any attempt to approach them. Taylor (1947) pointed out that those exposing without orgasm are shy and unassertive. This theoretical formulation presents a paradox — the shy, passive individual will show his genitals in a public place to a stranger. Such a bold attempt to assert one's masculinity seems aggressive enough and may even be construed as aggressive, and yet it is something that the normal socially adequate man would not do even if the desire was present. Langevin *et al.* (1979) examined assertiveness in exhibitionists and controls by using a variety of measurement methods and concluded that there is no evidence to support the notion that exhibitionists are unassertive or afraid of intercourse.

Summary of exhibitionism

Though the experimental evidence is inconclusive, Table 9.3 provides a summary of what we believe are the key motives and theories in the study of genital exhibitionism.

TOUCHEURISM AND FROTTAGE

There is very little literature on toucheurism and frottage *per se* and it is rare that these behaviours occur as a fixed erotic preference in their own right (Langevin, 1983). Frottage is rubbing against an unknown female, often with the genitals, whereas toucheurism involves more active use of the hands on the victim. Many sexually normal men cannot avoid touching or rubbing female strangers in the crowded transit system. Some sexually anomalous men we have seen, might selectively ride the subway at rush hours for the opportunities afforded to have 'innocent' or 'accidental' sexual contact with an attractive female. As with voyeurism, the line between normal and deviant is difficult to define. Sexually normal men may react to opportunities provided for toucheurism and frottage but they usually do not actively seek out situations to do so, whereas toucheurs do.

Toucheurism involving female strangers in *lonely* or *isolated* places may reflect an attempted rape aborted by the offender's own fears or inexperience, or by an unexpected reaction of the victim. A convicted 29-year-old rapist noted that he had engaged in exhibitionism and toucheurism. He did this when he was younger and uncertain about exactly what he wanted to do sexually. Exhibitionism was tried in the hope that the female would want to have sex with him. When this did not work, he became more active and grabbed a stranger's breast in the street late at night. When she screamed, he fled. In a later encounter when he repeated the 'toucheurism', the frightened female did not do anything and was raped. This case shows an expected theoretical association of courtship disorders predicted by Freund *et al.* (1983, 1984) but the exhibitionism and toucheurism were transitory and non-orgasmic. They resulted from inexperience and curiosity. One may also say the same about homosexual acts, voyeurism or toucheurism in normal heterosexual men. Because surrogate or exploratory behaviours such as toucheurism occur in men who present with a sexually anomalous preference such as rape, theorists attempt to link the unusual behaviours in a causal way. Unless a sound criterion of erotic preference is used, such attempts may lead to confusion both in understanding the etiology of the sexual anomaly and in clinical practice. In the case of toucheurism, it remains to be demonstrated that it is anything more than a surrogate for other more desired behaviour. Our previous studies (Langevin, 1983; Langevin *et al.*, 1985a) suggest that the most frequent association of toucheurism is with sexually aggressive behaviour and, if it is the only behaviour presented clinically, careful scrutiny of the individual's history of violence should be undertaken.

Toucheurism may also occur in the mentally retarded man who

has normal sexual desires but little restraint over his impulses and little concern for the inappropriate social context of such acts. For example, one of our clients, a 26-year-old retarded man, would approach women in a busy shopping centre, smile and say 'Hello!' If they smiled back and said 'Hello!', he considered them 'his girlfriend' and promptly touched their breasts.

The tactile stage of courtship represents both a greater degree of sexual arousal than the pretactile stage and it is a signal for permission to proceed to even more intimate personal contact. For the sexually aggressive male, particularly with frightened or submissive women, it may signal that he can get away with rape or sexually sadistic acts.

SEXUAL AGGRESSION AND RAPE

Rape is legally defined as vaginal penetration of a nonconsenting female by the male offender. It is associated by laymen with advancing armies or with desire for 'normal intercourse' and only involves an issue of consent. The frequent association of alcohol and rape (see Rada, 1978) suggests disinhibition of normal impulses. Feminist writers such as Brownmiller (1975) suggest that rape is part of the normal male's repertoire: 'It is the means by which all men keep all women in a state of constant fear'. Groth and Birnbaum (1979) support such a point of view, claiming that rape is always an aggressive act and never a sexual one. Anger and power over the victim are seen as the dominant motives.

More conservative writers (Freund, 1976; Rada, 1978; Langevin et al., 1985a) propose that rape is associated with a continuum from purely sexual desire through purely aggressive. In our clinical contacts with such individuals, we have had the opportunity to see cases in whom transitions occurred. To illustrate, a 35-year-old, well-socialised and non-criminal man came to our clinic because of his concern for escalating violence in his sexual behaviour. Initially he had sought out prostitutes for what he described as 'rough sex', that is, intercourse with bondage and lack of concern for his partner's comfort. This progressed to slapping and punching the prostitutes but again with intercourse and orgasm. The final stage that concerned him was paying large sums to prostitutes to tie them up and beat them close to death. He was sexually aroused and spent solely by the beating without orgasm. If one saw this patient in the earlier stage, one could theorise that a sexual motive was operative but if he were seen in the last stage, aggression could be considered the primary motive. In fact, a progression was noted. In any case, there have been very few systematic sexological investigations of sexually aggressive men and most empirical studies have been reported over the past ten years or so.

Following Gene Abel (Abel, Barlow, Blanchard and Guild, 1977), we have employed the term 'sexual aggression' to encompass all forms of forced body contact with unwilling women. This label includes rape but vaginal penetration is not a necessary requirement. Selkin (1975) noted that about half of the sexually aggressive men in his study did not attempt vaginal penetration but instead demanded oral or anal sex, which may be just as traumatising to the victim as forced vaginal intercourse.

Typically, in the case of many sexually anomalous men, there is no lack of an appropriate and consenting partner for sexual intercourse. Many sexual aggressives are married; in fact, they appear comparable in marital status to their age group in the community at large. Thus deprivation is not at question. It therefore seems unlikely that they would attempt to rape and face possible incarceration if deprivation were the motive for their rape. Two explanations for their behaviour are afforded by psychopathy and sexual sadism.

The term psychopathy has had many meanings and it is difficult to identify reliably. It is often confused with 'criminal tendencies'. About 40 per cent of rapists are labelled 'psychopaths' (Rada, 1978). Many more have a long criminal history involving theft, break-and-enter, and common assault on men in addition to their marker sexual crimes. Half are drinking at the time of their offences and about a third are chronic alcoholics. Violence pervades their background so that, even if they did not lack moral standards, aggressiveness would be a way of life for them, i.e. they are part of a 'subculture of violence' (Rada, 1978). Their lifestyle represents the anomie one sees during wartime when rape by 'normal men' may occur. Thus these antisocial individuals, seen during peacetime, take what they want — they steal, they indulge in alcohol and drugs and they rape. Since the psychopath does not incorporate social norms and mores, why should he be expected to incorporate sexual patterns of behaviour? However, psychopathy, by itself, cannot explain all sexually aggressive acts, otherwise all rapists would be psychopaths. Many rapists show preferences for sexually anomalous behaviour.

Rape appears to be a theft; it is so close to conventional sexual acts but it is stolen. A number of phallometric studies have shown that response to depiction of 'forced intercourse' is a good predictor of rape. Abel *et al.* (1977) contrasted sexual aggressives with other sexually anomalous men on penile tumescence responses to audiotaped descriptions of rape and consenting intercourse. The two groups did not differ in reactions to intercourse but rapists reacted more to rape stimuli. Abel *et al.* computed a 'rape index', which was the ratio of reactions to rape versus reactions to intercourse. Rapists had larger rape indices and their scores were correlated with degree of force used in the actual offences. These interesting results were replicated and extended with design improvements by others (Barbaree, Marshall and Lanthier, 1979; Quinsey *et al.*, 1981; Quinsey and Chaplin, 1982). When more refinements and controls were added, the effects reported by Abel were reduced or disappeared in some cases. In our own work (Langevin *et al.*, 1985a), rapists and non-violent non-sex offenders were compared on penile volume changes to audiodescriptions of rape, consenting intercourse, non-sexual assault and neutral or non-sexual non-violent stimuli. Rapists and controls did not differ but they all reacted similarly, and more so, to rape and consenting intercourse than to assault and neutral stimuli. The rape index did not correlate with reliably rated degree of force in the offences. Some other factors seemed important in rape. The rape index is presently considered controversial and experimental.

The fact that sex is stolen and that a stranger usually is being forced may provide the exciting elements for a sexually anomalous man, such as a sadist. We have also examined the Clarke Sex History Questionnaire in three separate studies (Langevin *et al.*, 1985a,c and unpublished observations). The results were surprising. Though sadism is considered a rare feature of rape, we found that 45 per cent of the 91 cases to date satisfied DSM-3 criteria for sadism. They were aroused to controlling and dominating females, witnessing the fear, terror and discomfort of their victims, torturing and, in some cases, killing them in a frenzy of excitement. Mutilation and, in rarer cases, cannibalism occurred.

Up to a quarter of the rapists dressed in female clothes and masturbated (transvestism). This is not in keeping with the popular stereotype of the sexual aggressive as a 'macho man'. The transvestism occurred in both sadistic and non-sadistic sexual aggressives and appeared mainly as a fetishistic attraction to the female clothes, usually to undergarments. However, the sadists as a group were significantly different statistically in showing signs of feminine gender identity or ambivalence on the Freund Gender Identity Scale (Freund *et al.*, 1977). Such a result would be expected more from trans-sexual or homosexual men. In fact, we are aware of two convicted rapists who are seeking sex reassignment surgery to become women.

Table 9.4: Summary of evidence for theories of rape and sexual aggression

Author	Motives/theory	Experimental evidence
Freund, 1976; Barbaree *et al.*, 1979; Holstrom and Burgess, 1980	Force is essential to rapists' sexual arousal	Authors are divided in their opinions. Rapist may be aroused *in spite of* woman's distress or he may elicit fear and pain for his sexual gratification
Groth and Birnbaum, 1979	Rape is not sexual. It is a pseudosexual act addressing issues of power more than passion	A political issue that may not be resolvable empirically. In spite of face valid evidence of sexual excitement and vaginal penetration it is argued that the act is *not* sexual. It is difficult to know what would qualify as 'purely sexual'
Levine and Keonig, 1980; Langevin *et al.*, 1985a, d	Rapists are sexually ignorant and have no understanding of sexual arousal	Negative. Objective tests of sexual knowledge show rapists to be well informed
Levine and Keonig, 1980; Langevin *et al.*, 1985a, d	Rapists hate women	Evidence is mixed. Attitudes to women, in unpublished data, suggest they are conventional. However, they do tend to be hostile in general
Rada, 1978; Langevin, *et al.*, 1985a, d	Mothers of rapists are rejecting, over-controlling and punitive but also seductive and overprotective	Mothers seem only strict and unaffectionate just like fathers are. However, only one controlled study is available. Both parents are often alcoholics.

Rada, 1978; Langevin, *et al.*, 1985a,d	Rapists had excessive handling of genitals as a child. They are often sexually abused themselves	Negative
Rada, 1978; Langevin, *et al.*, 1983, 1985a	Rape is a defence against homosexuality	Negative
Rada *et al.*, 1976, 1978, 1983; Langevin *et al.*, 1985a, d	Sex hormones play an important role in rapists' behaviour	Mixed results but mostly positive. More work clearly warranted. Other hormones than testosterone may be important
Williams, 1969; Ruff, 1976; Langevin *et al.*, 1985a	Sexual violence is associated with brain pathology, especially of the temporal lobes	Positive findings but more work needed. Sadists especially may show brain pathology
Brittain, 1970; Langevin *et al.*, 1985a, d	Sadistic rapists have 'effeminate' tinge/ feminine gender identity	Positive. Most seem indifferent to gender but some are feminine identified

Other findings suggest that brain pathology, endocrine abnormalities, substance abuse and a history of violent socialisation played some role in the sexual aggressive's behaviour, both for the sadistic and the non-sadistic types (cf. Langevin *et al.*, 1985a). The non-sadists showed greater levels of penile responsiveness than either sadists or controls to the same erotica in the laboratory. In conjunction with significantly elevated levels of adrenal androgens and a trend to higher levels of testosterone, the higher level of penile reactivity presents a partial biological explanation of why they rape. We know many are 'psychopaths'. With the added biological pressure to higher levels of sexual responsiveness, the rapist becomes a psychopath with a special sexual need, which leads to his particular sexual crimes.

Summary of rape and sexual aggression

Table 9.4 offers many more questions about sexually aggressive men than it answers. Recent work suggests that rapists may be more unusual than originally thought but much more replicative research is required for even a minimally satisfactory understanding of this sexual anomaly.

DISCUSSION

The courtship disorders show overlapping features; still their uniqueness is more noteworthy. Table 9.5 shows what we believe are the key factors and hypotheses in the anomalies examined in this report. The dearth of studies of voyeurism or toucheurism and frottage indicate the rarity of the behaviours as anomalies in their own right. They appear usually not to reflect erotic preferences *per se* but serve as surrogates for other acts, curiosity or, in the case of toucheurism, incomplete acts of rape.

Exhibitionism stands out as a narcissistic behaviour in which sexual gratification is derived from being watched and, by presumption, being admired. Transvestism also serves a need for admiration but, as in the case of rape, fetishism plays a role, usually earlier in the developmental stage of the anomaly.

Table 9.5: Features of the courtship disorders

Voyeurism
Most often a surrogate for a wide variety of sexually conventional and
  anomalous behaviour, especially for exhibitionism.
Not usually violent.
Masculine gender identity.

Exhibitionism
Primarily a narcissistic act in which admiration by a female is desired but
  without body contact.
Voyeurism is often a surrogate act in lieu of opportunities to expose;
  the male may imagine the female seen is exposing with erotic intent.
Not usually violent.
Masculine gender identity.

Toucheurism and frottage
Often associated with, or precursor of, rape, or may be linked to attempted
  or aborted rape.
May occur as inappropriate albeit 'normal' behaviour in mentally defective
  or socially inadequate men.
Rare as an exclusive sexual anomaly.
May be violent.
Gender identity uncertain.
Rarely presents as a preferred sexual outlet.

Sexual aggression and sadism
Desire for control of victim; her terror and bodily injury are prominent.
Sadism may be more common than suggested in uncontrolled studies.
Crossdressing and fetishism are noteworthy.
Disturbance in the sexual arousal mechanism ('hypersexuality') may be
  important in some cases.
Gender disturbance in sadistic rapists; they are feminine identified,
  ambivalent, or indifferent rather than masculine identified.
Violence common in sexual and non-sexual situations.

However, the gender identity of exhibitionists is masculine and they are not especially prone to rape, although some do engage in other forms of violence.

Sexual aggression, in our research, has been found to be more sadistic than generally suggested and it is not especially a desire for sexual intercourse as much as a sexual anomaly characterised by a need to control, humiliate and injure the victims. That is not to say rape is aggressive and not sexual. Rather sexual pleasure comes from an anomalous fusion of sexual desire and aggression. The rapists in general show sexual anomalies and the sadists show some gender disturbance.

The attempts to link the courtship disorders have shown that the association is weak. In fact, other sexual behaviour, such as transvestism, seems important but has been almost entirely overlooked. Perhaps this reflects a heterosexualcentric bias evident in sex research (Langevin, 1985). We see sexual anomalies as deviations from the conventional norm. We see these men wanting heterosexual intercourse but they are thwarted in their goals because of socialisation or personality deficits. We also assume what is masculine and feminine without benefit of empirical investigation. Exhibiting and rape are considered, of course, masculine and aggressive. The extent of transvestism, whatever its purpose in these groups, may therefore be overlooked. Examiners may not even ask about transvestism. It seems that our preconceptions need to be challenged and a thorough sexual history taken for each sexually anomalous person.

If we examine two questions, our profound ignorance about sexual anomalies becomes apparent: What are the *stimuli* (person's age, sex, etc.) that sexually arouse the courtship-disordered men? What sexual *responses* do they wish to engage in (expose only, injure, have intercourse, etc.)? Very few studies have attempted to map the stimulus-response matrix (Langevin, 1983) of sexually preferred behaviours and there are many gaps in our knowledge as a consequence. This has an important bearing on clinical practice. An attempt to determine erotic preference patterns will bring order to a chaotic clinical picture. When a man has exposed to 9-year-old boys and girls and also shows a history of cross-dressing and of rape, one must make sense of the behaviour. Until more is known, clinicians will remain puzzled. However, evaluating sexual preferences will be helpful (Langevin, 1983).

A psychological aetiology has frequently been assumed for the courtship disorders but biological explanations in terms of endocrine-developmental or of neurological factors have been neglected. Rada *et al.* (1976, 1983) and Langevin *et al.* (1985a) have found endocrine differences in rapists and controls, and Langevin *et al.* (1985a) have found that brain pathology, especially in the temporal lobes of sadistic rapists, may be important. Biological variables appear important and much more attention should be directed to these questions.

We propose here that there are two basic sexual anomalies within the domain of the courtship disorders — exhibitionism and sexual aggression. Voyeurism is a subclinical entity, misconstrued as primary and rarely seen as a sexual anomaly that stands alone. Usually it is a substitute for more desired primary sexual desires and it is seen to co-occur with almost every possible sexual anomaly. Like fantasies, it may be useful as an indicator of more active sexual desires such as rape or paedophilia, but in itself, it may be no more than a normal precursor of other sexual acts. Exhibitionism seems primarily motivated by interpersonal narcissism, a desire to be admired specifically in a sexual context. This desire may extend to younger females and appear paedophilic in nature, or even to males and seem homosexual. However the exhibitionist primarily desires the adult female and he would most like her to admire him and expose herself with automasturbation. His desire for admiration may be expressed in transvestism in which dressing as a female is used to stimulate the fantasy of being admired sexually. Exhibitionism is an anomalous response tendency and the stimulus conditions eliciting it may become quite diffuse, depending on the individual and his circumstances. Thus children and even men may occasionally be the victims of indecent exposure.

Obscene calls and toucheurism are also surrogate acts for a range of sexual needs, although toucheurism may lead to rape or injury of a victim. Sexual aggression should be scrutinised for the distinction between sadistic and non-sadistic rape. The sadist may or may not appear dangerous. He may be most preoccupied with control and entrapment. However, some, and they will not always reveal it, have a morbid interest in the injury and death of their victims. Obviously, identification of this group is important. The non-sadist may have a problem of managing his high sex drive. This is frequently complicated by substance abuse, antisocial tendencies or non-sexual aggressiveness, as well as possible brain pathology or endocrine abnormalities. We have come a long way from the earlier conceptualisations of the courtship disorders but it is clear that we have only begun to understand these sexual anomalies.

REFERENCES

Abel, G.G., Barlow, D.H., Blanchard, E.B. and Guild, D. (1977) 'The components of rapists' sexual arousal.' *Arch. Gen. Psychiatry, 34*, 895–903

Allen, C. (1949) *Sexual Perversions and Abnormalities*. London: Oxford University Press

Arieff, A.J. and Rotman, D.B. (1952) 'One hundred cases of indecent exposure.' *J. Nerv. Ment. Dis., 96*, 523–38

Barbaree, H.E., Marshall, W.L. and Lanthier, R.D. (1979) 'Deviant sexual arousal in rapists.' *Behav. Res. Ther., 17*, 215–22

Bastani, J.B. (1976) 'Treatment of male genital exhibitionism.' *Compr. Psychiatry, 17*, 769–74

Blair, C.D. and Lanyon, R.I. (1981) 'Exhibitionism: etiology and treatment.' *Psychological Bulletin, 89*, 439–63

Brittain, R. (1970). The sadistic murderer. *Medicine, Science and The Law, 10*, 198–207

Brownmiller, S. (1975) *Against Our Will: Men, Women and Rape*, New York: Simon & Schuster

Christoffel, H. (1936) 'Exhibitionism and exhibitionists.' *International Journal of Psychoanalysis, 17*, 321–45

East, W.H. (1924) 'Observations on exhibitionism.' *Lancet, ii*, 370–5

Evans, D.R. (1970) 'Exhibitionism.' In *Symptoms of Psychopathology* (ed. C.G. Costello), New York: John Wiley

Fenichel, O. (1943) 'The scoptophilic instinct and identification.' *Int. J. Psychoanal., 18*, 6–34

Forgac, G.E. and Michaels, E.J. (1982) 'Personality characteristics of two types of male exhibitionists.' *J. Abnorm. Psychol., 91*, 287–93

Freud, S. (1953) *Three Essays on the Theory of Sexuality* (1901–1905). The standard edition of the complete psychological works of Sigmund Freud. (vol. 7). London: Hogarth Press

Freud, K. (1976) 'Diagnosis and treatment of forensically significant anomalous erotic preferences.' *Canadian Journal of Criminology and Corrections, 18*, 181–9

Freund, K., Langevin, R., Satterberg, J. and Seiner, B. (1977) 'Extension of the gender identity scale for males.' *Arch. Sex. Behav., 6*, 507–19

Freund, K., Scher, H. and Hucker, S. (1983) 'The courtship disorders.' *Arch. Sex. Behav., 12*, 369–79

Freund, K., Scher, H. and Hucker, S. (1984a) 'The courtship disorders: a further investigation.' *Arch. Sex. Behav., 13*, 133–9

Freund, K., Scher, H., Racansky, I.G., Campbell, K. and Heasman, G. (1984b) 'Males who are prone to commit rape.' Unpublished manuscript, University of Toronto

Gebhard, P.H., Gagnon, J.H., Pomeroy, W.B. and Christenson, C.V. (1965) *Sex Offenders*. New York: Harper & Row

Grob, C.S. (1985) 'Single case study: female exhibitionism.' *J. Nerv. Ment. Dis.*, *173*, 253–6

Groth, A.N. and Birnbaum, H.J. (1979) *Men who Rape*. New York: Plenum Press

Hackett, T.P. (1971) 'The psychotherapy of exhibitionists in a court clinic setting.' *Seminars in Psychiatry*, *3*, 297–306

Harwick, A. (1959) *Aberrations of Sexual Life: After the Psychopathia Sexualis of Dr. R. v. Krafft-Ebing*. London: Staples Press

Hollender, M.H., Brown, C.W. and Roback, H.B. (1977) 'Genital exhibitionism in women.' *Am. J. Psychiatry*, *134*, 436–8

Holmstrom, L.L. and Burgess, A.W. (1980) 'Sexual behaviour of assailants during reported rapes.' *Arch. Sex. Behav.*, *9*, 427–39

Jones, E. (1953). *Sigmund Freud: Life and work*. London: Hogarth Press

Karpman, B. (1957) *The Sexual Offender and his Offences*. Washington, D.C.: Julian Press

Kinsey, A.C., Pomeroy, W.B. and Martin, C.E. (1984) *Sexual Behavior in the Human Male*. Philadelphia: W.B. Saunders

Kolarsky, A. and Madlafousek, J. (1983) 'The inverse role of preparatory erotic stimulation in exhibitionists: Phallometric studies.' *Arch. Sex. Behav.*, *12*, 123–48

Kolarsky, A., Madlafousek, J. and Novotna, V. (1978) 'Stimuli eliciting sexual arousal in males who offend adult women: An experimental study.' *Arch. Sex. Behav.*, *7*, 79–87

Kutchinsky, B. (1976) 'Deviance and criminality: The case of a voyeur in a peeper's paradise.' *Diseases of the Nervous System*, *37*(3), 145–51

Lang, R.A., Langevin, R., Checkley, K.L. and Pugh, G. (1986) 'Genital exhibitionism: narcissism or courtship disorder?' *Canadian Journal of Behavioral Science*, in press

Langevin, R. (1983) *Sexual Strands: Understanding and Treating Sexual Anomalies in Men*. Hillsdale, N.J.: Erlbaum Associates

Langevin, R. (1985) 'An overview of the paraphilias.' In *Clinical Criminology: The Assessment and Treatment of Criminal Behavior* (eds. M.H. Ben-Aron, S.J. Hucker & C.D. Webster), Toronto: M & M Graphics & Clarke Institute of Psychiatry

Langevin, R., Bain, J. *et al.* (1985a) 'Sexual aggression: constructing a predictive equation.' In *Erotic Preference, Gender Identity and Aggression in Men* (ed. R. Langevin), Hillsdale, N.J.: Erlbaum Associates.

Langevin, R., Handy, L., Paitich, D. and Russon, A.E. (1985b) 'Appendix C. Supplementary SHQ scales.' In *Erotic Preference, Gender Identity and Aggression in Men* (ed., R. Langevin), pp. 343–56, Hillsdale, N.J.: Erlbaum Associates

Langevin, R., Paitich, D., Hucker, S., Newman, S., Ramsay, G., Pope, S., Geller, G. and Anderson, C. (1979) 'The effects of assertiveness training, provera and sex of therapist in the treatment of genital exhibitionism.' *J. Behav. Ther. Exp. Psychiatry*, *10*, 275–82

Langevin, R., Paitich, D., and Russon, A.E. (1985c) 'Voyeurism: Does it predict sexual aggression or violence in general?' In *Erotic Preference, Gender Identity and Aggression in Men* (ed. R. Langevin), pp. 77–98, Hillsdale, N.J.: Erlbaum Associates.

Langevin, R., Paitich, D and Russon, A.E. (1985d). 'Are rapists sexually anomalous, aggressive or both?' In *Erotic Preference, Gender Identity and Aggression in Men* (ed. R. Langevin), pp. 17–38, Hillsdale, N.J.: Erlbaum Associates.

Lasègue, C. (1877) 'Les exhibitionistes.' *L'Union Médicale*, *23*, 709–14

Levine, S. and Koenig, J. (1980) *Why Men Rape: Interviews with Convicted Rapists.* Toronto: Macmillan

Macdonald, J. (1973) *Indecent Exposure.* Springfield, Ill.: Charles C. Thomas

McCawley, A. (1965) 'Exhibitionism and acting out.' *Compr. Psychiatry*, *6*, 396–409

McCreary, C.P. (1975) 'Personality profiles of persons convicted of indecent exposure.' *J. Clin. Psychol.*, *31*, 260–2

Malamuth, N.M. (1981) 'Rape fantasies as a function of exposure to violent sexual stimuli.' *Arch. Sex. Behav.*, *10*, 33–47

Mohr, J., Turner, R.E. and Jerry, M. (1962). 'Exhibitionism and pedophilia.' *Corrective Psychiatry and Journal of Social Therapy*, *8*, 172–86

Money, J. (1981) 'Paraphilias: Phyletic origins of erotosexual dysfunction.' *International Journal of Mental Health*, *10*, 75–109

Paitich, D., Langevin, R., Freeman, R., Mann, K. and Handy, L. (1977) 'The Clarke SHQ: A clinical sex history questionnaire for males.' *Arch. Sex. Behav.*, *6*, 421–36

Quinsey, V.L., Chaplin, T.C. and Varney, G. (1981) 'A comparison of rapists' and non-sex offenders' sexual preferences for mutually consenting sex, rape and sadistic acts.' *Behavioral Assessment*, *3*, 127–35

Quinsey, V.L. and Chaplin, T.C. (1982) 'Penile responses to nonsexual violence among rapists.' *Criminal Justice and Behavior*, *9*, 372–81

Rada, R.T. (1978) *Clinical Aspects of the Rapist.* New York: Grune & Stratton

Rada, R.T., Laws, D.R. and Kellner, R. (1976) 'Plasma testosterone levels in the rapist.' *Psychosom. Med.*, *38*, 257–68

Rada, R.T., Laws, D.R., Kellner, R., Stivastava, L. and Peake, G. (1983) 'Plasma androgens in violent and nonviolent sex offenders.' *Bull. Am. Acad. Psychiatry Law*, *11*, 149–58

Rickles, N. (1950) *Exhibitionism.* Philadelphia: Lippincott

Rooth, F.G. (1971) 'Indecent exposure and exhibitionism'. *Br. J. Hosp. Med.*, *5*, 521–33

Rooth, F.G. (1972) 'Changes in the conviction rate for indecent exposure.' *Br. J. Psychiatry*, *121*, 89–94

Rooth, F.G. (1973) 'Exhibitionism, sexual violence and paedophilia.' *Br. J. Psychiatry*, *122*, 705–10

Rosen, I. (1967) *Pathology and Treatment of Sexual Deviations.*

London: Oxford University Press

Rosen, I. (1979) 'Exhibitionism, scoptophilia and voyeurism.' In *Sexual Deviation*, 2nd edn. (ed. I. Rosen), London: Oxford University Press

Ruff, C.F., Templer, D.I. and Ayers, J.L. (1976) 'The intelligence of rapists.' *Arch. Sex. Behav.*, *5*, 327–9

Saul, L.J. (1952) 'A note on exhibitionism and scoptophilia.' *Psychoanal. Q.*, *21*, 224–6

Selkin, J. (1975) 'Rape.' *Psychology Today*, *8*, 71–6

Smith, S.R. (1976) 'Voyeurism: A review of literature.' *Arch. Sex. Behav.*, *5*(6), 585–608

Smukler, A. and Schiebel, D. (1975) 'Personality characteristics of exhibitionists.' *Diseases of the Nervous System*, *36*(11), 600–3

Stoller, R.J. (1975) *Perversion*. New York: Pantheon

Taylor, F.H. (1947) 'Observations on some cases of exhibitionism.' *Journal of Mental Science*, *93*, 631–8

Tollison, C.D. and Adams, H.E. (1979) *Sexual Disorders: Treatment, Theory, and Research*. New York: Gardner Press

Turner, R.E. (1964) 'The sexual offender.' *Canadian Psychiatric Association Journal*, *9*, 533–40

Williams, A.H. (1965) 'Rape-murder.' In *Sexual Behaviour and the Law* (ed. R. Slovender), Springfield, Ill. Charles C. Thomas

Witzig, J.S. (1968) 'The group treatment of male exhibitionists.' *Am. J. Psychiatry*, *125*, 179–85

Yalom, I. (1960) 'Aggression and forbiddenness in voyeurism.' *Arch. Gen. Psychiatry*, *3*, 305–19

10

The Sadomasochistic Contract

Christopher C. Gosselin

The study of sexual behaviour in humans differs from many other fields of psychological endeavour in that although a certain amount of information may be gleaned by direct experimentation, a great deal more data derives from clinical experience, from anecdote and case history and, thanks to today's comparative freedom of communication, from direct interview with those who need neither the clinician's modifications nor the psychoanalyst's couch. It would also seem that nowadays we are to some extent allowed to formulate some of our theories of sexuality on the basis of analogy from other areas of work: no psychologist has ever taken a group of male infants and systematically conditioned them into a later fetishistic obsession for gymslips or stiletto heels, even if Rachman and Hodgson's (1968) classic experimental induction in adult males of sexual arousal at the sight of a woman's high-heeled boot produced at least some temporary effect. Most of us thus seem content to accept, for instance, that the sexual pattern we acquire is at least partly the result of childhood conditioning, simply because we are pretty certain that people *can* be conditioned under the right circumstances.

This point is emphasised simply because although we may well recognise that our knowledge of the human sexual condition derives from the examination of data of many kinds, our individual natures and our individual psychological training almost inevitably cause us to prefer and trust some types of evidence more than others, and for reasons no doubt found in our personal case histories we may find the acceptance and even the countenance of other sources of information so difficult and so arousal-inducing that our perception of their value may become somewhat distorted.

What is more, nowhere is the danger of bias towards the preferential acceptance of one type of evidence more acute than in the study of variant sexuality. Deviation has classically been very much the stamping-ground of the psychodynamic, symbolutilising and interpretative approach so held in disdain by more statistically oriented researchers: the war between the two camps seems still to be continuing, even if the psychodynamicists seldom bother to reply to the Eysenckian hornets buzzing about their ears. Yet as far as the study of sadomasochism is concerned, any war is unfortunate, for it may interfere with our capacity to understand the variation properly. Sadomasochism is at the time of writing just beginning to come out of the closet, to be regarded as a form of sexual expression capable of giving enjoyment and amusement to the participants instead of driving them to the psychoanalyst's couch, the clinician's behavioural modification programmes or the loneliness of sexual isolation due to fear or guilt. As a result, the empiricist must beware of failing to take notice of the vast amount of non-clinical case-history material now becoming available from contented practitioners of 's/m', and must not discard it on the grounds that it is not always structured and is often unquantifiable or otherwise intractable to statistical analysis. At the same time, those who favour the generally psychodynamic approach must beware of failing to realise the implications of conclusions based on data stemming from those who find their alternative mode of sexual expression less a guilty torment and more a lot of fun.

One immediate advantage in adopting this wider approach to data-gathering in the study of variant sexual behaviour in general and sadomasochism in particular is (or has been for this writer at any rate) the realisation that a particular variant pattern is not entirely a once-and-for-all process that is completed entirely in childhood. True, some predispositions towards some form of sex variancy may well exist even before we are born, and the experiences of childhood and adolescence that we undergo doubtless do much to fixate the sexual preferences or obsessions that we shall later show. One only has to observe or be told of the numerous, sometimes almost pathetic examples of males (less than females, as we shall see later) who, however foolish they appear, allow themselves to be taken through some individualistic ritual of pain and humiliation in order to achieve sexual pleasure, to appreciate how powerful are the influences that have set the sadomasochistic pattern on its particular victim.

It is nevertheless also becoming more evident that these predispositions and pre-adult learning experiences are not all that produce the sadomasochist's behaviour. The greater tolerance shown by society and by individuals of both sexes has come to mean that s/m (a convenient shorthand) rituals are not limited to obliging ladies of pleasure giving 'special services', but are also performed between a fair number of very loving couples who realise that, for them at least, there are more paths to sexual pleasure than those listed in conventional marriage guidance handbooks. Society's tolerance seems surprisingly well marked, even if unevenly distributed. Comedians make jokes about s/m on television, rock groups and dancers appear on the small screen in s/m-symbolising costumes — sometimes even complete with whips and manacles — and one can even buy sadomasochistic-themed greetings cards to send to appropriate friends. More aware people, even if they are themselves totally uninterested in the world of s/m, allow that it seems less a nameless perversion carried out by sex-crazed psychopaths and their drug-numbed victims and more one of those vaguely odd activities that turn some people on and not others.

As a result, one of the answers to the question, 'Why do some people enjoy these practices?' can be seen to lie not in the past but in the present and future, in that it is for them a forward-looking strategy for pleasure, an expected source of arousal and an immediate means of giving and receiving sexual excitement of a unique kind.

Before developing such a premise, however, it would seem as well to describe something of the realities, i.e. not merely the fantasies depicted in relevant pornography, involved in sadomasochistic ritual, even if only to enable researchers to be able to select useful (as opposed to merely naive) hypotheses to test, while therapists of all types may profit by appreciating the sex lives of appropriate clients and thus avoid the looks of uncomprehending amazement and the tactless verbal blunders that, according to some clients, sometimes mar the interaction between them and those to whom they may turn for enlightenment about their condition. Admittedly, therapists are these days far less likely to have to deal with direct sexual sadomasochism, for protagonists are seldom interested in therapeutic help, except perhaps when that help takes the form of a Berneian permission to be themselves. More sadomasochists nowadays accept themselves as what they are, and it is indeed this greater self-acceptance that has enabled researchers to learn with more certainty of their world. We have come far (except perhaps in the minds of those who hold that sexual variation is *always* the outer symbol of psychopathological conflict) from the writings of a famous psychiatrist, whose reference I shall omit to spare his blushes, wherein he gives as his opinion fifteen years ago that 'without exception, those who possess such sexual patterns are at the root deeply unhappy people'. Perhaps any who still echo this view should visit the London night-club that opened about two years ago to cater exclusively for a fetishistic and sadomasochistic clientele and watch the hundred or so people of all ages, walks of life and sexual orientations chattering, laughing and joking, dancing and occasionally going through minor s/m rituals for their (and everybody else's) pleasure: in such a way they might realise that if such people are deeply unhappy, they either have an admirable defence mechanism or coping strategy, or the psychiatrist has a somewhat unusual definition of unhappiness.

BEHAVIOUR

A circumspect description of the behaviours that may be involved in an s/m session may not come amiss, because to both lay-people and psychologists it is sometimes difficult to believe that such behaviours occur in reality. The first and most universally known facet of an s/m ritual is that of beating, the intensity of which can be minimal or severe and the duration equally variable. It is nevertheless worth mentioning that the ritual may sometimes go on for some time: for those whose experience of punishment is limited to 'six of the best', it may come as a surprise to learn that an s/m beating is sometimes more like two hundred strokes, administered with a variety of instruments (apart from hand-spanking) ranging from warm-up paddle or tawse through cane or riding-crop to cat-o'-nine-tails or birch. The whip beloved of pornographic fiction is actually less often used, largely because its effects and landing areas are unpredictable and it is of course awkward to use in a smallish room. Strokes are interspersed with pauses during which the instrument of 'discipline' is drawn softly around the target area to sensitise it and create an anticipatory effect, whilst a verbal commentary dwelling on what is going to happen, the 'reasons' for the treatment or the sexual aspects of the ritual are used to the same effect. The action starts gently and works up in intensity, thus suggesting that pain tolerance increases with arousal level.

In using the word 'pain', however, it may be as well to point out that to some recipients the stimulus does not appear to be felt as pain in the proper sense of the word, but apparently resembles more the exhilarating effect produced by the birch-twig stimulation favoured by many sauna addicts. Such a contention is apparently more favoured by those who enjoy their beating rituals at a comparatively modest level.

Pain stimuli can of course be administered by other methods such as pricking or piercing, burning, pinching (the use of small spring clamps on male or female nipples seems popular) or the like, but a catalogue of methods is unnecessary here. The surprising thing is that this pain can reach quite epic proportions and still be welcomed: a case was brought to my attention in which the initials of one male masochist's 'mistress' had been branded by her on his buttocks as a mark of his submissiveness to her. For students of Eysenckian personality dimensions, her Extraversion and Neuroticism scores were unremarkable, but her Psychoticism score was 8 — approximately three times the normal score for a woman of her 23 years of age.

The second facet of sadomasochism is known as bondage, wherein the masochistic partner is tied up or restricted in various positions and by various means according to the protagonist's tastes. Of course, minor tie-and-tease activities are carried out from time to time by many sex partners without any colouring of sadomasochism being formally involved. S/m bondage is, however, very much more intense, and although the stressful positions beloved of s/m pornography are seldom indulged in for long except by some aficionados, complete immobilisation is commonplace and is frequently completed by the use of gag and/ or blindfold. Bondage rituals that are unassociated with other elements of s/m often puzzle those not involved, for it is hard to see what either partner gets out of them once restriction has been completed: there seems little one can do to continue the ritual and little for the 'victim' to experience beyond the continuing feeling of immobilisation. As a result, bondage is generally allied with some of the activities previously described, and the submissive partner is thus tied up and then beaten or otherwise stimulated.

There is nevertheless one form of the bondage-alone ritual that for some time apparently extends its pleasure for the submissive partner at least — and in some cases for the dominant partner as well, who gets visual and aural pleasure from witnessing the submissive's situation. This variation, known generally as 'occlusion', virtually always uses fetishistic material or garments in which the submissive is tightly swathed from head to foot, partially (though clearly not entirely) restricting breathing and denying sight, speech and hearing to the submissive whilst restricting smell and taste to the material involved: the subject will sometimes contentedly spend anything up to six hours at a stretch in what addicts of the process often term 'meditation'.

For psychologists and medical therapists this practice is of broader interest because of its resemblance to the sensory deprivation experiments inaugurated by Heron, Doane and Scott (1956), wherein subjects frequently developed high-intensity fantasies and hallucinations during their period of restricted sensation. The practice also bears resemblance to the carbon dioxide therapy once popular in some clinical situations, in which a controlled mixture of oxygen and carbon dioxide is administered to the patient and the consequent partial reduction of oxygen to the brain released material from the deeper recesses of the patient's mind. An intriguing but admittedly unproven parallel with these phenomena also exists in the numerous cases of pilots in high-flying aircraft whose oxygen supply is faulty and who consequently abandon any sense of responsibility and begin babbling fantasies quite freely. It may even be worthwhile citing a folk custom among Eskimos entitled 'flying to the moon', which occurs on the marriage night: before the groom progresses to the nuptial bed, his friends dress him in his parka with the hood up and hang him by the top of the hood from the ceiling. This is actually more comfy than it sounds, almost like being in a parachute harness: however, the hood almost closes round his head giving rise to oxygen and sensory deprivation, and the result is a sense of exaltation and considerable fantasy production — generally of an erotic nature because of the situation in which the ritual is enacted.

From this it is tempting to postulate that occlusion bondage is just one more way of releasing inhibition, with an added power derived from the fact that the occlusive material is generally the submissive's favourite and that the ritual is geared to the type of fantasy involved. Couple this with preparedness and expectancy effects, and the ritual is almost certain to have great power.

The last important facet of sadomasochistic behaviour is the humiliation aspect, under which may be subsumed the whole range of boot-licking, crawling, abuse-accepting and even scatophagic behaviour, or indeed anything that might be included in the more general category of forcing someone to do something that at least in principle they should not wish to do. Allied to this is a more mental approach, which may be carried out by pouring scorn or abuse upon the partner or by dressing him or her in a belittling costume in readiness for the performance of menial tasks. Alternatively, no physical or mental derogation or attack is involved: instead, acts of lovemaking are carried out via a quasi-formal ritual of commands and obeisances in which the enjoyment of one partner is at least in theory assured because he or she gets exactly what is desired, whilst the other partner obtains pleasure through fulfilling those desires.

This set of behaviours is of course interesting on two counts: first, we see its general acceptability in a limited form in the demonstration of courtly love manifested by the romantic poet or lover, especially of former times. Such a character freely proclaims his enslavement to his mistress, kneeling humbly before her, kissing her dainty foot, worshipping the ground she walks on and pleading (rather half-heartedly, let it be noticed) for release from the bonds of love that she has set upon him. Secondly, in many cases it appears that this almost symbolic sadomasochism is the only type of behaviour ever enjoyed by some couples. There are no beatings, no restrictions: the submissive partner is dominated only as the result of what the other commands.

Gentle or severe, however, the behaviour outlined is of course unusual, especially when it is remembered that the rituals involved are frequently conducted between loving partners in the course of, or by way of, lovemaking. The turn-on is in fact a matter of mutual activity rather than isolative fantasy, the ritual role-playing being intermingled with tenderness and reassurance. It is indeed this sense of caring, affection and trust that often permeates private *and even some professional* s/m relationships that leads one to the concept that however cruel, violent and one-sided the behaviour might seem, it is in fact a contract between the participants to which both agree.

This idea of an equable contract was well made by Smirnoff

(1969), who by analysing Sacher-Masoch's novel *Venus in Furs* together with parallel activities in Sacher-Masoch's own life demonstrates that a sadomasochistic ritual has to be an 'equable' partnership, for the last thing that the masochist wants is to be the victim of a really cruel person. The main theme of the novel is that of a man, Severin Kusiemski, becoming the sexual slave of Wanda von Dunajew, who beats and abuses him in a real but ritualistic way after Severin has offered her a contract delivering himself totally into her power. At the end of the story, Wanda's lover takes over the flogging while Wanda leaves the scene for ever. The lover takes his role seriously, but the flogging does not elicit any pleasure in Severin although theoretically he could not dream of a more satisfyingly masochistic situation than to be beaten by his triumphant rival: all Severin feels, however, is disgust, dismay and a clearly non-sexual humiliation. 'Because the lover fully and wholeheartedly enjoys his activity as tormentor, he cannot satisfy the masochist because he is not part of the real contract,' Smirnoff states. He goes on:

> Severin pretends that he has been cured by an excess of torture — an absurd claim coming from a masochist. He may be cured, not through punishment, but because he has been fooled in the process by Wanda's betrayal. What cures Severin is not the lashing, but Wanda's derisive laughter as she leaves the scene. She tells Severin that she has betrayed him by rejecting the treaty which stipulated that the executioner must be his victim.

Such a quotation, the interpretations of which are more by logic than from evidence, would be of limited value had its viewpoint not been much agreed with by many of the masochistic subjects studied in Gosselin and Wilson (1980). The consensus there seemed to be that where a working s/m relationship exists between two people (and, let it be said, it may not exist continuously, but may merely be invoked when both partners agree to play it, the interaction being at other times perfectly conventional) then both partners tacitly set out limiting conditions to that relationship, stating in effect, 'I wish to take a certain role involving activities X, Y and Z, and I would like you to promise to cooperate.'

Empirical studies of the s/m *relationship* — as distinct from studies of s/m behaviour — are virtually non-existent. It might be dangerous to extrapolate too much from Spengler (1977) to general statements, largely because the data was obtained from answering contact magazine advertisements, which by their very nature are searching for new contacts, presumably not being content with what relationships they may or may not have already. Such comment as exists concerning the relationship aspect derives largely from psychoanalytic writing: Panken (1967), for example, sees the variation in terms of 'interacting or relational reciprocities wherein the underlying motivation and intrapsychic dynamics differ for each partner', whilst Avery (1977) also infers that relationship is all-important, stating that 'sadomasochism is conducted under strict rules: both parties know precisely what the bursting point is: they believe that a wish for affection is equivalent to weakness or craven dependence'. One may doubt whether the last statement is necessarily true in every case; the idea of an affectionate relationship lying at the heart of apparently cruel behaviour must remain, even if one were only to take as evidence the number of marital couples who appear at s/m parties or visit the night-club previously mentioned. One must not judge the relationship by the s/m behaviour involved' — though I freely admit that after researching this topic for some years, I am still amazed when the gasps, hisses and real tears of the masochistic partner and the seemingly cold disdain and/or aggressive behaviour of the sadist change to smiles, soft words and caresses between bouts of action.

For this is the first fact that one must accept about sadomasochism. There is often confusion (especially in the media) between the sexual sadist and the psychopath, yet in general — given that there will always be the odd exception — the two species could not be more different in personality terms. The hallmark of the psychopath is an inability to feel compassion, caring or tenderness, even perhaps anger and fear. In contrast, the sexual sadist feels these emotions acutely and exults in them in every interplay with his or her masochistic partner.

The *masochistic* partner, notice: not any partner. The sexual sadist does care about those with whom the interaction takes place, and would be reluctant to do anything with anyone who was not willing, if not eager, to have those things done to them. True, persuasion helps to develop a ritual, but there is nothing of the violent coercion beloved of s/m erotica and witnessed so distressingly in cases of wife-battering. Indeed, it is probably this factor that has confused many coffee-table discussions about rape, for to take by *simulated* force against *simulated* resistance is very different from rape itself, even if the two are confused in the minds of those who might probably not attempt either.

Neither in this pattern of sexual behaviour is it by any means the sadist who makes all the rules: often it is the submissive partner who governs the action as well as the dominant one. As many conventional lovers know, to spend the occasional love-making interlude doing only what one's partner enjoys, moving to their desire and command alone, is often a most pleasant experience. To the masochist also, there is pleasure in giving as well as in receiving. So in the end the contract seems surprisingly well defined, and whilst one partner may agree to take a dominant, pseudo-brutal role towards the other and the other may avidly become the submissive, pseudo-victim of the domin-ant's attentions, each has the other's best interests at heart. Even in s/m literature, which is not all pornographic, much is written on suggestions for how a sex session might proceed, rather as a formal sex education manual might teach the mechanics of ordinary lovemaking. Some of this instruction consists of precau-tions — hygiene, prevention of abrasions, safety signals that separate the genuine from the artificial plea for respite.

Remember that a slave may suddenly start to cough or feel faint. If masked and gagged, choking or lack of oxygen may result in serious consequences within seconds. Always, there-fore, observe the following precautions:

Never leave a bound and gagged slave alone in a room. If you must depart (even for a minute) take out the gag or release the hands.

Before commencing a session, lay out a pair of scissors in every room in which the slave will be trained. Always place the scissors in the same position where you can grab them instantly. Remember it is better to cut through and destroy an expensive mask than face the coroner.

If using chains, make sure you have a strong steel wire-cutter in the Training Centre, just in case a padlock jams.

Even if the slave is not gagged, but is in bondage, do not go out of earshot. Do not drown a genuine cry for help by playing loud music or running a bath.

It is essential that gags, nostril tubes, enema pipes, rods and other insertions should be scrupulously clean and dipped into mild antiseptic (diluted Dettol, etc.) before use, and thoroughly washed and disinfected after use.

If the slave is to sleep in a heavy punishment suit and mask, and in bondage, the Master or Mistress should sleep in the same bed. Unless a very light sleeper, allow enough slack on the slave's chained wrists to allow her/him to adjust the breathing holes of the mask during the night.

Always have padlocks with the same key combination so that one key can open any padlock. Have a spare key in every room. If taking the slave outside with chains and padlocks, always carry the key, even if you have told the slave that the key has been left behind in the Training Centre.

During normal suffocation training, never wear heavy gloves: close the collar of the hood round the slave's neck with your hands, and never use a strap or chain which might impede instant removal.

In principle, do not use a gasmask as a suffocation instrument unless it has been adapted so as to give instant access of air.

When the slave is in bondage and wearing a gasmask for a length of time, make sure the filters are completely clear and clean. Dust and talc, over a period of time, can clog the filter.

When the slave is ordered to wear a mask which has no openings except two short nostril tubes, always allow her/him to clean the nose with tissues, then, with the mouth closed, take several deep breaths to ensure there is no obstruction. Preferably, a slave with catarrh should not wear this type of mask.

The M.M.A. recommend using wide leather straps for bondage. These cover a wider area of skin than ropes, and can be instantly loosened. However, for those who prefer ropes, the following tips should be observed:

Never use cheap or coarse rope. This has no 'give' and can quickly cause skin-sores, especially when the slave struggles to get free. Use soft linen rope, the thicker the better.

Thin rope will cut into the skin and very soon cut off the blood circulation. This will cause numbness and the slave may not realise that circulation has stopped. This is dangerous! Ideally, straps should be used to actually secure the slave and, if required for photographic or aesthetic reasons, the rope added, firmly but not tightly.

(From the Masters' and Mistresses' Handbook, 1980)

Thus, every couple that enjoys this sort of pleasure carefully and solicitously works out (if they don't already know) what both participants enjoy. The roles are pre-set and attitudes are fixed for both participants *for that session*: the last emphasis is made because some couples (but by no means all) like to swap roles from one session to another. Often the protagonists create a labyrinthine set of rules and conditions, behaviour that each must observe, even words that each must or must not use. To the outsider, indeed, the behaviour must seem (and perhaps is) a game of sexual dungeons and dragons, played with all the excitement, intensity and seriousness that hallmarks the devotee of either activity.

And this, of course, is what brings s/m behaviour into the world of loving couples rather than individuals out for terrifying kicks, for both partners want to please each other and to have the performance repeated on future occasions. Neither partner is going to want to annoy or upset the other. The contact is thus not one-sided except perhaps in one respect. Unusual sexual patterns seem in the present state of our society to develop less easily in females than among males. The reasons usually given for this are speculative (even if quite plausible), but the fact remains that women are seldom attracted to variant sex patterns as easily or as firmly as are men. As a result, since s/m requires a partner if it is to be anything more than a matter of fantasy, there is in theory a permanent situation of too many s/m-oriented men chasing too few similarly minded women. In fact, there seem to be so few women of a 'natural' s/m persuasion that most of the men concerned find themselves trying to persuade a more or less conventional woman into trying a little s/m play.

This, indeed, is where the relationship aspect becomes intriguing, for it is far more common in a heterosexual s/m session for the woman to be the dominant partner and the man to be submissive, than the other way round. This surprises and even attracts a number of women, so such as are interested will be content to play a game with their lover, They enjoy a parade of power, relishing 'permission' to get their own back on the conventionally dominant male — especially if they are fond of men but feel that their previous encounters with them have been less successful than they might have wished. They can also seize the opportunity to work off any aggression (some of which may be repressed or displaced) they may possess in any case into the bargain.

The situation additionally allows them to tell their lover, under the guise of a 'mistress's command' exactly what to do in order to please them sexually: traditionally, of course, the female is not supposed to be so forward or so open as to ask for anything sexually, yet given the role of dominatrix she can ensure that she gets the pleasure she wants, exactly as and when she wants it. At the same time, her lover may become especially turned on by the knowledge that he is pleasing her, so both of them are likely to get excellent sex out of the ritual.

Small wonder, therefore, that after a few games of this sort the female becomes conditioned operantly and acquires something of a taste for the activity. This is possibly a reasonable motive system for participating: a straw poll amongst aficionados of the behaviour (a pilot study for further research at present being carried out) shows that whilst the male motive is virtually always sexual, the female reward is frequently quoted as being 'a sense of power'.

The female enjoyment of power in this situation is especially interesting when one realises that the women who enjoy these rituals are neither male-oppressed in the traditional sense nor women with a high hostility towards the men they partner. Instead, both general impression and personality studies to be quoted later show them to be the sort of cool, competent, outward-going women who could run a business or a home as easily as they would run a sadomasochistic sex ritual. The enjoyment of power is nevertheless marked. For some, indeed, the enjoyment is so strong that each session is played for the woman's pleasure alone, *without* reference to what the partner may or may not enjoy!

AETIOLOGICAL CONSIDERATIONS

Given, then, that reward conditioning seems to play at least some part in the development of sadomasochistic behaviour in women, it is of course pertinent to deal with more fundamental causes for the behaviour in both sexes. Research data is scarce enough, and is scarcer when women are concerned than when men are concerned. Direct influences may nevertheless be discussed under different headings, as follows:

Genetic influences

Evidence of genetic predisposition towards s/m *per se* is scarce. In any case, it seems unlikely that genetic influence should predispose anyone towards a specific variant sexual pattern rather than versatility of sexual predisposition as a whole. On the other hand, it is not illogical to postulate that some genetically induced hormone imbalance or abnormality could produce in some males a greater tendency than usual to submit sexually, or a greater desire in some females to dominate a sexual encounter, either informally or formally. The second situation (female dominant) could manifest either as an aggressive lesbianism or as heterosexual female sadism: the first might appear as submissive homosexuality, heterosexual or homosexual masochism, or as femmiphilic transvestism.[1] As a result, it would seem to be more sensible to look for evidence of a genetic predisposition towards sadomasochism *or behaviours that can be shown to be associated with it*.

One such piece of evidence comes from a twin study in males conducted by Glenn Wilson and reported in Gosselin and Wilson (1980). The numbers of twin pairs involved were small — 14 pairs of identical and 14 pairs of fraternal twins — but when intra-class correlation for the incidence of appropriate fantasy and behaviour was measured, some evidence of a genetic influence appears, especially when one realises that the same study noted that 36 per cent of sadomasochists are also transvestic and 41 per cent of transvestites are also sadomasochistic (Table 10.1).

The correlations for sex drive and satisfaction are included to replicate the studies of Eysenck (1976) and Eysenck and Wilson (1979). The latter paper also includes evidence that homosexual

Table 10.1: Intra-class correlations of identical and fraternal twins on relevant fantasy items, self-rated sex drive and overall sex satisfaction

	Identical twins[a]	Fraternal twins
Being whipped or spanked	0.36	0.13
Wearing clothes of the opposite sex	0.80	0.43
Sex drive	0.42	0.02
Sex satisfaction	0.52	0.17

Note: [a] 14 pairs of twins in each category.

Source: Gosselin and Wilson, 1980.

orientation is to some extent predisposed by heredity, and this becomes interesting when one realises that male sadomasochists indulge in a significantly greater amount of homosexual fantasy and behaviour than do members of their control group of randomly selected age-matched men, that Spengler's (1977) study showed 38 per cent of his s/m subjects to be exclusively homosexual and a further 31 per cent to be bisexual 'to some extent', and a survey of 98 sadomasochists recently carried out by the secretary of an s/m organisation showed 32 per cent to be bisexual or homosexual in orientation. The figures differ because of differences in the type of sample, but the incidence of homosexuality seems in any case unexpectedly high unless homo/bisexuality and sadomasochism are associated. Could the genetic findings really be indicating a predisposition towards sadomaochism *and/or* homo/bisexuality *and/or* transvestism, i.e. towards sexual variation in general rather than just one?

Other Biological Influences

The difficulty raised in the last paragraph reappears here, in that it is almost impossible to decide whether data obtained from nominal sadomasochists is not referable to other variations, especially when the overlaps of interest between different 'clans' is often so high. The probability of one biological 'set-up' producing a predisposition towards any one or more sexual behaviours is further evidenced by the finding (Gosselin and Wilson, 1980) that transvestites, sadomasochists and fetishists alike are significantly more introvert and neurotic in Eysenckian terms than controls, and Eysenck (1970) has provided evidence for the view that these variables are at least partially biologically determined. On the other hand, there are a number of reasons why too much should not be read into the former findings, for the greater introversion and neuroticism of these variants may have nothing *directly* to do with the production of variant sexual patterns: instead, these variables may merely make the subject far more sensitive to stimuli in general and more likely to retain an alternative sexual pattern induced by conditioning (see later).

It may therefore be appropriate at this stage to enter a brief *caveat* against regarding innate predisposition of any kind as too strong a contender for aetiological explanations of the development of sadomasochism or indeed some other sexual

243

variations. Such contentions die hard: Krafft-Ebing's (1886) belief in the biological origins of sexual patterning is but one example of the strength of conviction that this concept can generate. His experience and wisdom cannot be gainsaid, yet he clearly was fatally biased by virtue of never having studied a control sample in whose families he might as easily have observed his 'neuropathic tendencies'.

Yet Krafft-Ebing is not merely a straw man in this context, for other clinical sources contribute — perhaps inadvertently — to the idea, simply by classifying sexual variations as 'neuroses' (e.g. Linford Rees, 1967). However, one should perhaps remember that a variant sex pattern may not of itself be a neurosis, but anxiety over the fact may be — and it is only those whose anxiety is unbearable to them who present clinically. It will, in fact, be interesting to monitor any changes in Eysenckian extraversion and neuroticism amongst sexual variants as society begins to accept their behaviour more readily than in times past. Such tolerance seems already beginning, even if only in fits and starts and with minor retreats: the neuroticism of the samples of variants studied in Gosselin and Wilson (1980) is already less than Eysenck's normative group of 'patients with sex problems' published five years previously (Eysenck and Eysenck, 1975).

Biological (or rather, biophysical) influences are also lastly invoked to explain why males are so much more prone to developing variant sexual patterns than are females. It has been postulated that three factors account for the bias, namely:

(1) the greater visual sensitivity and heightened susceptibility to erotic stimuli shown by males,
(2) the males's more efficient biofeedback for monitoring arousal via the sex organs, and
(3) the male's greater susceptibility to non-coital sexual arousal.

If, indeed, the male's greater proneness to sexual variations is due to these factors, then they may be considered more as biologically determined than otherwise. Money (1963), after concluding that men were significantly more responsive than women to visual stimuli (women being in his view more sensitive to tactile stimuli), asserted that the evidence from pseudohermaphrodites would suggest that the sensory proclivities are dependent on the early organising effect of androgen (see also Buffery and Gray, 1972, for evidence of a similar male visual sensitivity in other species). The remaining influences mentioned above are of course physical and need not be discussed here: it is nevertheless interesting that Peto (1973) gives a totally psychoanalytically phrased appreciation of the same three influences.

Traumatic experience

Although Freud abandoned his original concept that parental seduction causes later hysterical symptoms (see Hadfield, 1967 for a discussion of this point), such an event well exemplifies the type of one-trial learning experience involving an extremely high salience stimulus and a high arousal state that could lead to powerful conditioning. As Freud himself realised, the experience may be real, or imagined from partial or mis-read cues: in either case, such a scene may present to the young child elements of cruelty, pleasure in the acceptance of such cruelty, confused gender identification or fetishistic speculation, but offers no prediction of which (if any) of these elements he will internalise as a variant sex pattern, nor indicates why such an experience should produce in the budding fetishist a liking for leather, rubber or plastic instead of the materials associated with conventional lovemaking.

A trauma that is almost directly symbolised in the sex pattern later to be developed is not only in theory more plausible but forms the basis of Stoller's (1970) model of how a variant pattern is learned. Leopold Sacher-Masoch is himself a classic example of such a process in acquiring masochistic leanings: he was as a young boy a witness to one of his aunt's adulterous sexual relationships. The event was interrupted by her husband, whereupon the lady flew into a rage, chased everybody out of the room and, on discovering Leopold, beat him with a riding-whip. Sacher-Masoch's subsequent obsession with sex in the form of a woman who beats her lover whilst wearing (as his aunt had done at the time) a fur-lined jacket is well-known. However, the fact remains that the incidence and nature of traumas in variants and non-variants has never been compared, and until this is done, the ease with which variants confabulate early experiences renders research involving self-reports of early traumas virtually impossible.

Learning experiences

Whilst trauma can be regarded as a special case of learning experience, the more general field of upbringing contains other paradigms that may influence variant and non-variant alike. Clinical and other case histories (e.g. Cath and Cohen, 1967; Davison, 1968; North, 1970) give examples of backgrounds that might traditionally be expected to give rise to variant sexual patterns, but in the absence of control studies such details are of little scientific value. Additionally, there is the old problem of ascertaining whether a given behaviour has been learned as the result of a given set of experiences or independently of them: unfortunately, even the subject's word cannot always be trusted here, for confabulation once more over-easily becomes the enemy of research.

So, as was stated at the beginning of this chapter, our general view of how a sadomasochistic sexual pattern is learned comes by analogy (and sometimes pretty slender analogy) from experiments concerning fetishism and from our knowledge of conditioning processes in general. Even the work of Brown, Martin and Morrow (1964), in which it was later claimed that rats could be trained to develop masochistic behaviour is actually irrelevant here, for there was no attempt to link the willing acceptance of pain with sexual reward, only with an *eventual* escape from further punishment.

We can nevertheless first briefly discuss and perhaps discard one or two popular pieces of sexual folklore concerning how an s/m pattern develops. For example, there is the oft-stated belief that sexual variations tend to develop more easily when the mother is physically or emotionally dominant and the father is weak or physically or emotionally absent. Such a contention, however, is not supported by evidence: 72 per cent of Prince and Bentler's (1972) transvestites stated that the father's image was masculine, strong and good, whilst Gosselin and Wilson (1980) showed 93 per cent of their s/m group and 73 per cent of their transvestite group had a good image of their mother. The belief might have arisen because many variants now interested in the origins of their behaviour were children during the Second World War, a time when fathers were physically and emotionally absent and mothers had to become strongly family-directive, and attributed their sexual pattern to this remembered situation.

A second popular concept is that childhood experience of

corporal punishment allied to the inevitable arousal of fear is the cause of later s/m behaviour. Here research results are extremely confusing. A direct survey of 141 masochist men carried out on the writer's behalf by an s/m club tabulated the sources from which their members believed they derived their masochistic inclinations. Results showed (Table 10.2) that school punishment was the most frequently quoted source, but development 'of its own accord' had occurred more frequently than actions by older individuals, domestic discipline or the influence of other children. On the other hand, the Gosselin and Wilson survey showed sadomasochists to have estimated that they had received only a marginally greater amount of corporal punishment as a child than had the control group, and there was no particular correlation between the incidence of sadomasochistic fantasies or activities and ratings of punishment frequency.

The position among females may, however, be somewhat different. A survey by Gosselin and Wilson (1980) of 25 female sadomasochists (all, as it happened, self-styled sexually dominant women) and 27 sexually conventionally oriented women showed that although their experience of corporal punishment was not very different, the correlation between punishment frequency and the frequency of *sadistic* fantasies in the dominant women group and *masochistic* fantasies in the control group was surprisingly high (Table 10.3).

The third and last piece of 'folklore' to be dealt with concerns the age at which any conditioning towards s/m and allied behaviours takes place. In therapies involving a retrospective search for the supposedly repressed event that may have given rise to the variant sexual behaviour, a regression almost to babyhood is sometimes carried out: psychoanalytic literature often speaks of fetish objects as equivalent to Winnicott's (1953) infantile transitional object, the first object realised to be 'not me' by the child and containing me-odours and mother-odours, breast softness and body softness, a mother-substitute when the mother is absent. Case histories are sometimes reported that deal with *treating* very young children for fetishism or gender dysphoria (Bemporad, Dunton and Spady, 1976; Cohen, 1976; Galenson, Vogel, Blau and Roiphe, 1975), thus inferring that infantile maladaptive learning is almost the *sine qua non* of deviational development. Admittedly, the childhood inevitabilities of smacking, restriction by reins or pram straps, overheating,

Table 10.2: Source of masochistic inclinations among 141 self-styled masochist men

Source	Percentage of respondents
School punishment	27
Own accord	21
Actions by older individuals	18
Domestic discipline	11
Influence of other children	11
Books/magazines/cinema/television	8
Medical/dental treatment	3
Experiences in H.M. forces	1

Source: CMR Research Report No. 11 (first publication)

Table 10.3: Correlations of fantasy frequency with punishment frequency in women

Fantasy theme	Conventional	Sadistic	Masochistic
Dominant female group	0.48	0.50	0.06
Control female group	0.35	0.39	0.57

Source: Gosselin and Wilson (1980).

wetness, humiliation and a somewhat close association with female dominance are appropriate and therefore plausible conditioning agents: however, other popular s/m associations are very unlikely to have acted as direct conditioning agents in babyhood. Leather, rubber and plastic are still the most popular fetishistic fabrics — especially in black — but the rubber bed sheet has passed into history for today's young fetishists, and leather has never much figured in Mothercare shops. And what is one to make of the following as infant conditioners?

> Fur . . . amputations, deformities, squints . . . uniforms such as . . . traffic warden, ballet dancer, air hostess, bride . . . objects such as . . . roses, crystal, surgical callipers and crutches . . .

Of course, the psychodynamicist may well smile indulgently at such hair-splitting, for these fabrics, costumes and objects can of course symbolise the s/m and fetishistic learning experiences to which the variant has yielded. And perhaps the psychodynamicist is right, but it doesn't make the job of the experimentalist any easier!

Surveys of the age at which variants remember their first appropriate experience nevertheless show a remarkably late development in many subjects of a variant sexual pattern supposedly laid in at infancy. Forty-three per cent of Spengler's (1977) sadomasochists showed their first inclinations after the age of 19: the unpublished research previously mentioned and carried out by the secretary of an s/m organisation showed 47 per cent of first inclinations developing between 8 and 13, whilst exactly the same peak occurs for 48 per cent of the fetishists studied in Gosselin (1979). If the memories of the subjects in these surveys can be trusted, and if a number of years does therefore elapse between the supposed infantile conditioning and its manifestation, this presents something of an obstacle to any simple theory of conditioning in this type of interest.

If, however, such a simple theory is in fact inadequate, it may explain why the equally simple paradigms implicit in Rachman and Hodgson (1968), McConaghy (1970) and Halvorsen (1975) (who all used simple classical conditioning processes to produce sexual responses to fetishistic or even non-sexual objects) failed to produce anything more than a weak and transient response totally unlike the often obsessional devotion shown by fetishists and sadomasochists towards their preferred sexual behaviour.

One must nevertheless allow that a complex and often quite specific[2] behaviour cannot be expected to spring fully-fledged from nowhere, however strong any genetic or otherwise biological predisposition might be. Could it not be, then, that Freud was right after all when he referred to the child as 'polymorphically perverse', in that during childhood he acquires by quite gentle learning experiences *a potential* for a whole range of behaviours which only at puberty and adolescence become sexualised if the child finds them useful in the production of pleasurable sexual feelings? The boy or girl who experiences genital pleasure by squeezing a rope between the legs whilst climbing it in the gym may not necessarily later develop a taste for rope bondage unless other conditions and experiences persuade, but the concept is there for elaboration if required. The often highly fetishistic costumes and aggressive behaviours of many superheroes and superheroines seen in comic books and on television may not produce in every young reader or viewer a fetishistic or sadomasochistic sexual pattern, but the image is

popular and thus clearly attractive, and may even be prototypi-
cally arousing: indeed, Freeman (1967) clearly demonstrates the
similarity between comic-book imagery and the soft pornography of variancy.

Why, then, (apart from any innate predispositions) do some
interiorise the sadomasochistic or fetishistic patterns of sexuality
and others escape them? A clue might come from La Torre
(1980), who organised an experimental manipulation of male
egos in which 30 students were given feedback to the effect that
they had been turned down by potential girlfriends whom they
had selected from photographs, while another 30 students were
informed that the girls had reciprocated interest. The two groups
of young men were then asked to rate the attractiveness of
various pictorial stimuli ranging from an abstract design to
female nightwear, panties, feet, legs and a complete female. The
men who had been told that they had been rejected showed a
lesser interest in the whole woman and in the abstract design than
in the underwear, feet and legs relative to the ego-boosted men.
It is therefore possible that the choice or usage and development
of a fetishistic or sadomasochistic pattern (the over-valuation of
feet and legs and the undervaluation of the whole female could
be construed as masochistic and sadistic elements respectively, as
well as fetishistic elements in general) may depend on experiences in which the subject is rejected by others in sexually tense
situations.

Rejection can, of course, begin in infancy, but its overt and
potentially repetitive demonstration from peer groups in general
start when the child begins to have to learn to socialise at school
(where parents are absent and unable to help the child to
socialise painlessly) and continues until late adolescence, when
socialisation has either been achieved or not achieved. If the
male child is not accepted by peer group females during this
period, then (whether or not he retains his heterosexuality) he
may choose the easier, non-rejecting options of fetishism and
transvestism — for the garments and the fabrics do not reject, yet
give sexual pleasure — or sadomasochism, wherein either a
stylised revenge ritual or a stylised appeasement ritual, which
mirrors the very disdain of those who rejected him, is the source
of sexual excitement. Assisted by the powerful operant conditioning of masturbation to trial fantasies of this nature (see
McGuire, Carlisle and Young, 1965, for an elaboration of this
concept), the rejected male has a cast-iron guarantee of pleasure

far more telling than infantile classically conditioned associative learning: to some extent one is drawn to Stoller's infuriatingly untestable hypothesis that the chosen ritual and its resultant sexual excitement

> . . . depends on a scenario . . . on whose story line the writer has been at work since childhood. The story is an adventure in which the hero/heroine runs risks that must be escaped. Disguised as fiction, it is an autobiography that hides crucial intrapsychic conflicts, screen memories of actual events, and the resolution of all these elements into a happy ending best celebrated by orgasm.

If we now return to the idea of a (preferably) real-life relationship in which there exists a sadomasochistic contract, it can be seen that such a contract may be useful to both parties. Pseudo-revenge and the enjoyment of role-playing power for the female has already been mentioned. If the healing of rejection experiences in Stollerian terms is required, the s/m scene is perfect for the male, whether he prefers the sadistic or the masochistic role, for in the former he can 'force' acceptance upon his (actually already accepting) partner, whereas as his partner's 'slave' he both recognises the (artificial) rejection pattern yet correctly judges that in fact he is never rejected and is constantly needed by his 'mistress' to do everything for her while she is apparently almost permanently sexually turned on by her interaction with him. The s/m relationship thus begins to emerge as not merely a behaviour but also as a sort of therapeutic strategy, an adaptive process that is useful for some people even if anathematic to others.

It may, in conclusion, therefore, be helpful to restress in some measure the advantages of such a relationship to those who enjoy it, so that the concept of a forward-looking cause may not be too alien to aetiology. To begin with, an s/m relationship, even if limited only to the sexual sphere, has very definite rules that govern it, behaviours and attitudes that the participants must observe, roles and psychodramas that they must or must not play out. Most conventional relationships are comparatively devoid of rules, and the participants have to find their emotional way towards one another by trial and error. In such a situation, the inevitable mistakes that they make may well induce irrevocable tensions that mar the relationship to some extent without the participants being aware of the fact. The rather more overt rules inherent in the s/m system act as a means by which such mistakes can either be avoided, exorcised or even utilised (by turning them into an excuse for 'disciplining' the transgressor!) in developing the relationship.

It is next obvious that most lasting s/m relationships contain much more flexibility of behaviour and attitude than might seem to be the case. Many conventional relationships, on the other hand, never explore the variations in role that are in theory open to them. Clearly, some may have no wish to do so: the variable patterns of s/m behaviour (in which the roles of dominant and submissive may be voluntarily exchanged for a session) may nevertheless have something to impart to the development of the somewhat publicised 'fluid relationship' concept, in which traditional male and female roles are voluntarily abandoned in favour of more versatile and less stereotypic behaviour.

Perhaps it should be mentioned at this point, however, that some sadomasochists disagree with the concept of role-playing within their relationship. To them, their interaction with their partner is a total one untinged with mere role-playing, although some admit that the true analogy is with the so-called 'method' actor, for whom the part is as totally real as can be for the period during which the role is being played. There is nevertheless another point at which s/m role-playing and reality meet, and this occurs when the language of conventional sexual instruction and s/m command are compared. For example, a marriage guidance book might advise in somewhat delicate terms:

> The wife, too, should try to tell her husband of any fantasies she has, and the husband might, if practical, try acting out some of these fantasies for her pleasure.

It may only be a question of semantics (and, admittedly, intensity) as to whether such advice is not the same as the more explosive dictate from 'The Masters and Mistress's Handbook':

> The mistress should give clear instructions to her slave as to her desires, and the slave should unquestioningly fulfil those desires for her pleasure alone.

Every command is of course a permission to act in a way that the recipient of that command probably wants to act anyway but may be afraid to do so under other circumstances for fear of rejection or ridicule. The s/m system can thus produce permissions rather than restrictions, and the participants may be using that system not because they are afraid of commitment but because it enables them to break through their inhibitions towards a commitment that they could not otherwise reach.

The existence of definite (even if artificial) rules that pertain to the s/m scene also produce one other powerful advantage that can strengthen this type of relationship immeasurably as well as pointing a gentle moral for more conventional interactions. In any system with defined rules to which all participants agree, the confidence that arises from knowing exactly where one stands, even in a limited arena, imparts a great deal of emotional strength to the participants. Any organisation — the armed services, the nursing profession, the police, even perhaps the church — knows that to be sure of one's function, to know where one's responsibility starts and ends, to do what circumstances have empowered onc to do without too much soul-searching is both comforting and confidence-building. This is especially true for those who fit with the Gosselin and Wilson and the McGuire et al. finding for sexual variants of a comparative lack of sociosexual skill: the very clear sociosexual signals of costume, attitude and behaviour within the s/m scene may give the under-skilled participant a confidence and feeling of worth that he or she might otherwise not possess. Competence and confidence are of course admired and desired by most of us, not least when sex is concerned. During interviews with s/m subjects, it became clear that even the imbalance inherent in an s/m relationship had allowed the development of an interactional confidence that had spilled out from the confines of the sexual arena into the participants' general lives.

Such interviews also elicited other motives for s/m-oriented people to behave as they do. These included the reduction of sexual and emotional tension, guilt and non-directed aggression, the reduction of vulnerability and the increase of total sexual trust (especially amongst devotees of bondage rituals, as one might expect!). Motives like these are in some ways reparative: Alex Comfort has nevertheless gone further, postulating that the rituals of sadomasochism do not merely raise the sexual confidence of those who are less blessed with it to a normal level, but raise the consciousness of those who undergo its rites and ordeals to a level that would not otherwise be reached. Drawing parallels between ritualised sex and older religions, he postulates that the factors of special costumes, ritual, concentration, anticipation, worship and high arousal common to both activities produce states designed to allow participants to transcend their normal limitations and take upon themselves the mantles of gods and goddesses. Perhaps not all of us would easily go along with such a free-wheeling concept: however, surely one must confess to a sneaking regard to such a description of sexual ecstasy.

It is not of course claimed that the s/m impulse has any particular virtue that commends it over any other sexual lifestyle. Sadomasochists probably do not entirely choose to be what they are: instead, they are virtually stuck with the pattern they possess, admitting ruefully that it limits the number of potential partners with whom they can form anything but the most transient relationship, and demands a special attitude towards sexual activity from those partners that they do acquire. However, because patterns of aggression may lie within all of us, the s/m pattern may represent an effective way of coping with facets of that aggression; for others, meanwhile, it may throw light upon their own attitudes to sexuality and on those with whom they seek to live. Stoller (1970) came to the somewhat pessimistic conclusion that all sexual excitement arose partly from hostility, ending his paper with the following words:

> My theory makes sexual excitement to be just one more example of what others have said for millenia — that humans are not a very loving species and that is especially true when they make love. Too bad.

If such a gloomy possibility be true, the sadomasochists may be at an advantage: if on the quiet they agree with such a statement, then they have perhaps found a way to make the best of it, defusing the hostility into a play-game, strengthening their relationships as they go and, in the process, maybe having a little laugh at themselves — and the rest of us — into the bargain.

NOTES

1. Benjamin (1966) comes to the conclusion that there are two types of transvestite (t/v). The first is the fetishistic transvestite, who cross-dresses in an exotic, over-the-top fashion in fetishistic garments and fabrics: he has no real wish to be a woman but experiences excitement of

dressing as he does. The second is the nuclear or femmiphilic transvestite, who generally dresses more modestly, is more like a 'real' woman in appearance and wishes that society would allow him to express what he believes is the female in him. Other writers (and transvestites) go along with this distinction: interestingly enough, some research by Sybil Eysenck and myself (Gosselin and Eysenck, 1980) showed that the nuclear t/v becomes more extravert and less neurotic when 'en femme' for a day or two than he is when in his male role: the fetishistic t/v does not.

2. In the sense that many sadomasochists are attracted, not to the whole range of sadomasochistic behaviour, but to a fairly specific preferred ritual containing only one or two elements of the behaviours described earlier in this chapter.

REFERENCES

Avery, N.C. (1977) 'Sadomasochism: a defence against object loss.' *Psychoanalytic Review*, *64* (1), 101–9

Bemporad, J.R., Dunton, H.D. and Spady, F.H. (1976) 'Case report: the treatment of a child fetishist.' *Am. J. Psychother.*, *30* (2), 303–16

Benjamin, H. (1966) *The Transsexual Phenomenon*, New York: The Julian Press

Brown, J.S., Martin, R.C. and Morrow, M. (1964) 'Self-punitive behaviour in the rat: facilitative effects of punishment on resistance to extinction.' *Journal of Comparative and Physiological Psychology*, *57*, 127–33

Buffery, A.W.H. and Gray, J.A. (1972) 'Sex differences in the development of perceptual and linguistic skills.' In *Gender Differences: their Ontogeny and Significance* (eds. C. Ounsted and D.C. Taylor), London: Churchill

Cath, S. and Cohen, H. (1967) 'Elbow rubbing and the wish to be beaten: a study of a case and the possible genesis of perversion.' *Israel Annals of Psychiatry and Related Disciplines*, *5* (2), 185–97

Cohen, F.W. (1976) 'Art psychotherapy: the treatment of choice for a six-year old boy with a transsexual syndrome. *Art Psychotherapy*, *3* (2), 55–67

Davison, G.C. (1968) 'Elimination of a sadistic fantasy by a client-controlled counterconditioning technique: a case study.' *J. Abnorm. Psychol.*, *73* (1), 84–90

Eysenck, H.J. (1970) *The Structure of Human Personality*, 3rd edn., London: Methuen

Eysenck, H.J. (1976) *Sex and Personality*, London: Open Books

Eysenck, H.J. and Eysenck, S.B.G. (1975) *Eysenck Personality Questionnaire*, Sevenoaks: Hodder and Stoughton

Eysenck, H.J. and Wilson, G.D. (1979) *The Psychology of Sex*, London: Dent

Freeman, G. (1967) *The Undergrowth of Literature*, London: Nelson

Galenson, E., Vogel, S., Blau, S. and Roiphe, G. (1975) 'Disturbance in sexual identity beginning at eighteen months of age.' *International*

Review of Psychoanalysis, 2 (4), 389–97

Gosselin, C.C. (1979) 'Personality attributes of the average rubber fetishist.' In *Proceedings of the First International Conference on Love and Attraction* (eds. M. Cook and G.D. Wilson), London: Pergamon Press

Gosselin, C.C. and Eysenck, S.B.G. (1980) 'The transvestite "double image": a preliminary report.' *Personality and Individual Differences*, 1, 172–3

Gosselin, C.C. and Wilson, G.D. (1980) *Sexual Variations*, London: Faber & Faber

Hadfield, J.A. (1967) *Introduction to Psychotherapy*, London: George Allen and Unwin

Halvorsen, J.E. (1975) 'Conditioning a fetish in subjects who do not believe that they can be conditioned.' *Dissertation Abstracts International*, 35 (7–8), 3581

Heron, W., Doane, B.K. and Scott, T.H. (1956) 'Visual disturbances after prolonged perceptual isolation.' *Can. J. Psychol.*, 10 (13–16), 311

Krafft-Ebing, R. von (1886) *Psychopathia Sexualis*, Translation, 1965, New York: Stein and Day

La Torre, R.A. (1980) 'Devaluation of the human love object: heterosexual rejection as a possible antecedent of fetishism.' *J. Abnorm. Psychol.*, 89, 295–8

Linford Rees, W.L. (1967) *A Short Text-book of Psychiatry*, London: English Universities Press

McConaghy, N.B. (1970) 'Penile response conditioning and its relationship to aversion therapy in homosexuals.' *Behaviour Therapy*, 1, 213–21

McGuire, R.J., Carlisle, J.M. and Young, B.G. (1965) 'Sexual deviations as conditioned behaviour: a hypothesis.' *Behaviour Research and Therapy*, 2, 185–90

Money, J.A. (1963) 'Cytogenetic and psychosexual incongruities, with a note on space-form blindness.' *Am. J. Psychiatry*, 119, 820–7

North, M. (1970) *The Outer Fringe of Sex*, London: Odyssey Press

Panken, S. (1967) 'On masochism: a re-evaluation.' *Psychoanalytic Review*, 54 (3), 135–49

Peto, A. (1973) 'The olfactory forerunner of the superego: its role in normalcy, neurosis and fetishism.' *International Journal of Psychoanalysis*, 54 (3), 323–30

Prince, V. and Bentler, P.M. (1972) 'Survey of 504 cases of transvestism', *Psychological Reports*, 31, 913–17

Rachman, S. and Hodgson, R.J. (1968) 'Experimentally induced sexual fetishism: replication and development.' *Psychological Record*, 18, 25–7

Smirnoff, V.N. (1969) 'The masochistic contract.' *Int. J. Psychoanal.*, 50, 665–71

Spengler, A. (1977) 'Manifest sadomasochism in males: results of an empirical study.' *Arch. Sex. Behav.*, 6 (6), 441–56

Stoller, R.J. (1970) 'Pornography and perversion.' *Arch. Gen. Psychiatry*, 22, 490–9

Stoller, R.J. (1976) 'Sexual excitement.' *Arch. Gen. Psychiatry*, *33*, 899–909

Winnicott, D.W. (1953) 'Transitional objects and transitional phenomena.' *International Journal of Psychiatry*, *34*, 89–97

Author Index

261

Subject Index